THE NURTURANCE PHENOMENON

ROOTS OF GROUP PSYCHOTHERAPY

THE NURTURANCE PHENOMENON

ROOTS OF GROUP PSYCHOTHERAPY

Ruth R. Greenberg–Edelstein
Rutgers University
Newark, New Jersey

APPLETON-CENTURY-CROFTS/ Norwalk, Connecticut

0-8385-7062-3

Notice: The author(s) and publisher of this volume have taken care that the information and recommendations contained herein are accurate and compatible with the standards generally accepted at the time of publication.

86 87 88 89 90 / 10 9 8 7 6 5 4 3 2 1

Prentice-Hall of Australia, Pty. Ltd., Sydney
Prentice-Hall of Canada, Inc.
Prentice-Hall Hispanoamericana, S.A., Mexico
Prentice-Hall India Private Limited, New Delhi
Prentice-Hall International (UK) Limited, London
Prentice-Hall of Japan, Inc., Tokyo
Prentice-Hall of Southeast Asia (Pte.) Ltd., Singapore
Whitehall Books Ltd., Wellington, New Zealand
Editora Prentice-Hall do Brasil Ltda., Rio de Janeiro

Library of Congress Cataloging-in-Publication Data

Greenberg-Edelstein, Ruth R.
  The nurturance phenomenon.

  Includes index.
  1. Group psychotherapy.   2. Nurturing behavior.
I. Title.   [DNLM: 1. Group Processes.   2. Mental
Disorders—therapy.   3. Psychotherapy, Group.
WM 430 G7984n]
RC488.G65   1986   616.89'152   86-1190
ISBN 0-8385-7062-3

Cover Design: Paul Agule

PRINTED IN THE UNITED STATES OF AMERICA

This book is dedicated to
my two main sources of nurturance and intimate reciprocity:
my primary group of Ruth, David, Daniel, and June Edelstein
and my group in the beginning of Elsie, Nathan, Ruth,
and Lille Greenberg and Ella Schwarz.

Contents

Preface

This book is about the exchanges of nurturance which enable most human groups to endure. It forms a broad framework for group therapy and a discussion of the place and use of the small group in society. The perspective on groups is based on nurturance as an explanation for what transpires in the family, in small and large groups, and especially in the curative process in treatment groups. This is the basis for understanding the fundamental relationships that bind a group into a unique entity. It is of special interest to those concerned with understanding the functions of nurturance in groups within the overall social order, and those interested in remedying failures in achieving adequate involvement in the group nurturance process.

Out of our coexistence in time and place grows our very being and potential for becoming. This can happen only in a nurturing environment where we give and take at some level of reciprocity. The more we are able to transcend the limitations of a socially fixed world, the more we are able to develop alternative ways of nurturing each other that help us envision our human potential. This is why established theories of behavior that emanate from our times, or often from the past but applied today, also need to be transcended or fully recognized as simply language which allows us to communicate and understand each other within various contexts. In fact, the language of psychoanalytic, behavioristic, or humanistic theories of behavior can itself be nurturing. It gives us a sense of security and comfort to see that our behavior fits into a general scheme of human activities. The labeling of behavior, ironically enough, can be reassuring and confer authenticity and validity to what we are doing and to who we are. Burke has referred to psychoanalytic theory as a "secular conversion" since we can use psychoanalytic terms to perceive behavior and events from a new point of view.[1]

Reciprocity as a curative factor is usually dealt with in current theories of treatment, but the nurturance component is often not recognized as such. Each theory emphasizes the importance of certain behaviors and ignores others. Not one has placed major emphasis on the constellation of nurturing behaviors which unify people into groups. This is partly due to the reluctance of social scientists to acknowledge a characteristic and process, predominately associated with females, as being of major significance in social formations and treatment methods. It is also partly due to the way historians have interpreted events, paying little or no attention to nurturance as a compelling need throughout life, and its part in the formation and maintenance of societies. Nurturance has indeed been "the undercover of history" as have women.[2] Prominent in recorded history have been the accounts of power struggles and wars, the negative extreme of the nurturance dimension.

The competitive struggles of the daily world and the economic structure, which creates a grossly unequal distribution of goods and potentials for love and fulfillment, affect how nurturance is viewed and exchanged. The exchange of nurturance in the family has been overshadowed by the attention given to family power struggles. The family, seen by Lasch and others[3] as the "haven" away from the alienating force of the community and state, has itself reflected the mentality of the social order of which it is a part. Highly developed modern urban life seems to place major barriers in the way of our reaching out and caring and helping one another. Specialization and the formalization of relations contributes, in no small measure, to this impediment. To counteract this, throughout history people have banded together to form their own communities. In this way they have attempted to establish security, protection, and a caring, nurturing world of their own outside the mainstream of things.

Nurturance, given or received, can vary greatly. The nurturance system established for a group may place some members in subordinate receiving roles. It is remarkable that members who are voluntary participants in a particular group can become so enmeshed in the group that their voluntary status is lost in the throes of the psychological pull of the group. Within a complex society, social institutions, especially those of the workplace, create hierarchical relationships that can have a profound influence on our sense of self and our ability to participate in egalitarian relationships. The stratification by power and powerlessness and the corresponding distribution of positive and negative self-images, pervasive in our world, appear in most small group settings. Unless the harm of placing nurturance in the hands of one or the few is recognized, such cultural restrictions can continue to do their damage even in therapy groups.

Nurturance has taken a variety of forms during different historical periods. Religion at times has represented nurturing qualities.[4] At other times, women have been the nurturing force for societies in danger of becoming overriden and destroyed by unresolvable conflicts and threats to their existence.[5] The impact of history on our attitudes and beliefs is conspicuously evident in the general subversion of nurturance to an inconsequential phenomenon that is the peculiar domain of powerless women. These trends are the antecedents to the usage and meaning given to nurturance. In order to understand the value of nurturance systems and their use in small groups, we need to examine the origins of the role of nurturance in our value system today. The power of the small group to nurture, heal, and expand the meaning of existence depends on our ability to make some connections between what we do in our primary associations and what is happening in the society at large. Ultimately, the continued existence of the human race may depend on such expanded perceptions of our individual worlds.

The assumption that the nurturance phenomenon is fundamental to group psychotherapy alters some generally accepted propositions. The underlying premise is that a psychotherapy group will be effective if a reciprocal nurturance is achieved regardless of the apparent issues, conflicts, solutions attempted, and so-called covert meanings behind what is happening. For instance, a nurturance proposition about early group themes[6] would refer to the conflicting expectation of unconditioned and conditioned nurturance from the therapist. Instead of a proposition placing emphasis on the therapist participating as a person in order to appear human and believable,[7] it would read: the therapist participates in reciprocal exchanges in the group to model and enhance therapeutic exchanges. Instead of postulating the search for the process as "indispensable and a common denominator in all effective groups,"[8] the proposition would read: the nurturance exchange reflects the quintessence of group actions, and the intellectualizations and abstractions that uncover the "covert" meaning of a process destroy the value of the exchange. For instance, a group member expressing hostility toward another or others is usually reacting to inadequate or absent nurturance; she or he is expressing a sense of deprivation, whether the stimuli come from the past, the present, or fantasy. Accordingly a corollary proposition would read: a prominent source of anger is the group member's perception of others as not understanding him or her, or as not sharing themselves in a genuine way. While invoking explanatory and established theories of transference, resistance, displacement, or other theories that may assist, such interpretations are far from central or essential and can be at times impediments to the all important reaching out of people to each other.

To what extent have nurturance needs been allocated to a subservient place in our methods because they are associated with women, nonassertiveness, and noncognitive processes? How does reciprocal nurturance serve to hold people together and to heal? Does this process have potency of its own, or is it simply another form of communication? Can the generally accepted and respected theories of human behavior be realigned to accommodate reciprocal nurturance as the focal therapeutic method in group therapy? How does it manifest itself in groups, especially therapy groups which are deliberately created to help people and to rebuild shaken worlds?

The first four chapters center on the nurturance phenomenon, defining it, giving its origins, and describing its curative value. Activities that facilitate setting up the treatment group and formulating concepts of therapeutic nurturance are described in Chapters 5 and 6. Chapters 7 and 8 identify the nurturance components in the group structure and process. The final two chapters are perspectives on the place of nurturance in the community and history. Those primarily interested in group psychotherapy may first concentrate on Chapters 5 and 6, which start the group using reciprocal nurturance as a therapeutic agent. The earlier and later chapters can then be used to enrich the meaning of the therapeutic values of nurturance and to enable the reader to explain his or her group observations within the broader social contexts of the nurturance exchange as a fundamental human activity.

NOTES

1. Burke, K. (1965). *Permanence and change.* New York: Bobbs-Merrill, pp. 125–177.
2. Boulding, E. (1976). *The undercover of history.* Boulder, Colorado: Westview Press.
3. Lashe, C. (1977). *Haven in a heartless world.* New York: Basic Books.
4. Stuard, A. M. (1976). *Women in medieval society.* Philadelphia: University of Pennsylvania.
5. Toynbee, A. (1948–1961). *A Study of History* (Vol. 3). London: Oxford University Press.
6. Whitaker, D. D., & Lieberman, M. A. (1964). *Psychotherapy through the group process.* New York: Atherton Press, p. 63.
7. Yalom, I. (1985). *The theory and practice of group psychotherapy.* (3rd ed.). New York: Basic Books, p. 209.
8. Ibid., p. 143.

Acknowledgments

I wish to thank Professor Madeline Schmitt of the University of Rochester and Professor Ernice King of Bryn Mawr College for their detailed critical evaluations of the manuscript in its early stages. Their comments were thoughtful, comprehensive, and extremely helpful. Others who offered very significant comments at various stages in the development of this book were Professor Elizabeth Brophy of Loyola University, Professor Peggy Chinn of the State University of New York at Buffalo, Professor Ann Davis of the University of California at San Francisco, Professor J. David Edelstein of Syracuse University, Professor Marilyn Huelskoetter of St. Louis University, and Professor Ethel M. Rosenberg of the University of Central Arkansas. I want to thank my editors, David Gordon and Diane Baer, for their support and caring in their management and direction of this project.

I am most grateful to all the clients, students, and colleagues that I have known and deeply cared about at Bellevue Psychiatric Hospital, the Bureau of Child Guidance and the Public Health Department in New York City, Brooklyn State Hospital, Essex County Medical Center, Payne Whitney Psychiatric Clinic of Cornell University, Syracuse Psychiatric Hospital, and the Westchester Division of New York Hospital. I especially wish to acknowledge the richness of my life together in small groups with colleagues and students at Northern Illinois University, the State University of New York at Upstate Medical Center, Syracuse University, and especially Rutgers University.

THE NURTURANCE PHENOMENON
ROOTS OF GROUP PSYCHOTHERAPY

1
Nurturance Defined

Nurturance is transmitted between people in many different ways within any human enterprise. It is usually a process that occurs within the bounds of established norms. The nurturance experienced in therapy groups, however, goes beyond socially prescribed norms and depends on the norms that develop in the group. Concentration on this phenomenon frees the group to work on the most elemental meaning of the human being and to value its unique worth.

THE NURTURANCE PROCESS

Nurturance is the caring and helping that are fundamental to human relationships and groups. It includes any interactions that build unity and support. It may run the gamut, from exploratory nurturing remarks to intense personal exchanges. Nurturance includes aiding, comforting, confiding, nursing, exchanging, fondling, establishing solidarity, and promoting development and growth. It always moves in at least two directions and includes positive reactions by the person being aided, comforted, or confided in. It may occur any place: the nursery, school, home, workplace, hospital, political organization, legislature, or court room. Both strong peer relationships and group psychotherapy are based on egalitarian exchanges of nurturance.

Nurturance in therapy groups occurs at five levels, from one-sided giving or aiding all the way to the exchange that leads to solidarity with others and transcendency of self. Negative exchanges also can occur at five different levels, from one person simply ignoring another to an intense exchange of hostility and hatred. The rhythm of the group is made of alternating positive and negative reciprocity. Group focal conflicts, which are the center of the group process, emerge out of the struggles for nurturance, reciprocity, and solidarity and are solved progressively more effectively as the group increasingly utilizes the nurturance exchange.

The early experience of nurturance given by a caring adult helps establish a sense of constancy and an awareness of being a distinct person. The search in adulthood for a reliable and enduring source of nurturance leads to marriage contracts, membership in groups, and religious affiliations. The particular ways people learn to receive and give nurturance affect the way they live and whether they move primarily toward or away from people. Horney has observed that reaching out to others may be based on a positive attitude or it can be instigated by a desire to control or a fear of losing the other.[1] Although clinging to another for support has been considered a neurotic "incapacity for love,"[2] seeking out another always has some positive features and requires some capacity to give.

Awareness of self comes from identification with and internalization of the nurturer. These processes provide the means for an independent existence. The conscious and unconscious memories of early childhood nurturing are the sources of self-identity and the intrapsychic processes that help us differentiate ourselves from others. The struggle for differentiation characterizes childhood and adolescence, and occurs again and again throughout the adult years. Interaction with the internalized image of the nurturer helps move us to self-reliance. It is the means by which we move from dependence to freedom and creative growth, because the capacity to take the place of the other, the nonself, enables us to reason and attempt alternate ways of behaving.[3]

The most fundamental nurturance is nonreciprocal. It is predominantly a unilateral giving by which we comfort or help someone, and he or she does not respond. An example is the parent's care of the newborn. As soon as the infant actively responds, the situation changes and an elementary exchange begins to take place. The infant may momentarily take on a combined giving and taking role, when he or she is actively sucking at the breast, for the infant is taking from the mother while also stimulating her in return. A teacher who is primarily a giver of information, guidance, and support, usually receives something from the person who is the object of the giving. The student who learns well the lesson taught gratifies and therefore, nurtures the teacher.

When memories of negative exchanges predominate, there may be insufficient internal support for the building of nurturing relationships. There then develops a tendency to avoid contact with others for fear of rejection, or worse. The alternative is to be compliant and avoid all change. When the deprivation of basic nurturing is extreme, it is almost impossible to have meaningful exchanges with others without first having had some remedial, elementary contact with a nurturant person who is able to give without requiring much in return. This may be more easily achieved in therapy groups than in one-to-one relationships because the group can create the social norms that make the acceptance of nonreciprocal nurturance appropriate. The dyadic relationship can do this less effectively because group acceptance is lacking. In this matter, the needs of the adult are very different from those of the child, for the adult requires a social climate that will permit him or her to develop ways of meeting needs among peers.

Altruism is usually nonreciprocal nurturance prompted by empathy and compassion in specific situations. It refers to such acts as helping a stranger across the street. Researchers have considered altruism as different from nurturance.[4] A prevailing assumption appears to be that nurturance is primarily and perhaps, exclusively confined to early childhood rearing practices. Nevertheless, some have expanded the notion of altruism to include reciprocity and presented ideas that include the essence of the nurturance exchange.[5]

An elementary reciprocity develops when the recipient of the altruistic act becomes responsive in some way. The relationship still remains unequal, with one person in greater control and predominantly the giver. Social reciprocity is achieved when more active exchange takes place in accordance with accepted norms. There may be an exchange of addresses, of information, or a sharing of personal interests. Therapeutic levels of reciprocity are not likely to be achieved in exchanges between strangers. There is a high likelihood, however, that it will occur when strangers are united under catastrophic conditions, for when lives are threatened, as in natural disasters, survival depends on an active exchange of caring and helping.

NORM OF RECIPROCITY OF NURTURANCE

The term *norm of reciprocity* was coined by Gouldner to refer to the expected mutual helping and exchange that takes place between people within any social system. Reward systems are built to safeguard the continued conformity to particular norms of reciprocity.[6] Marx noted that,

> . . . you can change love only for love, confidence for confidence, etc. . . . Every one of your relationships . . . must be a definite expression of your *real, individual* life corresponding to the object of your will. If you love without calling forth love, that is, if your love as such does not produce love, if by means of an *expression of love* as a loving person you do not make of yourself a *loved person,* then your love is impotent, a misfortune.[7]

In his classic review of values in different preliterate societies, Hobhouse came to the conclusion that reciprocity is the "vital principle" in any society. In the family, clan, and tribe, the individual is so entwined in reciprocal acts, he or she has no existence as an individual.

> In the clan and the tribe . . . the individual has no legal position, scarcely even the possibility of existence, apart from the body to which he belongs. The family, the clan, or the village, or perhaps all three, are responsible to him for his safety, responsible to others for his wrong-doing, responsible . . . for his maintenance. His life is laid down by his place in them, his property is in the main a share in their property, his gods are their gods . . . His position in the group is, as it were, an exhaustive account of his existence, and he has little personal life apart from it.[8]

This was altered when the state came into being, for then individuals became their own agents. They were free to enter reciprocal relationships through contracts with whomever they wanted, do what they wanted with their property, or even leave their home or establish their own church. The responsibilities were then "taken over and even amplified by the state, which owes its members protection in the exercise of all rights which it recognizes. . . ."[9] In some respects, the replacement of the family by the state, permitted the development of a wide range of new reciprocally nurturing relationships of different intensities, durations, and levels, but it also led to a deprivation of nurturing arrangements that, although stultifying, were personalized, everlasting, and constant.

The principle of reciprocity operates to establish social equilibrium, a "reciprocity of service" that provides for giving and returning the equivalent.[10] In an integrated system, "expectation of the other is reciprocal or complementary . . . actions, gestures, or symbols have more or less the same meaning" for the participants. There is, then, a common culture, a "set of norms" through which the interactions are mediated.[11] In the community, it is the basis of essential services; at the workplace it enables the owner to stay in business and the worker to earn a living. The experience of the normalized exchange carries with it a sense of rectitude, that we are behaving correctly and properly. In this way, it functions in the service of conformity.[12] Moreover, the exchange is dependent on the place where it takes place, whether a kitchen in the home, a nursing office at the workplace, a government office in a federal building, or a meeting room at a community center.[13]

In stratified societies, the social system usually prevents reciprocity between people of different status. The more egalitarian the society, the more likely that the norm of reciprocity will prevail. Insults, aggressive acts, and other injuries are reciprocated in almost all social orders. Historically, it has been the negative forms of reciprocity that have been recorded, that is, the acts of retaliation, in which the emphasis is placed not on the return of benefits, but on the exchange of aggression and destruction.[14]

Class-ordered systems feature unequal, nonreciprocal relationships that are almost always exploitive. One commands, directs, forces, and the other complies, often by assisting, working, and supporting the other. Those who bear the subservient role gain some control by virtue of the eventual dependence of the other on the exchange. The nurturance phenomenon cannot be understood without its counterforce, as manifested in negative reciprocity. The dynamics of the human condition include alternating negative and positive exchanges that help maintain or regain equilibrium in social systems. Usually social norms prevent potentially abusive negative reciprocity.

> If the possible sexual exploitation of daughters by fathers gives rise . . . to mechanisms that serve to prevent this, then it would seem that *other* types of exploitation may also be controlled by other kinds of mechanisms. If the exploitation of women by men (or men by women) is worthy of attention, then also worth studying is the exploitation of students by teachers, of workers by management or union leaders, or patients by doctors.[15]

Household and familial arrangements and marriage contracts usually reflect the political system. When the system is democratic, marriage is based on reciprocity between the man and the woman. The more hierarchal a society with controlling and dependent groups the norms, the more likely will reciprocal exchange be rare in marriage.[16] Then, it is usually the wife who is the subordinate and follows orders. To the degree that a society is stratified into political and economically superordinate and subordinate groups, marriage systems function to prevent reciprocal exchange. Occasionally, the wife is a form of property that can be discarded or destroyed, as happens in India and other parts of the world.

Accepted, prescribed roles protect us from fears of isolation, but reliable sources of nurturance cannot depend solely on social roles, for not only do they change, they also end. With the change or termination of a role comes the possibility of loss of love, support, and other forms of nurturance that are inherent in the role. Self-nurturance can enable us to survive temporarily the loss of an important source of nurturance. Our personal internalized "network" can give us much support, but it can also foster rejection. We can have very negative views of ourselves, punish ourselves, and be ridden with guilt. Moreover, when the internal network becomes more important than the outside world, it can ripen into a pseudocommunity. The lack of external validation and consensus can produce delusions and hallucinations, sometimes negative and sometimes positive, but autistic and confined to the world of the self.

Care and support can be purchased at times when a personal relationship is not immediately available, internalized nurturance is insufficient, and daily social roles are not rewarding. It becomes a purchase of "love" when we try to get praise and favors and compliments on how we look and how we behave. We want to be called intelligent, good, beautiful, not because we love ourselves, but because these are ways of purchasing a simple form of nurturance, the equivalent of "the parental pat on the head."[17] This is especially so during periods of conflict and high anxiety. We are, however, discomforted by nurturance in the form of compliments and rewards when we feel we haven't actually "earned" them. May reported that clients will admit "they feel like fakers" when they are given public praise and acclaim, because they are being rewarded for behavior that is not genuine.[18]

A sudden and unexpected disability may precipitate the loss of important relationships and a new dependence on nurturance by strangers. For instance, at the onset of hospitalization, a client is subject to a series of activities never encountered before and is dependent on a number of strangers for personal care. The uncertainty of the role requirements often brings about withdrawal from playing any role. Giving the client a chance to play a familiar role is a precondition for his or her active involvement in the new situation.

SOME DETERMINANTS OF THE NURTURANCE EXCHANGE

Usually, nurturance is exchanged between specific people. Some persons are, however, catalytic to others and provide indirect nurturance by their mere presence. They are rewarding or supportive although no direct interaction takes place. A teacher communicating to a class the ramifications of a new idea may get the sense of support and encouragement from an unusually attentive class member whom he or she does not know, has never spoken to, and who does not speak up in class. The same happens to actors on the stage who feel support from the alert and responsive individuals sitting in the first few rows of the theatre. Similiar reactions occur when a person, known to be a supporter, is present. In the other direction, catalytic persons may be disquieting or threatening because they represent, in some way, criticism, disapproval, or indifference.

An increased number of people create the potentials for multiple and compound interactions. In a group of three, a strong relationship between two of the three will place the third person in a more receiving and subordinate position. When the group is as large as six persons, dyad, triad, and larger subgroup formations are possible. Intense reciprocity and interdependence within different dyads can influence the direction of the group positively or can dissipate the potential for intermutuality in the group as a whole. The formations within a group are likely to consist of the people who have similiar views or backgrounds, or whose behaviors are mutually complementary.

The vehicle for the nurturance exchange may be a dinner, a party, a work team, or a group therapy session. The exchange can occur at any meeting between two or more persons. Shared values and norms develop in a group in which the members feel close and share the same objectives. Interactions are influenced by societal values that give importance to authority, maintaining order, and protecting individuals who are struggling with uncertainty and fear of self-exposure. Some group members can assume authority roles and offer unilateral support, guidance, and concern to others. This requires some response from the others and usually represents social reciprocity between unequals.

Specific families give unique meanings to their nurturance exchanges and often maintain a characteristic dominant–dependent pattern. In a traditional patriarchal family, the father makes the decisions and is the one who supports the family economically. The members respond by obeying his dictates and maintaining solidarity with the other members by playing out expected roles. There are usually general norms, derived from the larger social group in the same subculture, which uphold the male as the authority in the family. When there is conflict between the norms of the subculture or community and the norms of the family, strong boundaries may have to be erected between the family and the larger group in order to maintain constancy in the family.

The duration of an action is a key to how significant it is. Behavior patterns that recur over and over again in many different circumstances have significant effects. Enduring nurturing relationships between members are typical of well-knit families. Pattern breaking is associated with commitments to ideas and alliances that are new and different and is a risk to the stability of the family group. If such actions are short-lived and transitory, they do not disrupt the integrity of the group, which cannot endure the strain of continuous change.[19] Nevertheless, short-lived, spontaneous reactions may be cathartic and contribute to the maintenance of the family system.[20]

At the workplace, relationships are usually unequal. They are based on social contracts and in most instances have to do with working for a wage. We are paid if our work contributes to the profits of the employer. This is a norm of unequal reciprocity because one party determines the circumstances of the reciprocity to a greater degree and gains more from the outcome. It is similiar to other conditions in which a group of people are subordinate to others who hold the power. People may share their common dissatisfaction with circumstances, and solidarity among them may become the means of gaining greater control. This is an example of a nurturance exchange among heretofore dependent persons that can lead to change in the power structure. Significant change in the behavior of groups always entails some negative exchanges that reach a crescendo, softened only by some form of a nurturance exchange.

A strong positive reciprocity between group members is the basis of power they cannot have as isolated and unrelated individuals. For some, mutual nurturance may be freely experienced in impulsive and spontaneous acts. The unconscious elements in some mass actions, when individuals feel an inexplicable unity with others correspond to peak experiences in therapy groups[21] that also have their foundation in the unconscious. A case in point is the coalescing of forces that occurs during an outbreak of "mass hysteria." First described by LeBon in the nineteenth century,[22] such behavior occurs when a considerable number of people feel a compelling unity with others and join in action with them without thinking about it. This might be seen as an overwhelming, unconscious urge of the participants to merge with each other in a unified action.

Such spontaneous action is periodically demonstrated by Malayesian women at the workplace. It tends to occur after management has imposed a speed-up and takes the form of one woman worker falling to the floor convulsing, after having seen a threatening "ghost." Her companion workers follow suit and the plant usually has to be closed to provide time for getting rid of the "evil spirits."[23] We might consider that the one who convulses first is the leader who, probably unconsciously, offers the heralding "call" for action. In effect, she is saying, that she is ready to stop and resist and ready to be the first to lead the others in doing this. The act of joining in the convulsions is based on a sense of communion and support. This is an informal, probably unconscious substitute for the protection and solidarity afforded by a union, since labor unions are outlawed in Malaysia. It may be an example of the social unconscious at work.[24]

The traditions and practices of the group to which we belong prescribe how nurturant we can be and with whom. Ability to interact with others in mutually acceptable ways comes from being able to play our own expected role as well as to accept the role of the other.[25] This is easy when we share the same reference group, but it is difficult, and perhaps impossible, if we do not. We also act occasionally in ways appropriate to one group, in another group where it is not. Fortunately, most of us shift fairly readily from one role to another. At times, we can be extremely nurturant and, at other times, we can be quite dependent on others for care and protection. We play different roles and put forth different aspects of ourselves in each group. When we are uncertain how to behave, we construct the best fit we can out of our experience; that is, we create roles when we find ourselves in situations for which we have no precedent. The roles we assume are affected by our feelings toward the others in the situations. For instance, if they are affectionate and considerate, we feel bound to carry out the reciprocal roles they expect of us. If, on the other hand, we perceive them as negative and rejecting, we may go out of our way to foil their expectations.[26]

Crises sometimes are handled by establishing entirely new behavior patterns. For instance, in Alcoholics Anonymous, alcoholics are oriented to the group's emphasis on sharing personal experiences concerning excess drinking. Return from a break with reality is facilitated by establishing close ties with peers and professional helpers who assist in establishing new ways of caring and relating.[27] In this respect, psychoanalysis has been considered a type of "non-religious conversion" when the treatment is seen as a means of "providing a new perspective that dissolves the system of pieties lying at the roots of the patient's sorrows or bewilderments." It presents a new system of terms that change painful experiences of the nurturing process by placing them in an acceptable conceptual framework.[28]

When new ways of expressing caring and exchanging nurturance are learned, some of the old ways may be lost temporarily. This can lead to difficulties with friends and relatives who expect a person to continue in the established ways. Therefore, such new behaviors may not necessarily be socially sanctioned. Finding a place for the new alongside the many other roles we play means determining its priority and reward values as compared to the other established demands and commitments. Standards may be lacking with which to measure its relative reward value and, therefore, have to be developed.[29]

NURSING AND NURTURANCE

Nursing exemplifies par excellence professional nurturance. It is humanistic care in which an empathetic bond between the nurse and client is reciprocally shared.[30] The nurse who fosters interpersonal nurturance usually has to struggle with the restrictions imposed by bureaucratic health care institutions. Occasionally, the most ingenious adaptation of institutional and therapeutic roles takes place.

Nurturance in nursing has often been bound into specific ways of caring and giving. Usually, institutional nurturance is restricted by rules and regulations and is given unilaterally by parental figures. Such limitations in the opportunity to exchange nurturance have been severely felt by neophyte nurses confronted with hospital regulations that place barriers in the path of creating nurturing exchanges. In some institutions, the primary nursing care approach, which provides for continuous care of a client by the same nurse during his or her hospital stay, alleviates this problem. In some instances, however, hospitals have saddled nurses with too many clients to make personalized care possible, and yet have falsely called this primary nursing.

Leininger emphasized that caring is "the most unifying, dominant, and central intellectual and practice focus of nursing."[31] She pointed out that evaluations can be made of the caring needs that exist and of the conflicts that may develop in attempting to meet those needs. She made the basic assumption that the universal need for caring is met in various ways by different groups[32] and observed that people were less dependent on others for care when individualism was espoused by the culture.[33] This conjures up the issue of rugged individualism versus group solidarity and suggests that groups may interfere with the independence of the individual. Democratic groups may, however, enhance the value of the individual, although not at the expense of the others.

Leininger included nurturance as one of 18 care constructs, using caring as the rubric under which all the other nurturing behaviors fall. However nurturance is the more inclusive term because it is a process that occurs at many levels and can take place without caring being present. Caring, on the other hand, is often simply a state of mind.[34] The etymological origins of nurturance are rooted in the words for the home and the maternal[35,36] and it has represented the fundamental processes of birth and growing. On the other hand, caring identifies the emotional underbase in forms of nurturance where concern is present. It has in its origins in words connoting sorrow, grief, and careful attention.[37]

Nursing is unique in that it frequently serves us when we have physical and psychosocial disorders. Because of this, it is a profession that is confronted with human beings undergoing the most severe strains on their capacity to give and receive nurturance. The therapeutic handling of these difficulties is part of the healing process. Most nursing care is at the elementary reciprocal level with the nurse the major source of nurturance to a client who responds with various degrees of acceptance, gratification, and appreciation. In some situations, as the client gains greater ability to function, he or she may reach a mutual reciprocity with the nurse that modifies or changes the personal perceptions and views of both participants.

Orem viewed nursing as a guiding force that assisted people in achieving as much self-care as possible.[38] In this respect, her stipulations have to do with the need for people to achieve independence from reliance on others. Within the context of nurturing needs, this would translate into the ability of people to be free to nurture themselves. Such a goal places a high value on the capacity of the person to be free of other persons. In some ways this goal is rational and valid, especially when we are concerned with incapacitated persons achieving greater control over their own functions. Yet in other ways this goal is isolating and possibly estranging in its espousal of freedom from brothers and sisters, peers, parents, and friends, who, in their capacity as resources for reciprocal nurturance, may enhance the "self-care" of all concerned.

At a time when this was not as fashionable as it is today, Peplau emphasized the central place of the democratic method in nurse–client relationships. She encouraged the full participation of the client as a partner with the nurse in identifying and assessing his or her problem[39] and noted the central place of elementary reciprocity in orienting clients to new situations that arouse the need for support, guidance, and nurturance. When this is provided, the way is paved for movement to more advanced relationships. The orientation is reciprocal in that the client informs the nurse as to who he or she is and what he or she needs, while the nurse offers information about the hospital, the clinic, and her or himself. This facilitates the development of needed support and nurturance through the use of nurse–client relationships and "the natural vehicles in nursing care, such as the bath, feeding, giving enemas, as new experiences in 'mothering' that displace earlier traumatic childhood experiences." In this way there can be "forward movement of the personality in ways that displace feelings of helplessness and powerlessness with feelings of creativeness, spontaneity, and productivity"[40]

The most direct reference to nurturance by Peplau is in her discussion of surrogate roles. In the nursing situation, the client is particularly likely to need nurturance as he or she has known it in the past.

> One nurse may symbolize a mother figure, another may stand for a sibling, still another may personify some other cultural figure outside the family constellation—such as a teacher, another nurse met earlier in life, and the like. Instead of relating to the nurse as he finds her the patient is likely to relate to her in terms of the older relationship.[41]

Such reactions may include nurturance exchanges. They are minimal at the socially prescribed level, and therapeutic if the nurse and client go beyond superficial observations perceiving the special qualities of each other.

NURTURANCE IN GROUP THERAPY

The curative value of the nuturance exchange is derived from what happens to the members when they discover themselves through egalitarian, symmetrical, and reciprocal interchanges with each other. In order that this happen, there must be interchanges of empathy, rapport within the context of candor and open communication, participation of the therapist as a person, and establishment of all members as cotherapists. The therapist and group members become participants in an intensely moving drama. They learn that perceiving one another as an emotional and thinking totality leads to perceptual breakthroughs and, occasionally, heightened, exhilarated peak experiences.[42] Significant outcomes of the exchange are the establishment of solidarity and a nurturance exchange network grounded in the experiences and understanding of each others's unique qualities. Whether the process can be explained by interlocking identifications and projections, reinforcement gratification, resolution of resistances, or some other existing theories is not important. What is important is the mutual exchange, especially at a highly personal level, and the development of the meanings of life that come from the group.

To comprehend some of the dilemmas we face we have to recognize that our knowledge of the real world is constructed from our experiences and interactions with others. Thus, we are in contact only with a conceptualized reality. The meaning of who we are comes from the social, economic, and political conditions in which we live. Since the self is dependent on external social factors most often outside our control, the self that evolves may appear estranged from our personal interests and concerns. Under these circumstances our own uniqueness becomes difficult to discern or elusive altogether. Without the rendering of new meanings and perceptions to our exchanges with others, we can become stuck in stereotypical deviant social roles that may give little pleasure or opportunity for growth and change.

Group therapy is based on the assumption that we all have the potential to continually create and recreate ourselves, and that we are not prisoners of our specific backgrounds and social worlds. The focus on nurturance as a central feature of the human condition permits the deemphasis of fixed interpretations and dogma and opens the way for a paradigm based on our capacity to create new ways of giving and receiving nurturance. It encourages freedom from the tyranny of well-established theories of behavior. This approach is the essence of praxis theory, which permits us to begin to free ourselves of a false consciousness imposed by the times, to understand the destructive forces that are part of our social world, and to develop ways of consciously influencing what happens to us.[43] A unique way of being is created by examining our way of reciprocally interacting, detached from the limiting and restricting socioeconomic elements and freed from fixed patterns that inhibit change.

In the beginning, the assumption of social ways of nurturing, such as being an advice-giver, a mother figure, a teacher, a cohelper, and a cotherapist, helps members overcome the isolation and separateness experienced in new groups. The enactment of roles in the group is influenced by the therapist's method of establishing norms, usually apparent in initial directions given to the group and in his or her reactions to the group's activities. It is also determined by the roles the members expect to play. There is a strong tendency at first for group members to expect to be highly dependent on the therapist and to look to him or her for direction, but member coleaders can emerge from the group fairly early.

Reciprocity in group therapy moves from the positive nonreciprocity of the opening session, where members express themselves superficially and usually disregard each other, to elementary positive reciprocity by which the members make parallel statements, sometimes on related topics, and take some notice of what others are saying in their effort to help the group get started.

The first session of a group of women senior citizens meeting at a community center began by the members making comments that had little to do with what the previous member had said. It was remarkable that these women, many of whom knew each other, could ignore one another so completely when they sat down in a formal group meeting. Persons present talked about areas of concern to themselves, such as a dying husband, how to celebrate the upcoming holiday, pulling down shades in an apartment to prevent exposure, search for a man, how well one of their mothers had handled old age, and fear on the streets. No one, except the group leader, offered support or verbally expressed interest in what the others were saying. They did show, however, some elementary reciprocity when they listened intently to what was being said.

In the next session, the members began to pay more attention to what each person was saying and focused on the conflict between the generations. Members showed their common dilemma by giving examples of negative encounters with younger people in the community. Social reciprocity was established when they remained with one topic, sharing incidents when their rights had been violated and when they had been insulted. It was evident early on that a particular theory of being old, based on their personal experiences, could be developed by the members. They had been called "old" and on occasion told to "go to an old age home." A theory was tentatively formulated to encourage members to listen more closely to what each was saying. It was proposed that the rejection they experienced made them very angry and this led to direct confrontation between themselves and people in their neighborhoods when specific incidents had occurred. A member proclaimed "But we don't know each other," indicating that the theorizing was premature, and the group needed to know the total person who happened to pull down her shades when afraid, or who shouted at her neighbors when they appeared to be critical of her.

An atmosphere of isolation and apprehension is created when the members remain hesitant, aloof, and avoid making any comments. The therapist can help the group over this hurdle by encouraging participation, often by soliciting the assistance of a member who is more ready to become involved. Silent anger should become spoken anger so that the meaning and implications for the group can be dealt with. If not redirected, this may progress to angry exchanges pertaining to socially sanctioned topics that warrant anger, such as remarks made by the members against working toward sharing ("It's none of my business what you do!"). If unchecked, this may further develop into more personalized attacks. Under proper direction, this can move to a positive reciprocity as the therapist helps members to establish group norms that foster self-expression, listening, and accepting. The group can utilize negative outbursts constructively when basic acceptance and efforts at understanding have become the established norms.

Negative exchange does not usually occur early in the life of the group. When it does occur, usually not before the third meeting, it can mean that the group members are making significant movements toward one another. The members usually become annoyed with the therapist for not telling them what to do and not directly "curing" them. The content of the actual message exchanged is probably less important than the experiences of the interaction that help establish the group as an entity. Negative reciprocity is most likely to occur between individuals who have strong reactions because they associate each other with significant persons in their lives (transferences).[44]

All groups experience antinurturant as well as nurturant forces. Occasionally, the movement away from or against the others is self-protective. An example of negative unilateral action is a member deliberately ignoring another, and that person not responding to this. This can be a way of preventing the other from being ignored first. Not responding to aggression can also be a withdrawal, a refusal to get involved. The more personalized the attack (i.e., the more the person's overall view of himself or herself is involved), the more likely that there will be an interchange of verbal attacks. If negative reciprocity proceeds unimpeded without some efforts at understanding what is happening, there is little likelihood for a therapeutic outcome. It is also unlikely that extremely negative behavior will develop in a therapy group, for the therapist and other members uphold norms that prohibit such extremes. Although hostility and aggression are useful in identifying barriers to mutual aid and understanding, they are too frightening and destructive if they occur in the beginning session. This prevents the formation of the therapeutic climate, essential for dealing with such manifestations. When the group has reached an advanced stage of solidarity, it can usually tolerate such reactions and use them to move the group toward greater understanding and the exploration of new ways of exchanging nurturance.

A typical early appearance of negative nonreciprocity occurred in a group of four women and one man who had been discharged from a state hospital and were meeting weekly in a community group. One woman dominated the group, talking frequently, interpreting what others said, and finally demanding to know what the group cotherapists were going to do for her. She rejected the leaders and tried to demonstrate what she thought they ought to be doing. It took the group and the cotherapists some time to offer the member, striking out and apparently attempting to dominate, the needed evidence that the members and the cotherapists were ready to try to understand and respond, although it was not clear how this was going to happen. By the third session, she felt she was beginning to "belong" and expressed concern and interest in the other members and the co-therapists. Her initial behavior had helped the group move rapidly into cooperative efforts and created an early cohesiveness. The initial impulse to reject the aggressive member was tabled as everyone accepted that she was reaching out almost wildly to everyone, albeit negatively, and the question was how to reach out to her.

Nurturance may be seen as occurring at five levels. Level 1 is a nonreciprocal relationship where one nurtures a mostly passive, receiving other. This level ordinarily does not occur in group therapy but may characterize the reactions of members to very withdrawn group members who, ostensibly, do not appear to respond. At Level 2, the recipient of the nurturance responds minimally. A frequent Level 2 reaction is the nonverbal response, such as a smile or positive gesture of a member in response to the efforts of other members to draw him or her out. Elementary reciprocity is not egalitarian when the members are assuming a cotherapist role in relation to a particular member. A more egalitarian elementary reaction occurs when members casually note each other's presence, nod recognition, and pay keen attention when any one of them speaks, each taking a turn expressing himself or herself. Social patterns of exchange characterize Level 3, where the give and take is socially prescribed for given situations and acceptable social roles are taken on; this may be based on equal or unequal status of the participants. This level often deals with general social cliches such as greetings, exchanges about general matters of interest, and the giving of impersonal information. If someone is accepted as an expert, for instance as a teacher or an experienced group member, he or she may assume higher status in the group at this level. At Level 4, democratic conditions prevail, the participants are equal, and exchange is personalized. It forms the heart of the therapeutic group and includes emotional and perceptual exchanges leading to changed views, attitudes, and behaviors. Level 5 is an in-depth reciprocity in which the involvement of the group in the uniqueness of each individual member is paramount; the barriers of self are transcended and nurturance potentials are released, thus exposing the core of each member. This is an advanced form of reciprocity that does not occur in all therapy groups. It is associated with peak and uncanny experiences in which the individual members experience each other fully and awarenesses merge. Because of its intensity and norm-transcending qualities, it is short-lived but may have enduring effects.

In any active session, negative forms of these levels appear and give substance for working on the barriers that block exchanges of information, perceptions, and caring. Tables 1–1 and 1–2 show the levels of negative and positive reciprocity that develop in groups. Whereas one level is apt to characterize a group at any particular time, there is usually movement between levels during one session. Some time after the second session, it is likely that negative social roles will appear: members may express "opposition" to the leader or demand accountability from the leader or others in the group. When negative levels do not occur, it is highly likely that little group process is taking place.

Under proper guidance, the working out of negative reactions provides the basis for positive reciprocity. For instance, when Fred finds Tom revolting because he uses four letter words frequently and Tom sees Fred equally as unbearable because he is very polite, the group helps them perceive the artificialities that surround their persons and that somewhere beneath these behavioral facades lies the person. Frequently an intense exchange of hostility is the result of global transferences[45] which are primary instruments of the therapeutic process in groups. First and foremost, the task of the therapy group is to clear the rubble on the surface that blocks the entrance to

TABLE 1-1. LEVELS OF POSITIVE RECIPROCITY

Level	Reciprocity[a]	Nurturance
1	Not present	One shares, tries to help; the other does not respond
2	Elementary	Persons respond to each other minimally
3	Social	Prescribed social roles
4	Therapeutic	Personalized exchange
5	Transcendency of self	In-depth exchange: unity and solidarity

[a]At Levels 2 and 3 the exchanges may be asymmetrical or democratic. At Levels 4 and 5 there is equal exchange between the participants.

TABLE 1-2. LEVELS OF NEGATIVE RECIPROCITY

Level	Reciprocity[a]	Nurturance
1	Not present	One ignores another; other does not react
2	Elementary	Superficial rejection
3	Social	Prescribed disapproval and rejection based on social codes
4	Rejection	Personalized disapproval and rejection
5	Destruction	Highly personalized exchange of hostility and hatred

[a]At Levels 2 and 3 the exchanges may be asymmetrical or democratic. At Levels 4 and 5 they are democratic.

the world of the person who lives below. The underparts are the sources of the therapeutic and in-depth reciprocal exchanges that can relocate lost persons and enrich lives.

CONCLUSIONS

Nurturance occurs in interactions between people. The earliest experiences of the child are of nonreciprocal nurturance. Elementary forms of reciprocity begin when the child starts to respond. As the child, or the less powerful person, is able to have more direct impact on the exchange, the process becomes increasingly reciprocal. When the interaction is between people equal in power and status, an egalitarian give and take is possible. This is the precondition for achieving intense mutual caring and peak experiences.

Altruism and social roles help group members to begin to accept and help each other. An elementary, positive reciprocity occurs when people are affected by each other's presence and reactions. Socially reciprocal relationships are achieved when this develops into an ongoing interaction on a socially sanctioned level. These include listening, helping clarify what is being said, sharing, and reflecting. Groups move beyond this when knowledge of each member and genuine caring and understanding lead to experiencing what it is like to be the other.

Accepted, prescribed roles protect us from fears of isolation, but reliable sources of nurturance cannot depend solely on social roles, for, not only do they change, they also end. Nurturance in professional nursing practice is most often at the elementary reciprocal level and provides formal support, sometimes at the nonreciprocal level, to clients unable to take care of themselves. The orientation, planning, and intervention phases of nursing can achieve various levels of reciprocity.

Nurturance in groups occurs at five levels: from nonreciprocal relationships in which one participant does not respond, to in-depth mutually reciprocal interchanges in which members are able to appreciate the uniqueness of each one. Negative group exchanges also occur at five different levels: from one person simply ignoring another to a highly personalized exchange of hostility and hatred. They give needed substance for working on the barriers that interfere with the members opening up and knowing each other.

NOTES

1. Horney, K. (1937). *The neurotic personality of our time.* New York: W. W. Norton & Co., Inc., p. 107.
2. Ibid., p. 110.
3. Kahler, E. (1961). *Man the measure.* New York: George Braziller, pp. 11–12.
4. Wispe, L. (Ed.). (1978). *Altruism, sympathy and helping: Psychological and sociological principles.* New York: Academic Press.
5. Trivers, R. (1971). The evolution of reciprocal altruism. *Quarterly Review of Biology,* 46:35–7. Garrett, H. (1971). *The limits of altruism.* Bloomington: Indiana University Press.
6. Gouldner, A. W. The norm of reciprocity: A preliminary statement. *American Sociological Review,* 25:172–3.
7. Marx, K. (1953). *Die Fruhschriften.* Stuttgart: Alfred Kroner Verlag, pp. 300–1; translated and quoted by Fromm, E. (1955). *The sane society.* New York: Holt, Rinehart, & Winston, p. 132.
8. Hobhouse, L.T. (1925). *Morals in evolution.* New York: Holt, Rinehart, & Winston, p. 61.
9. Ibid., p. 62.
10. Gouldner, A. W., op. cit., p. 162.
11. Parsons, T., & Shils, E. A., (1952). *Toward a general theory of action.* Cambridge, Mass.: Harvard University Press, pp. 105–6.
12. Harris, M. (1979). *Cultural materialism.* New York: Random House, p. 176.
13. Simmel, G. (1966). The spatial relations of social forms. In N. J. Spykman (Ed.), *The social theory of Georg Simmel.* New York: Atherton Press, pp. 144–6.
14. Gouldner, op. cit., p. 172.
15. Ibid., pp. 166–7.
16. Harris, M., op. cit., p. 173.
17. May, R. (1953). *Man's search for himself.* New York: W. W. Norton & Co., Inc.
18. Ibid.
19. Sorokin, P. A. (1947). *Society, culture, and personality.* New York: Harper & Brothers, p. 44.
20. See discussion on spontaneity in Chapter 4 under Moreno.
21. Discussed further in Chapter 3.
22. Le Bon, G. (1960/1895). *The crowd.* New York: Viking.
23. Fuentes, A., & Ehrenreich, B., (1983, August). The new factory. *Multinational Monitor* 4:5–9.

24. Foulkes, S. H., & Anthony, E. J. (1965). *Group psychotherapy*. Baltimore, Md.: Penguin Books, p. 42.
25. Mead, G. H. (1934). *Mind, self, & society*. Chicago: University of Chicago Press, pp. 152–64.
26. Shibutani, T. (1962). Reference groups and social control. In A. M. Rose (Ed.), *Human behavior and processes*. Boston, Mass.: Houghton Mifflin, p. 141.
27. Ibid., p. 142.
28. Burke, K. (1965). *Permanence and change*. New York: Bobbs-Merrill, p. 125.
29. Goffman, E. (1961). *Encounters*. Indianapolis, Ind.: Bobbs-Merrill, pp. 85–152.
30. Leininger, M. (1973). Humanistic issues in mental health nursing. In M. Leininger (Ed.), *Contemporary Issues in Mental Health Nursing*. Boston, Mass.: Little, Brown, p. 168.
31. Leininger, M. (1978). *Transcultural nursing: A new and scientific subfield of study in nursing*. New York: Wiley, p. 13.
32. Ibid., p. 35.
33. Ibid., p. 37.
34. Morris, W. (Ed.) (1973). *The american heritage dictionary of the english language*. Boston, Mass.: American Heritage Publishing & Houghton Mifflin, p. 203.
35. Thass-Thienemann, T. (1973). *The Interpretation of language* (Vol. 2). New York: Jason Aronson, pp. 41, 123.
36. Thass-Thienemann found that from these words the verbs to think were derived. The Latin verb pensare, which means to think, also means "nursing, feeding, fostering, taking care." The French verb, penser, which means to think, also was the source of the word, panser, which means "to care, to dress." The French verb, savoir, to know, also "refers to the internalized image of the 'Nursing Mother.' "
37. Ibid., p. 240.
38. Orem, D. E. (1980). *Nursing: Concepts of practice* (2nd ed.). New York: McGraw-Hill.
39. Peplau, H. E. (1952). *Interpersonal relations in nursing*. New York: G. P. Putnam p. 19.
40. Ibid., p. 32.
41. Ibid., pp. 51–2.
42. Maslow, A. H. (1970). *Religions, values, and peak-experiences*. New York: Viking Press.
43. Hoffman, J. (1975). *Marxism and the theory of praxis*. New York: International Publishers p. 17.
44. See Chapter 3 for discussion of transferences.
45. See Chapter 4 for discussion of global transferences.

2

Origins of Nurturance

The potency of the nurturance exchange in the therapy group can be diminished by prejudiced views of its nature and origin. It is a complex phenomenon which includes all giving and receiving, all passive and active acts between people. Links of nurturance qualities to women, who have been the prototypical nurturers, have distorted its universality and therapeutic possibilities.

HUMAN POTENTIAL

There is an innate reservoir of nurturance potentials that all people possess. This nurturance core is the source of early attachments and adaptations. Its potency rests on these two features: its value as a source of support, caring, and security, and its reinforcing qualities for moulding any other behaviors.

The inherent capacity of a group of children to build their own nurturing systems is demonstrated by six preschool-aged children who were moved together from one concentration camp to another when they had lost their parents shortly after they were born in Nazi Germany. Anna Freud and Sophie Dann were in contact with these children when they came to be housed in a nursery in England at the age of three. They reported that the children showed toward each other "a warmth and spontaneity which is unheard of in ordinary relations between young contemporaries. . . ."[1] They had the strongest feeling for each other, but cared very little for anyone else. They were very uneasy if anyone of the group was absent for even a few minutes.[2] For these little children, a maturity of support and caring for each other emerged from the extraordinary circumstances of having been together without a constant adult to rely upon almost from birth.

Contemporary theories of instincts assume that the social setting affects which instincts will develop, which will remain dormant, and how they will manifest themselves. Nevertheless, Fletcher viewed the sexual instinct as primarily organically rooted and less subject to the effects of learning, whereas the social instinct was associated with the unraveling of the interpersonal and the symbolic.[3] In Fletcher's schema, the social instinct represents our proclivity to attach ourselves to a group and to develop deep-rooted feelings of belonging to a certain place and a certain social tradition, while the sexual instinct includes nursing, fondling, breast feeding, playing and caring for the child. It seems obvious that these two concepts are united in the nurturance phenomenon, only one refers to reactions of the infant and the other to people in general.[4]

I believe that the nurturance core is more basic than the unbridled antisocial aggressive forces in Freud's id or pleasure principle that reside primarily in the unconscious or background of awareness. In Freud's view, however, loving and caring are not inborn, as he thought aggression is, but rather social developments made possible by moral values transmitted to the child by the parents. He saw them as adaptive processes that help prevent the eruption of innate antisocial tendencies emanating from the pleasure principle. To him love is the "great teacher" that builds ego and superego functions, for he believed that the human being learns because of "love for those nearest" to him or her.[5] He hypothesized that the capacity to nurture is derived from the internalization of the ego ideal. In his formulation, a nurturance need is not the driving force behind human development and society. Instead Freud singled out the aggressive instinct as the predominant force.

Refuting the notion of innate aggression that Freud hypothesized resides in the pleasure principle, Thompson considered aggression a learned behavior, a reaction to the wish for nurturance thwarted. She commented that, if destructiveness and violence "are to be understood, they must rather be dealt with as reactions to being obstructed in living."[6] In a similiar vein, Fraiberg identified the lack of bonding as the forerunner of adult aggression and noted that "the potential for violence and destructive acts was far greater among—bondless men and women. . . ."[7] In refuting the notion that the restraint of the pleasure principle is foremost in social development, the British psychiatrist, Ivan Suttie, saw social behavior as derived from the early forms of play.[8] Miller and Dollard substituted the reinforcement principle for the pleasure principle, thus also using the need for nurturance as the impetus for building effective behavior patterns.[9]

Murray distinguished 20 manifest needs. Seven of these represent core aspects of nurturance because they have to do with giving or receiving sympathy and gratification, participating in social activities and erotic relationships, and generally enjoying reciprocal relationships with others. He called them acceptance, affiliation, assistance, nurturance, play, sex, and surrorance; he did not recognize that they constitute part of a central core of nurturance needs.[10,11]

A wide range of derived needs appears as socialization takes place. Some of these are learned ways of avoiding nurturance possibilities because extremely negative experiences have thwarted its fulfillment. Examples of these reactions are avoidance, apathy, fantasy, seclusion, and narcissism. Learned reactions that engage others and have as their objective to actively move away or to passively submit include abasement, aggression, dominance, exhibition, and rejection. Finally, learned socially positive reactions are ways of experiencing nurturance in culturally acceptable ways, and they include achievement, altruism, conformity, flexibility, and understanding.[12] It is important to note that asocial reactions such as fantasy and seclusion can also be the base for creative reactions and, therefore, have their place in the life of the fully developed person. It is only when these activities severely impede opportunities for nurturance exchanges that they become harmful.[13] (See Figure 2–1.[14])

Maslow viewed self-actualization as the highest level of need.[15] It is dependent upon deep, reciprocal relationships. The needs for belonging and esteem call for mutual arrangements and exchanges. Physiologic and safety needs can be met in mutual support of one individual by another or one group by another, but they also are met in the unilateral support of an independent person for another person who is more dependent. Those who have fulfilled their needs for belonging and self-actualization are more likely to be ready to help others. Those still struggling for basic survival usually seek support from others.[16]

Faith and trust are central to Erickson's schema of life stages. Early parenting meets the baby's nurturance needs and gives the child a basis for developing trust and eventually a self-identity. In this way, there is conveyed to the child the importance of caring and loving.[17] This becomes distorted if the child's nurturance needs are not met and excessive regulations are imposed.

Our capacity to express nurturance grows throughout life and slowly increases in complexity as we begin to know different kinds of people under different circumstances. During adolescence, nurturance experiences become a range of exchanges with peers, adults, and younger children. In young adulthood, intimacy and isolation become central themes. We seek to exchange our very selves with another and thus achieve unity and a new identity. This will be affected by the capacity to make "significant sacrifices and commitments" that can only be made if we have been able to establish a fairly solid concept of self.[18] At this time, we are eager and willing to enter partnerships and make ethical commitments.[19]

During our early years, we depend on the nurturing climate of the

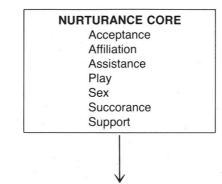

NURTURANCE CORE
Acceptance
Affiliation
Assistance
Play
Sex
Succorance
Support

DERIVED NEEDS (Examples)		
Social		Asocial
Positive	Negative	
Achievement	Abasement	Avoidance
Altruism	Aggression	Apathy
Conformity	Dominance	Fantasy
Flexibility	Exhibition	Seclusion
Understanding	Rejection	Narcissism

Figure 2-1. The constellation of nurturance needs as core. Inadequate fulfillment of nurturance needs leads to the establishment of derived needs which are predominantly culturally determined. Thus the superstructure of needs that society fosters are presented as alternate means of attaining basic nurturance. Terms used are based on some of Murray's formulations of manifest and latent needs and internal factors.[14] However, he did not use the terms altruism, conformity, and flexibility.

family. Later, in puberty and adolescence, we seek support from our peers in groups and dyads. The elderly, often disengaged from work and responsibilities for others, are the most free to practice unconditioned loving as well as to continue to work on refining self and developing new nurturance potentials. We experience ideal and inadequate nurturance throughout life. Ideally, we receive unconditioned nurturance in infancy, learn to incorporate the image of the nurturer, are able to carry out nurturing behaviors, form reciprocally nurturing relationships with peers, and, in adulthood, are able to form in-depth relationships, engage in a wide variety of nurturance exchanges, and refine the self in accordance with our exchanges with others (see Table 2–1).

When nurturance is not adequately given, a child may continue to seek it into the later childhood years. The accounts of the children's difficulties, presented by parents meeting in group sessions, suggested a relationship between inadequate nurturing and the learning problem.

TABLE 2-1. IDEAL AND INADEQUATE FORMS OF NURTURANCE THROUGH THE LIFESPAN

Age	Ideal Form	Inadequate Form
Infancy	Unconditioned loving parental figure: rapidly growing, responsive	Discontinuous loving parental figure; slow growth and responsiveness, learns nurturance uncertain
Preschool childhood	Parent nurtures by helping child to learn rules; by learning child shows love	Rigid rules imposed, over-regulates self in fear of loss of love
Early elementary school	Parental image incorporated; child offers support and caring on own	Parental image insufficiently incorporated; difficulty caring
Later school	Peer sharing and caring; learning is source of nurturance	Relating to peers via aggression, competition; problems learning
Adolescence	Nurturing peer groups	Antisocial peer groups or isolation
Young adult	Uniting of self with another	Relating to another at superficial level
Adult	Wide variety of sharing and caring	Sharing limited; relates via aggression and manipulation; limited caring for infant
Senior citizen	Unconditioned loving of others; caring for self refined	Limited sharing; incomplete acceptance of others; limited trust

An adaptation of Erickson's concept of nuclear life conflicts for the purpose of identifying nurturance components.[20]

In one instance, the mother of Richard, a 9-year old of average intelligence, described his dilemma in the learning situation. "He bursts into tears when he can't read the word. I try to help him relax." When asked what about reading upset him so, she replied, "Richard says he can't read it. He cries and says he can't do it." When asked, "What do you do. What happens before he cries and gets upset?" She explained, "I tell him I could read when I was in the second grade and he is now in the fifth grade and can't read. Then he starts to cry." Was he afraid of learning to read because, if he succeeded, he would never be able to receive the primary nurturance that younger children get, or after he had given it his all, was he thrown into a hold pattern because his mother's withdrawal would have been too devastasting?

A mother of 11 children stated outright that her Nicholas, a 10-year-old boy of average intelligence wanted her attention too much. Dividing her mothering among her 11 children had been a real problem. This was having a seriously negative effect on the development of Nicholas. She said, "Nicholas wants attention. His teacher has too many children and can't give it. He sits in school and does nothing." When a comparison was made between the large number of siblings and the large number of classmates, the mother said, "But he wants all my attention. I think each child should help the other . . . When he came, I felt

I had to accept assistance by my oldest girl, but he wouldn't take it. He wants my attention. By the time Nicholas came, I was tired and wasn't able to give as much attention." Then she gave another source of Nicholas' frustration. "I also have to give so much attention to my little boy who has polio."

An inadequate experience of nurturance can have serious effects. The base for developing mutual relationships with others is then missing and the struggle to achieve them is doomed to failure. Even once developed, they can be lost and then there is a struggle to regain them. Erickson observed that "the attempt to recover social mutuality" is evident in adults who develop schizoid and depressive states.[21] The objective of most therapies is to facilitate such a recovery.

Occasionally, social mutuality through solidarity is incorporated into group rituals, often taking the form of initiation and rites-of-passage ceremonies. This is usually institutionalized at a symbolic level. For instance, symbolic group murder (e.g., in Haitian voodoo, an animal is sacrificed to the gods by the group) is a way of establishing solidarity with a powerful god.[22] Freud considered the sacrificial animal a substitute for the father. Thus the destructive ritual can also be symbolic of rejecting controls from above, and the beginning of shared, and more democratic controls among peers. This theory applies to treatment groups, for most groups need to "destroy" the therapist in order to achieve such control.

Fixed modes of relating and control by power groups interfere with the development of a universalistic group consciousness and nurturance exchange. The stratification of people into higher and lower status prevents an egalitarian reciprocity between classes and places the majority into unequal and inferior positions. Davis and Moore believed, however, that social inequity was inevitable because certain positions in any society require talented people who have had special training, and nobody will want to undertake the sacrifices associated with getting the training unless they can expect to achieve privilege and higher status.[23] Many others do not consider social inequity and stratification as inevitable. Tumin considered stratification destructive because it produces an unequal sense of significance and an unfair predominance of unfavorable self-images among the lower class.[24]

Sorokin identified sensate and ideational cultural mentalities that emphasize different forms of nurturance. Sensate people are able to accept "transcient values" and experience a "full-blooded sense of life, joy and grief."[25] They are likely to have democratic relationships and enjoy reciprocal nurturance. In contrast, people with the ideational orientation are detached. When active, they seek to reform the world "along the lines of the spiritual reality."[26] This is likely to be a compensatory striving for a nurturing world that they feel they lack or have lost. Also, they emphasize past values and authoritarian or parental forms of nurturance.

It is the flexible sensate mentality that has the potential for fitting Habermans's vision of a "universalistic ego structure" that can fulfill the needs for meaning and authentic love in a complex society. The emphasis is on the replacement of the self-centered identity of the past with a "universal reciprocity" that transcends the self. This view anticipates the development of a more humane and caring world.[27]

SEXUAL BASIS OF NURTURANCE TRAITS

Nurturance has been discredited as a passive process and a feminine function. The tie of the masculine to the active and feminine to the passive is based on the notion that gender determines behavior. Shainess has challenged the passive–nurturance connection. Whereas nurturance is a natural and essential feature in human societies, passivity is neither natural nor a state that should prevail for any length of time. As a matter of fact, a persistent passive mode of being is pathological; growth and creativity can take place only in an active person. At a somewhat concrete level, it is apparent that the female can be as active in seeking to be penetrated as the male is active in seeking to penetrate.[28] Fried also reasserted the basic need for activeness and attacked the myth of female passivity.[29] Nurturance can be actively given or passively received, and a ready assortment of both forms would seem desirable. At any one time, an individual could be mostly active or passive, whether male or female, but most enduring relationships involve alternating as well as sharing these action modes.

A dynamic view of human potential assumes that "active and passive are forces that function in harmony with one another and that they are totally interrelated, like the tides and the moon."[30] Fromm went so far as to think of "penetrating" another as the way of discovering the other as well as discovering the self. The penetrating person, however, isolated from the person being penetrated, engages primarily in a biophysical event. Without mutual exchange between the participants, the sexual act, like any other interaction, is self-indulgent and exploitive.

Exaggerated loving roles and those that have been characterized by aggression have become stereotyped as female and male. This confuses the fact that we all are nurtured and learn to nurture, and that we all learn how to be aggressive. The overwhelming number of adults do not assume predominantly nurturant or aggressive roles continuously or for very long periods of time, just as they are neither introverted or extroverted continuously.

The placement of nurturance and aggression on two different scales permits a more realistic assessment of nurturance behavior in both sexes. If aggression and nurturance are considered dualistic behaviors rather than at opposite ends of a bipolar scale, it is possible for an individual to be high on both or low on both. When aggression is viewed as determined by circumstances, it is possible to account for the same individual being aggressive in one situation and nurturant in another.

Spence and Helmreich demonstrated that men and women who have high levels of both traditionally male and female traits also have higher self-esteem. Previously, it had been thought that the androgynous person, characterized by having an array of masculine and feminine characteristics, was rare. We know this not to be true. There is, however, much "role playing and self-deception" by both sexes as we live out our lives along prescribed roles that sometimes violate our potentials and preferred ways of being and behaving.[31]

A study based on a Preference Inventory indicated there still remains a tendency for young women to be significantly more interested in nurturing behavior than young men. These differences were most marked in relation to child care and activities involving psychological support. Nevertheless, interest in giving physical care and assistance to the disabled and distressed was not significantly different. A person's major area of study (business, liberal arts, or technical subjects such as engineering) appeared to make no difference, but interest in nurturing activities, based on cross-sectional samples, tended to become progressively lower as students spent more time in college.[32] Perhaps as people become more attuned to scientific paradigms, there is a lessening of altruism and compassion. Becker and Geer found that medical students lose their idealism during the 4 years of medical school. Although as freshmen, the students were filled with the desire to help and understand their client, they were preoccupied with techniques and had become cynical by the time they reached their fourth year.[33]

The division of traits between the sexes occurs early. Bardwick observed that boys are required to give up dependent behavior earlier than girls. Moreover, she thinks they are less accepted by adults because of their "impulsive, aggressive" behavior. Since, however, girls present more approved reactions, they "have less need to look within themselves for rewards and esteem, and they continue to depend upon others for feelings of esteem. Compared with boys, there is a delay in the girl's development of an independent sense of self."[34] Consistent with this reasoning, a girl's compliant behavior entitles her to greater nurturance and , as a result of this, she has no need to struggle for independence. In other words, boys receive conditioned nurturance based on how they behave whereas girls receive what amounts to unconditional nurturance because they tend to behave well almost always. Nevertheless, it is far more likely that the nurturance from the parent of the same sex becomes the model for the girl's behavior. It could be that mothers nurture boys less and boys thus take the hint that such behavior has nothing to do with them. Kagan noted that mothers spend more time talking to female infants.[35]

Chodorow believed that feminine characteristics, which include nurturance and dependency, were born in the so-called preoedipal years, probably the first 3 years, as were also the masculine characteristics, which include aggression, dominance, and autonomy. She observed that

> A boy must learn his gender identity as being not-female, or not-mother . . . therefore it becomes important to men to have a clear sense of gender difference, of what is masculine and what is feminine, and to maintain rigid boundaries between these . . . Boys and men come to deny the feminine identification within themselves and those feelings they experience as feminine: feelings of dependency, relational needs, emotions generally.[36]

Because the male identity is based on a struggle to develop a "me" and "not me" distinction, he is then more apt to develop a sense of autonomy and an experience of separateness from the mother. The female, on the other hand, develops a less fixed "me" and "not me." She has no problem with the "I" that is continuous with, and similiar to the mother. Her problem begins when it becomes negative to be a female in the society in which she lives and when the mother is conflicted about her mothering and femininity. Chodorow described men and women as not qualitatively different, but rather that gender was "processual, reflective, and constructed." To see men and women as significantly different kinds of people, she held, was "to reify and deny *relations* of gender, to see gender differences as permanent rather than created and situated."[37]

A number of studies with monkeys and baboons indicate that the sexual basis for nurturance is doubtful. Williams summarized a wide range of animal studies on sex differences that point to environmental influences.[38] For instance, maternal behavior was directed toward litters of pups by both male and virgin female adults whose gonads had been removed.[39] After being given several fresh litters of pups, some males' aggressiveness was replaced by nurturing behavior.[40] When a preadolescent rhesus monkey is paired with a monkey of the opposite sex, the females are more nurturant and the males very much hostile toward infants.[41] Nevertheless, males will be nurturant if the females are absent.[42] Male baboons seem to be instinctively nurturant.[43]

Maccoby and Jacklin's review of studies of sex differences in behavior reveals the lack of evidence that nurturance is innately a female trait.[44] Thirty one studies of helping and donating to charity behavior, and 14 sharing behavior studies were reviewed. Of eight findings dealing with directly helping and supporting another child, two indicated that girls (ages four and five) were more helpful: in four there were no differences between girls and boys. In 66 studies of aggression in children, 94 findings were reported. Of these, 52 showed more aggression in the male, whereas 37 indicated no differences between the sexes. The remainder found greater aggressiveness in the female. Girls seem to "have a great deal of information about aggression that they may never put into practice." They summa-

rized their survey of research on attachment, affiliation, and positive reaction by concluding that there is 'surprisingly little sex difference . . . the
picture that emerged is one of high 'sociability' in both sexes."[45] It was
suggested that boys tend to associate more often with larger groups in which
dominant behavior is more likely to occur, and that girls prefer small groups
where they do not have to compete.

Whiting and Pope also reported that girls, ages three to six in six different cultures, tend to show more help-giving behavior than boys of the same
age, but the differences are small and insignificant. Among older children,
ages seven to eleven and more influenced by their culture, there is significantly more helping, as well as emotional support, offered by girls. Hartup
and Kellner's work demonstrated a *reciprocal system* in helping behavior in
which there were no sex differences in giving affection, help, or reassurance
in children ages three to four. They stated "It is worth noting that the children
who most often gave help and affection to others were the same children who
most often *asked* for help and affection from others—in other words, helping
behavior was part of a reciprocal system. The nurturance-giving children,
however, were significantly *unlikely* to engage in the more passive form of
proximity seeking, that is, simply remaining close to others. Thus, help giving
is distinctly not a passive process."[46]

Clearly, the interaction of biology and environment is the only acceptable explanation for the development of nurturance and aggression, but it is
the environment about which we can do something. What turns out to be
male behavior in one society can turn out to be female behavior in another,
and, in still another, it may be equally practiced by males and females alike.
The rigidification of what we are permitted to do on account of our gender
is reflected in sexual confusions in persons with serious behavioral problems.
Generalized difficulty in functioning is often first manifested in this sensitive
area.

Sex Roles in the Therapy Group

In the early stages and periodically later on, the therapy group serves as the
locus for unconditional acceptance, attachment to others, and the building
of primary contacts. It has been likened to the cultural image of the mother
in its capacity to give elementary support and to be a source of identity.[47]
The early support and cohesiveness of the therapy group has been considered similiar to the unconditional love received during infancy.[48]

This fantasy of eternal love is aptly described by a young Korean
woman, who fantasied a mother whom she had never seen. She said,
"Surely she would be the most beautiful and unselfish woman . . . My
mother lived in the framework of my longing love, more vividly than if I had
been familiar with every line of her face, and I became always lonesome for
her. I thought of her when I was very hungry or cold."[49]

The search for unconditioned nurturance and the paradise lost[50] may be
one of the forces behind the hope for a future ideal society. It is based on

the hopes for a loving parental figure that is blind to "good" and "bad" behavior and accepts all as equally lovable.[51] Timelessness or eternity has been associated with feminine archetypical forms by Jung[52] and with the sacred by De Chardin. The latter regarded the feminine as a mode of perception that illuminates the universe and gives unity to life. He said it gives us "a consciousness of being one with the cosmos in a dynamic passive–active relationship."[53] In contrast, paternal nurturance has been associated with achievement, discovery, and new awarenesses. It is conditioned and withheld until some visible accomplishment is attained. It is dependent on our ability to work and gain status by adapting ourselves to the dilemmas of the past, present, and future.[54] To use nurturance in group therapy effectively, these versions of nurturance need to be desexualized and accepted as variants of the same phenomenon.

Our sexual identity influences how we lead therapy groups as well as how we behave in other groups. Although male therapists are apt to be more nurturant than other males, they are not likely to consider themselves nurturant. As mentioned earlier, it is apparent that nurturance is rejected as a prime therapeutic agent because of its association with females and early childhood rearing. Some female therapists also reject it because of its connection with inferior status and because adherence to masculine-oriented theories of behavior and therapy appears scientific, professional, and, most of all, is more "respectable."

Sexual identity affects how male and female cotherapists develop groups together, how therapists interact with male and female group members, and how male and female members interact with each other. Some therapy groups serve to retain sexual stereotypes and prejudices because the members and the therapist have not examined the insidious pressures of sexism on their personal lives. This may be considered not a personal matter, but a social issue that does not belong on the therapy group's agenda. Nevertheless, sexual prejudices and myths enter the group's themes, fantasies, and interactions. Of vital importance is that, without analysis of the sexual roles and their relation to the division of labor in the group, what is happening in the group may not be fully understood.

For instance, a group member in great conflict over her homosexual tendencies can be the impetus for the group to get to know each other's clashes with social standards and appreciate the social restrictions and rigidities that exist. One method the members might use is to increase their awarenesses of their own experiences with behavioral restrictions and to determine how these pressures can be diminished. Another approach would be to accept the community prejudices and concentrate on understanding and supporting the individual's attempt to adapt to social "reality." For feminist and radical therapists, the latter would be considered a "cop out." Group members often seek to increase their behavioral versatility, and group therapists need to have experimented with many possible ways of behaving and not be bogged down by sexual and social stereotypes.

In the therapy group, the total acceptance of all members becomes the therapeutic force that propels members and therapist forward to new experiences and personal and social growth. We move from unconditional nurturance to conditioned nurturance that becomes the passageway to gain once again unconditioned nurturance, but this time in the mature form that can occur between adults.

Identification with power, predominant male behavior, or personality determinants may lead to nonnurturant, aggressive probing tactics in the therapy session. This may be true of a member as well as the therapist. It may appear under the guise of trying to know someone or through a false notion of the way a person "lets others in." This happens when one or more members relentlessly pursue one aspect of a member's life demanding information and clarity despite the member's evident reluctance to disclose more. It can be an attack even though it is also a way of getting to know someone. It is consistent with the "scientific" method of getting at significant empirical data as soon as possible and regardless of cost to the "subject." The asking of focused, probing questions may seem clever, even brilliant. This might be so in a court room, but not in therapy. Probing is associated with the disciplinary actions of parents, teachers, and bosses. It may increase a member's critical examination of self, but in all probability reinforces his or her inferior, subordinate status in the scheme of things. To produce therapeutic encounters, seeking personal information has to be a caring, supportive endeavor, not a destructive and malevolent assault on the person's values, purposes, and sanity. Each person does this in his or her own way. A barometer to measure the quality of our inquiries of others is to ask ourselves: Why am I asking this question? How much do I really care about this person? Am I really interested in knowing more about this person? Am I asking the right kind of question for someone who doesn't know this person and is uncertain whether I can or will care about this person? Is my questioning aimed at satisfying my curiosity or at humiliating this person? Does the revelation of "secrets" or "sins" by someone else make me feel superior?

NURTURANCE IN SOCIAL CONTRACTS

Nurturance may be provided by arrangement. Although the family is the medium in which giving and exchanging nurturance is intense and has continuity, contractual relationships are limited in duration and intensity, and are "directed to getting either mutually some pleasure or service or profit or utility from the other party or even to getting as much as possible for as little as possible . . . the contractual relationship is inseparable from a great deal of freedom of each party from the other. . ."[55] The familial relationship is more apt to be tied to absolutes than not, to keeping relationships permanent and continuous rather than reaching out to new and different relationships. The individual and his or her ego are illusion, a surface phenomenon.

"The reality is the total 'we' of all the participants . . . All are one, and one is a part of all . . . if an individual tries to hurt the other, to cheat, to coerce, to exploit, to impose harm upon the other, he is cheating and harming himself as an inseparable part of the collective oneness."[56]

In contractual relationships, the nurturance exchange is often superficial and determined by role rather than person. Contractual relationships that formally arrange for certain levels of nurturance apply to social arrangements at work, home, and the market place.[57] They are based upon utilitarian and hedonistic considerations, often carefully calculated, artificially established and rationalistically bargained.[58] They are usually conditional and short-lived. While therapy contracts are similiar, they are also dynamic in that they are not fixed but are continually modified to meet new needs and goals over time.

People who fail to individualize their existence depend completely on the familial network to nurture and support them. Nurturance exchange is then confined to a limited number of individuals and does not reach a dynamic, transferable state appropriate to living in the modern world. Sometimes this is expected, other times it is considered malfunctional. In the modern era the familistic relationship has increasingly become contractural in nature with the dissolution of marriage contracts by divorce a common occurrence. Although voluntary and contractual in formation, a therapy group may take on characteristics of compulsory interactions for short periods of time mimicking the family.

Antagonistic relationships characterize some compulsory interactions. One party may go so far as to seek to destroy the other party. As Sorokin put it, in a less extreme way, they may seek to "inflict pain, damage or fines . . . When one of the interacting parties imposes upon the other certain forms of conduct, certain duties and functions *contrary to the desire and inclinations of that party* (Sorokin's emphasis), and subjectively and objectively not for its welfare . . . and forces their realization exclusively by application of various forms of physical and psychophysical coercion, the social interrelation is compulsory in its nature."[59] This type of interaction is inherent in a socially stratified society or group in which one or more individuals have greater power and control and the rights and wishes of the others are ignored or not even allowed expression. It is a good example of nonnurturant or negative unilateral relationships and disdain for the individuality of the other.

CONCLUSIONS

Nurturance is an innate potential that is dependent on the "social facts within which the individual is born, grows, and develops." It is a constellation of needs that include such manifest needs as affiliation, succurance, support, play, and sex, which are intimately related to one another. Although potential to nurture and to receive nurturance may be relatively uniform, when social facts are kept constant, we vary considerably among ourselves in the ability to utilize this potential. This variation contributes largely to the differences in personality structure that are apparent in most human groups. Our capacity to express nurturance grows throughout the life span and nurturing activities slowly increase in complexity as we begin to know different kinds of people under different circumstances. Nurturance between ourselves and others forms the basic framework for the trust and security that gives meaning to our lives. Without this meaning, we are subject to the paralyzing frustrations that lead to an inability to function within a society that constantly threatens our existence as working people, as members of a viable family, and even as physical entities.

A reciprocal system of behavior in which there are no sex differences has been observed in young children and the evidence suggests that there is a high potential for reciprocal nurturance in both sexes. The imagery of whole generations has been affected by the association of the male adult figure with giving conditioned love dependent most often on a reward for achieving some culturally sanctioned goal, and the association of the female adult figure with giving unconditioned love. This has determined our notions of how work should be divided between men and women and influenced the personality development of our children. It has not only inhibited the potential developments of individuals by forcing them into sexual stereotypes, but has restricted the use of the nurturance potential in building a more caring society.

Contractual arrangements, which can affect even familial relationships, often determine how we enact social roles and the types and levels of nurturance in which we partake. Therefore, the prevalent social arrangements need to be considered when we attempt to understand our anxieties and conflicts. It seems inevitable that prevalent personality types at any one time in history reflect the mores of the period. In working with specific groups of people, we are confronted with "ideal types" suitable to our hierarchal, competitive society. However, relationships based on competitiveness and winner-take-all economics are incompatible with the genuine reciprocal and egalitarian relationships fundamental to group psychotherapy.

NOTES

1. Freud, A., & Dunn, S. (1967). An experiment in group upbringing. In Y. Brackbill & G. G. Thompson (Eds.), *Behavior in infancy and early childhood.* New York: The Free Press, p. 494.
2. Ibid., p. 497.
3. Fletcher, R. (1968), *Instinct in man* (2nd ed.). London: Unwin University Books.

4. Ibid., pp. 302, 306.
5. Freud, S. (1958). *On creativity and the unconscious*. (J. Riviere, Trans.). New York: Harper & Row, p. 85.
6. Thompson, C. (1950). *Psychoanalysis: Evolution and development*. New York: Hermitage House, pp. 54–5.
7. Fraiberg, S. (1977). *Every child's birthright: In defense of mothering*. New York: Basic Books, p.48.
8. Suttie, I. (1935). *The origins of love and hate*. New York: Penguin.
9. Dollard, J., & Miller, N. E. (1950). *Personality and psychotherapy*, New York: McGraw-Hill Book, p. 9.
10. Murray, H. A. (1938). *Explorations of personality*. New York: Oxford University Press, pp. 144–46.
11. The other 15 manifest needs listed were: abasement, achievement, aggression, autonomy, counteraction, defendance, deference, dominance, exhibition, harm avoidance, infavoidance (avoiding humiliation), order, rejection, sentience, and understanding. Murray also listed latent needs he described as repressed versions of abasement, aggression, cognizance, dominance, exhibitions, sex, homosex, and succorance and that appeared as passivity/masochism, hate/sadism, voyeurism, omnipotence, exhibitionism, repressed heterosexual sex, repressed homosexual sex, and anxiety of hopelessness.
12. See Table 1–1.
13. Horrocks, J. E. (1964). *Assessment of behavior*. Columbus, Ohio: Charles E. Merrill Books pp. 539–44. Women have been significantly higher on succorance, nurturance, and affiliation, whereas men have been significantly higher on dominance, autonomy, aggression, and achievement, according to the Edwards Personal Preference Schedule, a well-established measure of Murray's needs.
14. Murray, H. A., op. cit., pp. 144–45.
15. Maslow, A. (1954). *Motivation and personality*. New York: Harper & Row.
16. Cunningham, C. H., Wakesfield, J. A., & Ward, G. R. (1975). An empirical comparison of Maslow's and Murray's needs systems. *Journal of Personality Assessment,* 39 (6):594–96.
17. Erickson, E. H. (1963). *Childhood and society* (2nd ed.). New York: W. W. Norton & Co., Inc., p. 249.
18. Ibid., pp. 263–66.
19. Ibid., p. 255.
20. Erickson, E. (1950). *Childhood and society*. New York: W. W. Norton & Co., Inc., pp. 247–74.
21. Ibid., p. 290.
22. Freud, S. (1918). *Totem and taboo*. (Brill, A. A., Trans.). New York: Moffat, Yard, p. 133.
23. Davis, K., & Moore, W. (1970). Some principles of stratification. In E., Lauman, P. Siegel, & R. Hodge (Eds.), *The logic of social hierarchies*. Chicago, Ill.: Markham, pp. 124–31.
24. Tumin, M. (1953). Some principles of stratification: A critical analysis. *American Sociological Review,* 18:387–94.
25. Sorokin, P. A. (1938). *Social and cultural dynamisms* (Vol. 1). New York: American Book, p. 97.
26. Ibid., p. 73

27. Habermas, J. (Spring, 1974). On social identity. *Telos*, 19:19–103.
28. Shainess, N. (1966). A reassessment of female sexuality and erotic experience. In Masserman, J. (Ed.), *Sexuality in women*. New York: Green.
29. Fried, E., (1970). *Active/passive*. New York: Grune & Stratton.
30. Mander, A. V. (1977). Treatment toward equality. In E. I. Rawlings & D. L. Carter (Eds.), *Psychotherapy for women*. Springfield, Ill.: Charles C. Thomas, pp. 285–99.
31. Spence, J. & Helmreich, R. L. (1978). *Masculinity & feminity: Their psychological dimensions*. Austin, Tex.: University of Texas Press, p. 112.
32. Greenberg-Edelstein, R. R. (1979). Preferences in giving child care, psychological support, and physical support among male and female college undergraduates. Unpublished paper, Rutgers, The State University, Newark, N.J.
33. Becker, H., & Geer, B. (1958). The fate of idealism in medical school. *American Sociological Review*, 23:50–6.
34. Bardwick, J. M. (1971). *Psychology of women*. New York: Harper & Row, p. 207.
35. Kagan, J. (1971). *Change and continuity*. New York: Wiley, p. 107.
36. Chodorow, N. (1979, July–August). Feminism and differences: Gender relation and difference in psychoanalytic perspective. *Socialist Review*, 46:63.
37. Ibid., p. 67.
38. Williams, J. H. (1977). *Psychology of women: Behavior in a biosocial context*. New York: W.W. Norton & Co., Inc., p. 148.
39. Rosenblatt, J. S. (1969). The development of maternal responsiveness in the rat. *American Journal of Orthopsychiatry*, 30:36–56.
40. Rosenberg, K. M., Denenberg, V. H., Zarrow, M. X., & Bonnie, I. F. (1971). Effects of neonatal castration and testosterone on the rat's pup-killing behavior and activity. *Physiology and Behavior*, 7:363–68.
41. Chavove, A., Harlow, H. F., & Mitchell, G. D. (1967). Sex differences in the infant-directed behavior of preadolescent rhesus monkeys. *Child Development*, 38:329–35.
42. Harlow, H. (1962). The heterosexual affectional system in monkeys. *American Psychologist*, 17:1–9.
43. Kummer, H. (1968). Two variations in the social organizations of baboons. In P. C. Jay (Ed.), *Primates—Studies in adaptation and variability*. New York: Holt, Rinehart, & Winston.
44. Maccoby, E. E., & Jacklin, C. N. (1944). *The psychology of sex differences*. Stanford, Calif.: Stanford University Press.
45. Ibid., p. 226.
46. Whiting, A. W. M., & Pope, C. P. (1973). A cross-cultural analysis of sex differences in the behavior of children aged three through eleven. *Journal of Social Psychology*, 91:171–88.
47. Slater, P. E. (1966). *Microcosm*. New York: Wiley; Scheidlinger, S. (1974). On the concept of the "Mother Group." *International Journal of Group Psychotherapy*, 24:417–28.
48. Fromm, E. (1956). *The art of loving*. New York: Harper, p. 39.
49. Kang. (1931). *Human relations area file*. Koreans 3:116,119,159.
50. Fromm, E., op. cit.
51. Ibid., pp. 125–26.

52. Jung, C. G. (1959). *Collected works* (Vol. 9). London: Routedge & Kegan Paul, pp. 1–110.

53. O'Connor, C. R. (1974). *Woman and cosmos: The feminine in the thought of Pierre Teilhard De Chardin.* Englewood Cliffs, N.J.: Prentice-Hall, pp. xi, 23.

54. Korzybski, A. (1948). *Science and sanity* (3rd ed.). Lakeville, Conn.: Institute of General Semantics.

55. Sorokin, P. A., op. cit., Vol. 3, p. 34.

56. Ibid., p. 133.

57. Ibid., p. 34.

58. Ibid., p. 35.

59. Ibid., p. 34.

3

Curative Value of Nurturance

Our coexistence in time becomes possible when we make true contact with each other. This is the precondition for a therapeutic exchange of nurturance. Another precondition is the release from social roles and the freedom to enter each other's world. Group transferences interfere with the therapeutic exchange since they are based on seeing others as objects, i.e., broken down into parts of themselves and, therefore, not as unique human beings. Nevertheless, a range of elementary, asymmetrical, and socially prescribed exchanges[1] become possible through the enactment of transferences. The establishment of elementary asymmetrical exchanges of nurturance is fundamental to the effective treatment of severely psychotic persons.

SOURCE OF COEXISTENCE

Nurturance exchanges may very well be the hallmark of what it is to be fully human. It is the close encounter that enables us to transcend the "prison of our separateness."[2] We gain a sense of identity and permanence of self by internalizing images of the people who nurture us, a process that begins in infancy. This continues in adulthood as we grow and change. Internalized nurturers are the models and ideals governing our interchanges, and it is these exchanges that furnish the substance of what we call reality.[3]

To be reciprocally nurturant is to be enroute and active,[4] enjoying "the uniqueness of another while at the same time affirming a life together."[5] It means to be open, available, and free to have hope[6] and to search for meaning and purpose.[7] To assume that others are like ourselves is the beginning of a willingness to make close contact. When we are finally able to know the elements of another person, we begin to expand our own perceptions.[8] Our self-awareness is realized through the process of having others come to live in us and we in them.

An idealized version of reciprocal nurturance between adults is the I–Thou relationship described by Buber. The other is not seen as belonging to some general category, such as women or doctors, but rather is accepted as a totally independent person who can give and receive personal "gifts" of caring and attention. Yet, the very experience of the self is dependent on the ability to exchange with others subjectively. The full awareness of our own existence rests on our support and caring from another and our support and caring of them. The essential element in this awareness is a genuine reciprocal relationship. It is in this way that we experience being a person who exists.[9] "The basic movement of the life of dialogue is the turning toward the other . . . the reciprocal essential relationship."[10] On the other hand, in I–It relationships, the others are objects who are labeled as fitting a particular category or even a series of categories. We then react to them as if they do not even have an independent existence from the category they represent. Such interactions keep us isolated in our own worlds, perceiving others as extensions of ourselves.

Scheler placed great importance on the reciprocal quality of the intense relationship. He proposed that it propagated a unique perception of reality and particularly pointed out that "intentionality occurred within the context of the common participation in the being of the other." It is "our common experience" that is "the foundation upon which our insight into the other is built."[11]

The exchange of nurturance takes place in a temporal and spatial frame requiring the ongoing presence of the reciprocators. We interchange with each other because we coexist together at a specific time and place. The coexistence experience can be a fantasy as well as "real" experience. We create a time together that is uniquely "our time" increasingly to improve our responsivity to current situations.[12] What if no coexistence is experienced, as happens when a person is confined to a prison or an isolated location? In fact, Frankl used memories and imagery to help himself and others through that period when they were cut off from the world in a Nazi concentration camp during World War II. "A man who becomes conscious of the responsibility he bears toward a human being who affectionately waits for him, or to an unfinished work, will never be able to throw away his life. He knows the 'why' for his existence, and will be able to bear almost any 'how'."[13] Frankl managed to live in the presence of his close ones through his imagination and taught others to do the same. It enabled them to survive the absence of meaning and purpose in their daily existence. It was his idea that the person can remove himself or herself from time to time in order to escape the rigidities of the present and in order to find some sort of future self or "real self" that is not hemmed in by the tyranny of the present.[14]

Coexistence can also be an alienating experience, since the presence of the other brings to awareness the possibility of our own object status in relation to the being of the other. Therefore, coexistence can lead us to lose sight of ourselves in the presence of the other or others. Sartre put it this way, "By the mere appearance of the Other, I am put in the position of passing judgment on myself as on an object, for it is as an object that I appear to the Other."[15] To transcend the tendency to see one another as an object is to seek to know and be known and to merge our subjective selves in reciprocal mutuality.

Self-awareness and reality elude us when we fail to coexist with others in a specific time frame.[16] One way to handle this is to create a pseudocommunity, where imaginary figures coexist with us in a fantasy world. This becomes an autistic community that is wholly structured in terms of imaged activities. It is a substitute for the lack of meaningful exchanges with others. While certainly not the same, Frankl's use of memories and imagery to bring close ones back into our world does bear some resemblance to this process.

Buber focused on the interhuman "sphere of the between" in which human dialogues unfold and where the flow between us takes place.[17] When we truly give to each other in an exchange, expressing ourselves without reserve, something happens that is unique and repeatable. We experience a togetherness, a coexistence in a space we simultaneously occupy. This happens when the burdens of conventional social customs no longer prescribe what we can say. Therapeutic nurturance in groups is the exchange of appreciation and acceptance between the members and all their efforts to become free to grow, change, and enjoy life to the utmost.[18] Buber called it "unfolding the dialogual" and "the between" space where people make contact, touch, and live together. Most central to this process is our awareness of each other as whole and unique individuals. This becomes impossible if we observe and analyze the other. The other has to become present as a person, as someone to relate to.[19] It is not a matter of

> . . . looking at the other, but a bold swinging—demanding the most intensive stirring of one's being—into the life of the other . . . this can only take place in a living partnership, that is, when I stand in a common situation with the other and expose myself vitally . . . if mutuality stirs, then the interhuman blossoms into genuine dialogue.[20]

We exist only in each other's presence and "what humanity is can be properly grasped only in vital reciprocity." The confirmation of the other does not mean that we approve of the other but rather that we affirm him or her as a person.[21] Genuine dialogue is hampered whenever we cater to superficiality or present ourselves as holding specific roles or positions.

When we impose our opinions and attitudes on others, seeing ourselves as "right" or meaningful, we try to manipulate them to win them over to our way of thinking. It is a "means of winning power" over others by depersonalizing them, and the serious thing is that when we are taken in this way, we may not realize it. We may instead have the "illusion of autonomy" when, in fact, we have lost it.[22]

The moments of peak reciprocity in group therapy mentioned earlier are precisely I–Thou interactions experienced by the therapist and the members. It is a mutual experience of fully living in the presence and mutual exchange of the other. It does not characterize the therapeutic relationships in general, but at peak moments it does. Maslow described peak experiences as consisting of reverence for life, a loosening of the differential between figure and group, and a more objective detached view of the world.[23] This epitomizes the self-actualizing attitude. It is an experience that unifies not only the individual with the other, but with the universe as well. Comparisons and judgments are abandoned, and the aspects of reality that are normally hidden, overlooked, or smothered in social restrictions, strikingly shoot forth. Such personal encounters occur in isolated moments rather than within a continuous flow of time. While short-lived, it can have lasting effects and help increase the presence of electrifying relationships in our lives. Even the most egalitarian and self-managed communities do not consist primarily or very often of I–Thou relationships. Hopefully, however, they do create the atmospheres that made such experiences possible.

Martin Buber and Carl Rogers discussed the implications of the I–Thou for psychotherapy in a dialogue that took place at the University of Michigan in 1957.[24] At that time, Buber did not accept the I–Thou as the basis of the therapeutic relationship because he believed psychotherapy to be inherently unequal, with the sick or needing person coming to a healthy person for assistance. Rogers proclaimed, however, that he entered the therapeutic relationship "as a subjective person, not as a scrutinizer, not as a scientist." He explained that he was most effective when he was "a relatively whole" and "transparent" person. Granting that he did not bring all aspects of himself to the therapeutic relationship, he felt that what did come forth was transparent. The other person is then viewed "from within" him or her. He said he develops a willingness for the other person to be what he or she is. He wrote,

> I call that "acceptance". . . . I am able to sense with a good deal of clarity the way his experience seems to him . . . Then, if in addition to those things on my part, my client or the person with whom I'm working is able to sense something of these attitudes in me . . . there is a real, experiential meeting of persons, in which each of us is changed.[25]

Nevertheless, Buber insisted that the therapist was able to do things that the client was not able to do; that they were not equals and could not be because neither the therapist nor the client looked at the therapist's experience. Buber conceded that in psychotherapy there occurs a direct contact, a "tangent which may not last but one moment. It is . . . not the situation of an hour; it is a situation of minutes." He maintained that it was made possible by the therapist and not the client, but he admitted that it would never occur without equal participation of both.[26]

The application of Buber's ideas to group therapy means emphasizing real giving and taking, the exchange of genuine caring, which is transmitted in real listening and real talking. Friedman held that group unity could not accomplish this.[27] Yet, the I–Thou relationship is the foundation of any "we" that may emerge. "He who existentially knows no Thou will never succeed in knowing a We." Even the disrupted ways of being exist in the interhuman space between people. In the group, it is not just the I–Thou, but I–Them, and I–They, and I–Two Others, and I–Therapist, etc. The group as a whole would seem to be only a form of "it," since it is not a person. Yet, there is the reality of what is happening in a group, its prevalent focus, dominant theme, or particular array of positive and negative valences that can be perceived by the members. In contrast, the group may be viewed only as it fits into a particular member's perceptions, needs, or pseudocommunity. The I–It reaction to the group would then be a self-nurturant egocentric stance, whereas the I–Thou would be based on reciprocity and an openness to the others.

NURTURANCE AND TRANSFERENCE

The quest for love and acceptance activates the transference dynamic where the group member reacts emotionally to the therapist or another member as if they were one of the significant persons in their past or present. According to Freud, such

> impulses will inevitably be roused, in anyone whose need for love is not being satisfactorily gratified in reality, by each person coming upon the scene . . . it remains a mystery why in analysis the transference provides the strongest resistance to the cure, whereas in other forms of treatment we recognize it is the vehicle of the healing process, the necessary condition for success.[28]

One type of transference comes from the emergence of repressed needs that have been placed in the unconscious because the possibility of their being fulfilled in reality has appeared nil. Freud saw such reactions as stopping or interferring with the free associations necessary for the analysis. Therefore, the transference–resistance can be a way of avoiding further disclosure, but it is also useful in that it brings unconscious needs and complexes related to them into the conscious.

In the group, primitive and repressed portions of the self may also come to the fore as part of the desired exchange. Reactions to another group member or the therapist is usually, at first, merely a repetition of patterns already established and represent either formal roles or established transference reactions. In this way, we strive to retain these patterns and to assert their primacy as a way of being. Thus, based on a habitualized behavior, the transference can also become a way of resisting change. It also can, however, be the vehicle for an important new experience, an experiment in working out a reciprocally nurturing relationship. The bridge from resistance or habitualized behavior and the new may be the direct struggle to create the interhuman space between ourselves and others and to grasp the meaning of the coexistence of the moment. To do this, the group activity needs to be directed at understanding the barriers created by the established patterns.

Whitaker and Malone observed that resistances protect us from anxiety and from having to discover the feelings and reactions of new people. "Resistances thus occupy a central place in the beginning phase of therapy, and require a bilateral relationship for their resolution." Of significance is the fact that all the other group members and the therapist bring their resistances to the therapy session. The resistances "function to provide protection against rejection . . . A new rejection would be more painful than the mere recall or reenactment of past rejections."[29] Resistances are most likely to diminish when intense involvements start to develop. This can only happen when the therapist and group members relinquish their social masks and various established roles, including relinquishing the "professional" role of the therapist for that of a catalyst–model group member.

We all acquire, as Freud pointed out, "by the combined operation of inherent disposition and of external influences in childhood, a special individuality" that makes up "cliches" we repeat over and over again as much as we can, when circumstances and availability of love objects permit. The transferences in the group are born in these "cliches." This repetitive pattern can be intercepted, given sufficiently striking circumstances and the desirability of establishing alternative ways of being with others. The repetitive patterns we cling to are limited ways of dealing with reality. Other possibilities may be realized in fantasy or "may remain completely buried in the unconscious so that the conscious personality is unaware of its existence." In intense relationships, however, there is a release of unconscious elements and, in fact it is the combined activation of the unconscious and conscious that makes relationships so intense.[30] The in-depth exchange of nurturance is the interaction in which the unconscious of two or more people meet. It is similar to two or more minds embracing. This reaction is creative and new and leaves the rudimentary interactions of the transference to die in the past from whence it came.

Thus, transference, a term that originally described the client's emotional reactions to the psychoanalyst, needs to be expanded in meaning. In the group, emotional reactions are directed toward one, two, or more people. Besides, there are reciprocal reactions also occurring all the time. The group situation then produces an overall intensification of transference because the emotional feelings are multiplied and intensified. The transference in the group has been called irrational, but this is not quite so. It is the enactment of established patterns with people whom we do not know. When we get to know them, a new creative and spontaneous interaction emerges. The countertransference of the therapist which is the emotional and personalized reaction to the client, becomes the usual and the expected between any of the members in the group. In an active therapy group, we experiment with and develop ways of being ourselves, sharing ourselves, and giving and receiving forms of nurturance, sometimes superficial, sometimes meaningful, and on occasion intense and transcending the boundaries of the self. The phenomena of transference and countertransference take different forms in the group because of the reciprocity that develops between the group members and the therapist. "Problems of the therapist are more easily hidden in individual therapy."[31] Transferences may be seen as resistances to change. It has been suggested that there need be no client resistance,[32] but when we are struggling to move beyond our well-established ways we must encounter some resistance to potential change. If we did not, the awareness of self-consistency over time would be missing. Resistance to change is positive evidence that there is an awareness of self as a clear entity.

Mullan and Rosenbaum identified four characteristics of group transferences: "multiple, variable, fragmented, and labile."[33] In the multiple form, a client may relate to the therapist as a father figure, may view another client as his daughter, and still another client as his mother. A variable transference is based only on a specific aspect of the person. In the fragmented form, a client may attach the negative components of a relationship to one person and confine all the positive aspects to another person in the group. A labile form of transference would not confine specific interactions to any one person, but rather, would involve transference components of the moment regardless of the object. This is most likely to happen when what a particular person is saying and doing takes precedence over any enduring characteristics of that person and his or her relationship to the individual. The group is particularly unique in providing the opportunity for a variety of exchanges at these different levels.[34]

One of the most important problems surrounding an extremely positive transference in groups is the tendency of the cohesive group to surrender to a togetherness and closeness that preserves the past and throws an almost insurmountable barrier in the way of movement toward greater reciprocity, independence, and mutual integrity of the self. This is a way of guarding against the anxieties of loneliness and becomes a "denial of distance".[35] The group members may be dominated by fear of being alone and therefore may deny their individuality.[36] They may hold on to each other in an encapsulated isolation from the rest of the world, rejecting the outside world in favor of this isolated community of people who have no real fundamental relationship with each other outside the therapy group. This is an enticing situation and is particularly apt to occur if the therapist falls into the trap of feeling "flattered" at being so indispensable.[37]

Yalom has recognized the individual member's tendency to see the therapist as nurturing. This can lead to a transference in which the member "incompletely differentiated himself from the therapist: their ego boundaries—[may be] blurred."[38] Furthermore, such members may "carry the therapist around with them," with images of the therapist observing their actions and engaging them in "imaginary conversations." This can be an important step in the therapeutic process. Yalom was concerned with the unbalanced roles of therapist and group members, noting that the therapist is much more important to the members than they are to him or her. He raised the question of how much does the group and the individual members mean to the therapist personally. Yalom held that this can "threaten the very frame of the psychotherapeutic contract . . . [and represent the] inherent cruelty of psychotherapy."[39] While distance may be necessary for a particular therapist at a particular time and with a particular group, this is clearly not the model that dominates when mutual reciprocity is a group goal. It is not unreasonable to hypothesize that the more aloof the therapist and impersonal his or her attitude toward the group members, the more they will be held back from achieving mutual reciprocity. The therapist and the members have to be important to *each other*.

RECIPROCITY VIA THE UNCONSCIOUS

Whitaker and Malone provided a good description of the reciprocal nurturance that develops in therapy between the unconscious of the self and the other or others. The interaction of the unconsciouses of the therapist and group members are symbiotic experiences in which body images and enactments of the "intrapsychic family" are shared.

Difficulties arise as the client compulsively repeats actions that in the past always ended unsatisfactorily. This happens because internalized images of basic infantile relationships remain unchanged. The group member seeks positive, nurturing parent figures who can offer the support needed. This is the means by which a satisfactory parental image is established and the basis laid for the development of the ability to be parent as well as child, giver as well as receiver. In the group, as in individual sessions, the group member achieves the gratification of certain infantile needs when he or she is totally accepted by the other. The remarkable thing is that individuals, needing parental nurturance, can nevertheless provide it to others, although they may not necessarily be able to engage in mutual reciprocity with the same person. Relationships in the group build and culminate in a phase of symbolic relationships in which fantasy predominates. The members become increasingly removed from reality and deeply and pervasively involved with each other as they join together in a "joint fantasy." These relationships may be described as "bilateral symbolic relationships."[40] The experience itself can be highly gratifying and provide the basis for a deep feeling of trust and hope. Buber's I–Thou may essentially be the touching and mingling of personalized fantasies that are the essence of the private self.

Whittaker and Malone identified five stages of treatment in which the core therapeutic experience takes place in the fifth stage. This is when the intense relationship at a deep symbolic level occurs.[41] The interchange between the therapist and the group members at the unconscious level is an in-depth relationship that may transcend the social entity of the individual. In the treatment group this core experience can occur between any two persons, but it is most likely to occur first between the therapist and a group member. Eventually, the group may become a richly broadening experience when the members experience this with each other.

NURTURANCE OF PSYCHOTIC CLIENTS

Nursing has been associated with the archetypical mother–woman who is compassionate and nurturing. Such enduring myths, and the prejudices that surround the concept of nurturance, need to be demystified in order to study the range of nurturing behaviors and their therapeutic uses. There is little doubt that problems confronting clients relate to their unfulfilled need for love and security and their inability to develop reciprocity at the peer level. Creative nurses who have transcended the narrow limits of feminine nurturance have drawn from the universal concept of caring and nurturance to develop client care methods that are built on knowledge, spontaneity, and interchange of the self with the other. These methods are utilized not only in the one-to-one relationship, but in the handling of groups. It is among those completely withdrawn into a psychotic world that the work of nurturance and the break through frozen waters is most vividly seen. Unfortunately, there has been concern among some nursing writers that the "nurturance connection" to nursing has been a handicap because the scientific method, heralded as the road to autonomy and professional success, emphasizes instrumental, dispassionate, and coldly neutral or indifferent behavior.

Schwing, a Swiss nurse psychoanalyst, published a book in 1940, *Ein Wegzur Seele Des Geisteskranken,* that described her therapeutic approaches to psychotic clients. Working with Federn, known for his work on ego psychology and the psychoses,[42] she placed emphasis on the therapeutic effect of motherliness. Her ideas were based on an understanding of psychosis as caused by "unresolved, buried conflicts which have become decisive for the client's later fate." Their failure to adjust is characterized by deeper and deeper regression, "until they have regained the period before their conflicts existed." Schwing noted that,

> Freud has taught us to pursue the cause of severe psychotic illness not so
> much in the present-day reality conflicts, but to go back through the long
> chain of disappointments in the life of the client to his earliest childhood.
> These primal conflicts are always most intimately connected with the
> mother. . .[43]

Having turned away from the world, these clients are typically mute or
excited and appear inaccessible to treatment or any kind of support and
caring. She believed that, ". . . we are dealing here with clients who have
lacked the experience of motherliness," which she noted might mean that
they had in fact lost their mother in infancy. Two of her clients, whose
mothers died at birth, had been left without any adequate mothering figures
to replace the mothers and two others seemed to have similiar situations as
the result of the mothers being "preoccupied outside the home."[44]

She distinguished between mother love and motherliness: mother love is
"something primary, natural, and 'instinctual'. . . [she] does not love her child
as an *object,* she loves it exclusively *as a part of herself.*" On the other hand,
motherliness "is the product of sublimation . . . Its aim is the merging of the
ego with the object through an almost complete conversion of ego libido into
object libido."[45] "Mother love" then is a narcissistic self-nurturance that has
no object and therefore there is no possibility of reciprocal nurturance. On
the other hand, "motherliness" depletes some of the ego libido, which is
directed toward the other, and a situation is created that requires a return of
nurturance from the object to replenish the depleted ego libido.

The essence of work with the psychotic client is initially motherliness
and then a strong positive reciprocal relationship.

> Only inasmuch as, and for as long as, the psychotic client loves us and
> trusts us does he permit us to guide him . . . for the psychotic client, as is
> with children, is helplessly exposed to the power of the unconscious . . .
> We help the growing child . . . to separate the ego from the id, to subordi-
> nate the demands of the id at first to the educator, later on to the superego
> and still later to the ego. Likewise, we must help the psychotic client to
> reestablish his own personality . . . The essential goal—the reestablish-
> ment of the borders between the ego and the id, and between the self and
> the external world—can be accomplished with the client only when his
> narcissistically cathected rigidity is loosened and when he can again trust
> and love.[46]

The long hours that Schwing spent with her clients in order to make
contact, conveyed to them devotion, compassion, and caring. Eventually,
they were able to reenter the world again. Relating this behavior to early
reactions to mothering acts may have some validity, but it can hardly be
sufficient explanation in itself. We suffer severe shocks to the adult homeo-
static mechanisms and frequently experience loss of sense of self when current relationships are destructive. The defects that make us likely to avoid

this world altogether may not necessarily be acquired in the early ego building stage of infancy, but in much later stages of ego development. The most serious limitation with the theoretical position taken by Schwing (not with her clinical work that would be seen by anybody as outstanding and excellent examples of nurturance), is that it confines narrowly intense caring and nurturing to clients who are severely psychotic.

Tudor's work resembled closely that of Schwing. She described her intensive involvement with psychotic clients in creating a nurturing social context and particularly made note of the direct influence of her work on the positive reactions to her clients by others working in the psychiatric hospital.[47] Mellow, then at Boston University, called her method *nursing therapy*. Her primary work with psychotic individuals was to "restore ego integrity by becoming an identification figure" offering clients the "opportunities to participate in a corrective emotional relationship." She noted that,

> strategic advantages are 'inherent' in the onging nursing care process because of the intimacy intrinsic to nursing: emotional closeness and physical care expressed through sharing the basic needs of feeding, bathing, clothing, work and play . . . It is this naturally given *experiential* realm of the ongoing nursing situation that must be transposed and shaped by the nurse into a therapeutic medium . . . If the nurse can succeed in extending herself to the client in such a way that he is willing to enter into a relationship with her, then the door is open for structuring their shared experiences into a corrective emotional relationship.[48]

Most significantly, Mellow noted that no matter how strange and removed a person may be, he or she will respond to "genuine human caring." She placed importance on "intuition, warmth, and spontaneity in the everyday situation."[49] Mellow's nursing therapy provided the rationale and clinical basis for the first doctoral program in nursing in 1960.

Schwing and Mellow clearly differentiated between the treatment during the acute stage of illness and the postacute phase. To the acute stage belongs the intense nurturing by the therapist and the development of some aspects of reciprocal nurturance; to the postacute stage belongs the analytic process that emphasizes the development of insight and mastery over conflicts. They failed to recognize that nurturing, support, and caring are deeply involved in all aspects of intense relationships between people and that conflicts and transferences are complex forms of struggling to fulfill the needs for nurturance and support.

Bowlby's description of phases of infant attachment and nurturance seeking include passive acceptance and active seeking out.[50] Different stages of nurturance seeking also are experienced by adults in treatment. The tracking eye movements and grasping and reaching movements of infants can be likened to the behavior of psychotic individuals making efforts to receive nurturance. Like the infant beginning to concentrate on one specific figure, the psychotic adult may need a special person continuously present and carrying out a repertoire of parenting behaviors. Just as the infant builds faith and trust when he or she is able to depend on someone, so does the psychotic person require closeness with someone to develop a sense of security. Because, however, we are dealing with an adult, it is possible the group may act as a facilitating agent, for it is not a brand new support system that is sought, but an old one that needs to be reestablished.

The eternally loving mother image has been fraught with contradictions, for nurturance and destruction have been seen as combined in the same figure.[51] Like the myth of the fickle mother, the group is seen at times as supportive and caring, while at other times, destructive and rejecting. For instance, although the group process may at times represent loving nurturance, at other times it stresses enactment of norms and goals that are threatening and anxiety provoking. The continuous human conflict between good and bad prompted Freud's speculation that there was early conceptual unity between God and the Devil in one figure that contained opposite attributes.[52] As a matter of fact, all human thought is dualistic in nature and is represented in the never ending conflict between opposites.[53] Individuation may become associated with loneliness and the bad group, whereas participation and bonding may be seen as related to the good group.[54] In this dualistic dilemma, nurturance becomes suspect as a front for the eventual destruction and death of the eternal bond. Meanwhile, we can at least dispel the narrow view of nurturance as child care, and expose the futility of the reasoning that has disconnected early nurturance from all later forms and from the nurturance–destruction continuum. Nurturance and destruction are in dialectical opposition. The dynamics of their relationship are impoverished by equating them with feminine and masculine stereotypes. The nurturing–destructive parental figures reappear symbolically over and over again throughout life, at work, in the community, and in therapy groups.

GROUNDED PRAXIS

Although all theories can be helpful, we need an approach that gives meaning to the past on the basis of what is happening now. The focus on nurturance as a central feature of the human condition permits the deemphasis on fixed interpretations of what is happening, and opens the way for a paradigm based on what is happening to a particular group of people at a specific time. The praxical approach concentrates on developing a connection between the experiences of the group. What is fundamental reality and existence then comes from the group. The group struggles with the real and the rational, what is happening, and what it means to the members.

Hoffman noted that ". . . the champions of praxis insist that we are of the world we study and cannot possibly be expected to theorize in some kind of detached, neutral manner. An essential ingredient in the praxis process is the exchange of ideas, which, in the end, is the basic source of the meaning of being and existence."[55] Group therapy is praxical activity oriented toward doing something about problems, and unifying behavior and theory in the struggle for a more intense contact with others. It allows the emergence of explanatory theories that grow out of our struggles in the group. There is a tendency for most people to view the social order as being permanent. In contrast, the members of a therapy group can free themselves from the prevailing social dictates by trying to understand the basic forces surrounding them and by developing ways of gaining control over them. The person is "neither the helpless plaything of external forces nor a slave to sinful appetite, but a being *who makes himself*. One whose human nature is actually created in the source of praxis: a being who is in a continual process of change."[56]

Occasionally, alienation in isolation by oneself is replaced by a type of group "alienation" with others. By virtue of being a member of a group, we automatically engage in some forms of social exchanges and nurturance. Also, acceptance of metapsychological, religious, and scientific theories may be equally effective in breaking the gloom and devastating effects of alienation. They may enable us to survive and function, for they provide us with a form of authoritarian nurturance that comes with fixed, stable ideas to live by. They do not, however, provide the free development of a self-identity and a release from the alienation imposed by our world. They allow us only to join the hordes of others who gather around various banners to follow charismatic or totalitarian leaders.

Nevertheless, the "loss of self-identity and control, cannot be overcome in practice unless it is also overcome in theory."[57] The subjective experience needs to be united with the objective world, a world that then becomes connected to the personal. Through spontaneous theory generation in the group, ideas become part of being and consciousness part of the sensory or physical world. This is a process enabling each person to say his or her own word and name the world. It is a "practice of freedom," the means by which men and women deal critically and creatively with reality and discover how to participate in the transformation of their world.[58] It is the difference between reproducing the norms and expectations of the past or establishing norms for the future. We make our own truth by opening up to each other and by joining together in acts of discovery.

The oppressed of the world are deprived of their will when they are persuaded to follow the prescriptions of their oppressors. Those with socially deviant behavior are implored to follow the norm of the majority. When reciprocal nurturance is used in a democratic setting, in which therapists and clients alike are subjects, knowledge comes from "unveiling reality."[59] In group therapy of this sort, the members and the therapists disengage from the dominant culture and take the chance of embarking on uncharted waters. They practice a freedom of expression unencumbered by social roles and established theories. It means discovering important parts of themselves that have been dormant, unknown, long repressed, or ignored. Most important, it means that the group develops a knowledge base and theories that come from its experiences as a group. Out of the therapy sessions come new awarenesses and consciousnesses and, hopefully, the ego integrity to deal with the social world that exists.

CONCLUSIONS

Intense exchanges of nurturance can lead to a unique perception of reality. The "common participation in the being of others" is based on the coexistence of one with the other that permits a "transpersonal system of temporality" to develop. The concept of reciprocal nurturance fits Buber's I–Thou relationship of mutuality and boundless present and the notion that hope is embodied in the creative community. The "unfolding dialogual" and the development of "the between" in the dialogue "where people truly live together" or coexist characterizes the nuclear element of group therapy. Buber's protest that therapy cannot effectively utilize the deep mutuality of the I–Thou does not hold for group therapy because the asymmetrical relationships of individual psychotherapy can be virtually eliminated.

The transferences in the group may represent various levels of nurturance exchanges and constitute an important aspect of the treatment in themselves. Resistances can be a protection from the fear of involvement in a mutual exchange which, in the past, has lead to rejection or nonresponse from others. The close interchange between group members and between therapist and group members at the unconscious level represents the essence of reciprocal nurturance. In the treatment group, this core experience can occur between any two persons in the group, but it is most likely to occur first between a group member and the therapist.

Some nurse psychotherapists have demonstrated the effectiveness of intense nurturing and some aspects of reciprocal nurturance in treating persons. Praxis theory goes beyond that by establishing practice as the basis for developing insights, understanding, and theory. The group becomes the means by which knowledge is created by "unveiling" the reality that is relative and unique to the group.

NOTES

1. See Chapter 1 for a discussion of these terms.
2. Fromm, E. (1956). *The art of loving.* New York: Harper & Row, p. 29.
3. Sadler, W.A., op. cit., p. 99.
4. Sadler, W.A. (1969). *Existence and love.* New York: Charles Scribner, p. 106.
   Marcel, G., (1951). *Homo viator.* Chicago: Henry Regnery, pp. 29–67.
5. Scheler, M. (1973/1912). *The nature of sympathy.* Hamden, Conn.: Archon Book, Shoe String Press, p. 52.

6. Ibid., pp. 111–12.
7. Ibid., pp. 113–14.
8. Scheler, M., op. cit.
9. Buber, M. (1970). *I and thou.* New York: Charles Scribner.
10. Buber, M. (1965). *Between man and man.* New York: Macmillan, pp. 16, 209.
11. Scheler, M., op. cit., pp. 57,59,62.
12. Ibid., p. 71.
13. Frankl, V. (1963). *Man's search for meaning.* New York: Washington Square Press., p. 127.
14. Ibid., pp 115.
15. Sartre, J. P. (1953). *Being and nothingness.* (S. E. Barnes, Trans.). New York: Washington Square Press, p. 302.
16. Heidegger, M. (1949). *Existence and being.* Chicago: Henry Regnery.
17. Buber, M. (1965). *The knowledge of man: A philosophy of the interhuman.* (M. Friedman & R. G. Smith, Trans.). New York: Harper & Row, p. 75.
18. Ibid., pp. 74,87.
19. Ibid., p. 80.
20. Ibid., p. 81.
21. Ibid., p. 85.
22. Ibid., p. 82.
23. Maslow, A. (1970). *Religions, values, and peak-experiences.* New York: Viking Press, pp. 59–68.
24. Dialogue between Martin Buber and Carl R. Rogers. In Appendix. Buber. op. cit., pp. 166–84.
25. Ibid., pp. 169–70.
26. Ibid., p. 177.
27. Freidman, M. (1963). Dialogue and the essential we. In M. Rosenbaum & M. Berger (Eds.), *Group psychotherapy and group function.* New York: Basic Books, p. 611.
28. Freud, S. (1950). *Collected papers* (Vol. 2). (J. Riviere, Trans.). London: Hogarth Press, pp. 313–15.
29. Whitaker, C. A., & Malone, T. P. *The roots of psychotherapy.* New York: The Blakiston, p. 76.
30. Ibid., p. 313.
31. Weigart, E. (1970). *The courage to love.* New Haven: Yale University Press, p. 186.
32. Ibid., p. 76.
33. Mullan, H., & Rosenbaum, M. (1978). Transference and countertransference. In H. Mullan & M. Rosenbaum (Eds.), *Group psychotherapy* (2nd ed.). New York: The Free Press, p. 182.
34. Ibid.
35. Weigert, E., op. cit., p. 233.
36. Ibid., pp. 233–34.
37. Ibid., pp. 234–35.
38. Yalom, I. D. (1975). *The theory and practice of group psychotherapy* (2nd ed.). New York: Basic Books, p. 199.
39. Ibid., p. 213.
40. Whitaker, C. A. & T. P. Malone, op. cit., p. 99.
41. Ibid., p. 81.

42. Federn, P. (1952). *Ego psychology and the psychoses.* New York: Basic Books.
43. Schwing, G. (1954). *A way to the soul of the mentally ill.* New York: International Universities Press, p. 49.
44. Ibid., pp. 51–3.
45. Ibid., p. 52.
46. Ibid., p. 58–9.
47. Tudor, G. (1952). A sociopsychiatric nursing approach to intervention in a problem of mutual withdrawal on a mental hospital ward. *Psychiatry,* 15:193–217.
48. Mellow, J. (1966). Nursing theory as a treatment and clinical investigative approach to emotional illness. *Nursing Forum,* 5:67.
49. Ibid., p. 68.
50. Bowlby, J. (1969). *Attachment and loss.* New York: Basic Books.
51. Jung, C. G., op. cit.; Neumann, E. (1955). *The great mother.* (R. Manheim, Trans.). New York: Pantheon Books. Sullivan, H. S. (1953). *The interpersonal theory of psychiatry.* New York: W. W. Norton & Co., Inc.
52. Freud, S. (1953). *Standard edition of the complete psychological works of Sigmund Freud* (Vol. 19). (J. Strachey, Trans.). London: Hogarth Press pp. 85–6; referred to by Bakan, D. (1966). *The duality of existence.* Boston: Beacon Press, p. 46.
53. Bakan, op. cit., pp. 46–7.
54. Ibid., p. 67.
55. Hoffman, J. (1975). *Marxism and the theory of praxis.* New York: International Publishers, pp. 16–17.
56. Ibid., p. 17.
57. Ibid., p. 19.
58. Shaull, R. (1968). In P. Freire, *Pedagogy of the oppressed.* (M. B. Ramos, Trans.). New York: Seabury Press, p. 15.
59. Freire, P. (1968). *Pedagogy of the oppressed.* New York: Seabury Press, p. 56.

4
Nurturance in Group Therapy Models

The exchange of nurturance occurs in all effective group therapy, but its curative value is not generally recognized. This chapter examines the nurturance strategies in some group therapy models.

Supportive and caring interactions tend to be subordinated by therapists and theoreticians to the metapsychological reconstruction process and intrapsychic explorations. These approaches trivialize the effect of reciprocal interactions as building blocks for creating a meaningful social world. The nurturance process as a fundamental aspect of "reconstruction" is often missed. There is general recognition that group therapy is useful in providing a suitable social environment for learning new social behaviors. Nevertheless, the therapeutic potency of the interactive exchange in a nurturing climate is often ignored in favor of "higher dynamics."

INTRODUCTION

The term group psychotherapy is meant to convey the "process of therapy," the "process of change,"[1] and the use of the group as a treatment entity. Therapeutic models range from the metapsychological to self-help formulas that make the assumption that cure can be obtained from neighbors, friends, and untrained strangers. Professionally run groups are more theory based and are apt to concentrate on group process and leadership by the therapist. Some therapists work primarily with models of reciprocity and mutual aid and base their work on the healing qualities of democratic climates and egalitarian relationships. All therapeutic group models depend on the power of dialogue to produce perceptual and behavioral changes. Anthony defined group therapy as a practice based on "periodic research evaluations on the efficiency of its treatment." He noted that provision for the integration of new findings into practice is essential; there always is a danger of establishing rigid dogmas and petrified treatment models.[2]

Nurturance is usually ignored as a therapeutic agent because it is so basic to human interaction that its manifestations are often regarded as mundane and irrelevant. Nurturance is as taken for granted as breathing, sleeping, and eating, and is therefore seen as the underbase for behavior. However, those of us unable to give, take, or exchange suffer from having to live dull, empty, and meaningless lives.

We feel nurtured by the therapist who diligently tries hard to make appropriate interpretations or to manipulate our behavior through group "games." This is generally a parental type of nurturance and reflects the type of exchange in which the participants are of unequal status. In some groups, the therapist is the prime dispenser of assistance and the group members are primarily recipients, although they usually respond with sufficient acceptance to encourage the therapist's efforts. This form of reciprocity is similar to that found in a college seminar. The group members are appreciative, learn their roles, and attempt to follow and apply the theory espoused by the therapist or teacher. This is often the forerunner to the eventual involvement of all members in interpreting each other's behavior and therefore to a more egaliatarian form of reciprocity, in that many parental figures, who may not agree, may come to the fore.

In a peer-oriented therapy group, the members live out a small part of their lives together. This is apt to happen in a setting where the goal is to experience genuine encounters. A leader-dominated group is less likely to lead to active involvement of the members with each other. A demanding and controlling leader can lead, however, to members banding together outside the formal group. This is also prompted when members are anxious about "the refusal" of the leader to lead. Occasionally, alternate leaderless group sessions or meetings right after the session are arranged by the leader in order to provide this opportunity for the members to coalesce. This method was initiated by psychoanalytically oriented therapists,[3] but it has been used by therapists with other orientations.[4]

Clearly, there are many shades of exchange in groups, but in one way or another, all therapy groups engage in some form of reciprocal nurturance. Its level, duration, and intensity depend on the characteristics of the participants, the level of group development, and the therapist's theory and personality. Most group therapy models foster some interchange between the group members and place power in the therapist.

In Bach's classic on group therapy, published in 1954, he presented the group as central to meeting human needs, for it is in the group that we increase our knowledge of ourselves and gain greater understanding of others. He placed major importance on the development of the group climate, since the group could dissipate itself by sinking into unproductive activities such as "defensive self-assertion, exhibitionism, psychological voyeurism, or sadomasochistic direction-giving and 'analyzing.' "[5] Similarly to other psychoanalytically oriented leaders in group therapy at that time, Bach did not view a work climate as consisting of reciprocal nurturance, but rather one where analysis and interpretation predominated.

THE PSYCHODRAMA MODEL

Moreno's introduction of psychodrama in the 1920s spearheaded the idea of the group as a therapeutic agent. He belongs somewhere between the group analysts and mutual aid theorists. This is so because the therapist–director runs the "show," using psychoanalytically-related concepts, although it is the client–protagonist who is on the stage doing the acting. The behavior of the protagonist and the auxillary egos selected by the protagonist are subject to the direction and interpretation of the director. The spontaneity and creativity given such prominence in psychodrama are confined within the boundaries set by the director. The therapist selects, or allows the group to select a member to be the chief actor or protagonist. The protagonist is then guided in portraying an aspect of his or her personal world. The protagonist acts out on a stage episodes related to difficulties he or she may be encountering.[6] The director exemplifies the nurturing patriarch or matriarch while the participants play the parts of people in the protagonist's life, helping to clarify, expand, and carry out a more supportive, peer-oriented exchange during the drama portions and afterwards. The protagonist and the participants, called auxiliary egos, are partly dependent on the director's interpretation of the situation that is unfolding. Within the confines of the drama being enacted, they may experience personal exchanges of nurturance and support. High sensitivity to what is happening to the protagonist is the key to being an effective director. In some ways, this is more difficult to do in the psychodrama than in group therapies because the director must make quick, spontaneous judgments in alliance with the protagonist.

Moreno saw spontaneity as fundamental to the psychodrama and to creative adaptation in life. He deplored that fact that it is frequently unavailable because of cultural restrictions to free response and believed that many behavioral problems resulted from this.[7] Unlike the displacement notion that characterizes the various psychological mechanisms of defense, Moreno held that spontaneity "functions only in the moment of its emergence just as, metaphorically speaking, light is turned on in a room and all parts of it become distinct."[8] He believed that the mechanisms of defense (through which behavior is constantly being regulated and diverted by unconscious directives) suppress spontaneity. Such spontaneity could very well be explained in terms of freeing portions of the unconscious bound up in maintaining what Moreno called "cultural conserves" and using parts of the self that have remained hidden and inactive.[9] The development and refinement of nurturing behaviors is partly dependent on the opportunity for free and spontaneous expression. The spontaneity–creativity interaction theory highlights the arousal state necessary for people to create new works of art, new machines, new social orders, and new awarenesses of others. An alert attentiveness arouses us to move toward others, to seek out their ideas, their ways of seeing things, and their reactions to us. Psychodrama may be seen as a vehicle for arousing an intensified exchange of nurturance that propels people toward each other.

Remarkably, spontaneity is so rare in our lives that special situations have to be created to allow it to be activated. It is very difficult to be spontaneous when we are constantly afraid of being reprimanded or punished for doing what we want to do. After all, we have tranquilized and physically restrained people because their acting out may be harmful to themselves or others. Hence, what do we mean by spontaneity? There is a difference between impulsive acting out and spontaneity–creativity, but their differences are slim. The differences are primarily temporal, for impulsive acting out the first time can be a discovery of what it is like to do something outside the realm of social control. If impulsive acting out becomes a pattern, it loses this discovery component and becomes instead a rejection of people. For instance, a 34-year-old hospitalized woman evinced a pattern of impulsive, autistic behavior. She responded to no one, insulted everyone within her visual field, urinated on the floor, and, on occasion, threw or destroyed objects available to her. She rejected the world about her, while conveying messages of what she thought about it. Some of these acts can be of the spontaneity–creativity caliber, as when she ate the cake belonging to the only person she thought might possibly care about her. Amid a pattern of renunciation, this might be a spontaneous effort to communicate.

Spontaneity–creativity can be fostered in a stage setting where people dramatize, create, and share their world. In doing this, they pay attention to what might ordinarily be fleeting impressions, images, and fantasies. It is a way of saying "look this is the way I see it or imagine it could be like. This is the way I care for and help and support these people in my world and this is what they do to me . . . This is the way I see it and, as I enact it, I already create a new me and a new situation!" The enactment before an audience demonstrates the forms of nurturance exchange experienced, desired, or felt to be absent. In this way, the psychodrama can both highlight a problem area and also be the means of working on it.

In some institutional settings, psychodrama sessions are regularly scheduled. They are the means by which clients and staff interact in spontaneous ways and discover each other in ways that would not happen otherwise. One client, a withdrawn, delusional 45-year-old man, was unable to communicate one clear thought to anyone on his unit. As an observer of a psychodrama enactment, he became alert and reacted to the actor–client being shouted at by one of the client–actors assisting in performing the prescribed scene. From the audience he exclaimed suddenly and clearly, in a burst of empathy, "I'll help. I don't want him to do that to him."

THE ANALYTIC MODEL

In the traditional, analytic group emphasis is on the individual rather than the group and the interpersonal relations between the members. The therapist plays a prominent role in interpreting resistance to change, analyzing tranferences, setting limits, and directing the working through of conflicts. Freud observed, however, that group suggestion "is not exercised only by the leader, but by every individual upon every other individual," and reproached himself for "having unfairly kept the factor of *mutual suggestion* too much in the background" (emphasis added).[10] He referred to Trotter's herd instinct, also called gregariousness, as an "analogy to multicellularity and as it were a continuation of it." He explained the nurturing force of the group:

> From the standpoint of the libido theory, it is a further manifestation of the inclination, which proceeds from the libido, and which is felt by all living beings of the same kind, to combine in more and more comprehensive units. The individual feels 'incomplete' if he is alone . . . Opposition to the herd is as good as separation from it, and is therefore anxiously avoided.[11]

Throughout the ages, a parental nurturance, loving and caring on the one hand, and autocratic and destructive on the other, has been the way nurturance is first experienced. For Freud, the compelling nurturance factor in group psychotherapy *was unidirectional and came from* the father–therapist who held the group together and who served as an authority figure in new clothing. It is not possible to substitute "mother–therapist" as the alternate parental-type leader, for his analysis emphasized the traditional dominant and powerful father in the family. He described the leader as superior to the group and noted that,

> the members of the group stand in need of the illusion that they are equally and justly loved by their leader; but the leader himself need love no one else, he may be . . . absolutely narcissistic, but self-confident and independent.[12]

The group leader was then seen as the symbol of the "dreaded primal father" and as representing the great force, control and authority sought by the group members. He saw the group as reenacting the primal horde, noting that,

> The leader of the group is still the dreaded primal father; the group still wishes to be governed by unrestricted force; it has an extreme passion for authority; in Le Bon's phrase, it has thirst for obedience . . ."[13]

A charismatic group leader tends to be associated with the controlling patriarch of childhood. This leads to the members' dependence and submission. The coercive atmosphere diminishes and disappears only when the group members develop a brotherly–sisterly group in which a dominant leadership is no longer needed. It might be considered that what the group does in behalf of its own therapy is to create a more democratic, nurturant, or "motherly" love by which caring for each other becomes the reason and purpose of its existence. Slater noted that the ruling patriarch is dethroned by the solidarity that develops among the "children" of the same "mother group."[14] He made the assumption that the mother is symbolic of a nurturance that creates democratic relationships whereas the father symbolizes a conditioned nurturance that encourages competition and struggle for control.

Freud hypothesized that being a member of a well organized group can be a replacement for a neurosis since he believed that individuals develop neuroses when they are not members of any viable group. The therapy group then serves as a substitute for inadequate or absent nurturing and caring relationships. It can give the support and direction that is otherwise unavailable. It has the potential for filling a vital need which, if not eventually met outside the treatment group, may have to be provided on a permanent basis. A "permanent therapy group" is, however, a family of sorts. The term therapy is not suitable to a relatively permanent arrangement that becomes an essential part of our daily existence. Some individuals have need of a "therapy" group for the rest of their lives, for they are unable to develop, or do not have available to them family or community groups.

Slavson presented the central role of the therapist as the parental figure shared by the group members. Group therapy was seen as an extension of individual therapy only, instead of one client, there were two or more being treated simultaneously.[15] In fact, he called it "interview group therapy" and said that the group was not an entity itself but only a means of "activating individuals."[16] Although the individual is seen as the product of a multiplicity of relationships, it is through the therapist–client dyad that multiple social relationships are reenacted and examined. (This is in accordance with Sullivan's view of the individual therapy session.)

In the 1950s, Slavson wrote further about the importance of planning group psychotherapy, including the careful selection of patients. He believed that the patients in a group should have "similiar personality problems and [be of] . . . the same social and intellectual level." Therefore, "a therapy group cannot be a chance conglomerate of persons who happen to have emotional or personality difficulties."[17] In a later work in 1956, he did note that a nuclear problem developed in the group, enabling all group members to get something out of the group work and accelerating the treatment. He noted that the group was then "in effect one patient."[18] This differs from Whitaker and Lieberman's group focal conflict, discussed later in this chapter; they emphasize the origins of the conflict in the group experience while Slavson is concerned with the similarity of conflicts between individuals.

Later, Slavson admitted that the group can be a therapeutic agent since release and catharsis were more intense and reactions flowed more freely. Moreover, perceptual distortions are more readily expressed and the group acts as a source of protection when negative reactions against the therapist come to the fore. In this way, transference and sibling rivalry are intensified.[19] Slavson's emphasis was then on the use of sharing and support among group members as the means of developing a more intense relationship between each member and the therapist. Nevertheless, nurturance exchanged between members is discounted in favor of the theory that it is primarily in the therapist that therapy resides. It is the expert therapist who behaves in such a way as to open the doors to change. The group becomes the background or medium within which the therapist manipulates the foreground.

During the 1940s, Wolf utilized the methods of psychoanalysis in analytic group therapy, i.e., use of transference, dreams, free association, and the past. He believed that the group setting permitted deeper psychoanalytic study than did individual psychoanalysis because the support of the "group ego," experienced by each of the members facilitated analytic probing. The group setting was seen as potentially nurturing and reassuring to the individual members who might feel alone and much more resistive to probing in an individual session. In this sense then, the group also helped place individuals into a more "vulnerable" position and more likely to be willing to take a risk. Contrary to the practice of free association in psychoanalysis, Wolf attempted to direct group treatment by programming therapeutic tasks in a series of preconceived stages. As in Slavson's approach, group nurturance was instrumental to the probing, but it was the probing that was considered the focus of therapy. Other group analysts, for example, Bion and Foulkes, concentrated on the group as a social entity and a process and, therefore, are not included in this section.

MODELS OF RECIPROCITY AND MUTUAL AID

Most therapists work on the assumption that theories are subject to modification based on new findings and that they always require adaptation to be suitable to the particular individual at a specific time and location in his or her life. Hopefully, the forcing of observations to fit the specific theory is limited to beginning therapists who have had limited clinical experience and therefore need contained theories and general directives of how to proceed. On the other hand, beginning therapists will be more therapeutic if they study and apply their capacities for nurturance exchanges and cease being fenced in by orthodox concepts of behavior. One of the reasons therapists with many years of experience generally do better than those who identify themselves with a specific theoretical orientation is that it takes a few years to get rid of the handicaps imposed by too strict adherence to specific theories of treatment. We learn how to be therapists as we learn to be parents and teachers, by replicating given roles, but specifically we imitate respected therapists and adapt our personalities, feelings, and thoughts to fit their model. Unless we also develop critical acceptance and the ability to adapt theories to observations, rather than observations to theory, we set ourselves up for the life-defeating mission of trying to perpetuate the past and conducting treatment relevant to a culture and people who no longer exist.

Burrow, one of the first psychoanalysts in the United States, was a forerunner of the sensitivity-encounter movement of the sixties. In the 1920s, he provided a model for democratizing the group process that permitted the development of reciprocal nurturance at several planes: between member and members, member and member, members and therapist, and member and therapist. Some several years after Freud wrote on the group, he discovered that he was very uncomfortable with the position of analyst with one of his students and came to the conclusion that there was something wrong with a situation that placed him in a superior position to his client. He believed the privacy surrounding psychoanalysis had no other "counterpart in any sphere of scientific procedure." He compared it to privatization of the investigation of medical pathology, which he called absurd. Burrow came to the conclusion that the social unity between group members was integral to the human being, and that isolating a person from the group for therapy violated the inherent organic unity of his or her place in the social world.[20]

Personal Exchange Model

The exchange of information, feelings, and experiences can be superficial or intensely and deeply moving. In therapy groups, candor is considered the major vehicle for therapeutic communication. Conflicts attributed by psychoanalysts to the oedipus complex or castration anxiety, become failures in communication due to the maintenance of family secrets according to the personal exchange theory. Some are really "open secrets" about which everybody is informed although the subject is not discussed; others represent situations of "suspected awareness." Each of these categories represents a form of impaired communication, either blocked or distorted. The concern is with failures in communication and their rectification through the achievement of candor rather than insight.[21]

Open communication is associated with the ability to empathize, have rapport, the capacity to be altruistic, and to develop self-awareness. Thinking itself is an act of communication, since it requires the ability to introject the position of the other and then respond to it internally. The internal dialogue is also the means by which we store memories and build personal symbols. The development of self through the other is partly a type of exchange of information. Awareness is built out of interchanges between people, for the substance of awareness of ourselves comes from others. When others react to us, we become aware of our effect on them and of "ourselves from the standpoint of others . . . By taking the position of the other toward ourselves we become an observer of ourselves."[22]

Shainberg described our interchanges with others as the circle of relationships that creates our presence.[23] He saw new ways of relating as a source of tremendous energy. There is real change obvious whenever we interchange at a very personal and intimate level with another. "We feel a difference, we *care and that is a difference which makes a difference . . .*" (emphasis added).[24]

Leavy stressed the "intensely personal nature" of the psychoanalytic dialogue above and beyond the place of psychoanalytic theory.[25] It is the humanistic and personal aspect that contains the therapeutic event. Whereas the exploration of the unconscious remains an objective of psychoanalysis, the most elementary human encounters during the therapeutic dialogue are more significant. They are "the means by which we become no longer strangers to one another." Therefore, the root of positive change is the process whereby we "*acquire one another's words* and accordingly *live in one another's world* . . . (emphasis added).[26] Therapy takes place through an interchange.

Leavy noted that Freud's emphasis on the processes of transference and countertransference placed the therapist in the realm of the client's world, no longer "outside the illness," but instead an intimate part of it. The unconscious images of clients and therapists interact when they gain fuller awareness of each other.[27]

The asymmetrical and symmetrical aspects of psychoanalysis reflect the contradictions inherent in the analytic process. The process is asymmetrical when we recognize that much of the analyst's reactions that parallel the clients are not spoken, and therefore hidden from the dialogue. Regardless of this, Leavy proclaimed that analysis is a way of becoming, and every moment in analysis is a lived moment. He failed to grapple with the fact that the client's experience of the other (the therapist) depends almost wholly on the unspoken that remains secret behind the assumed analytic role. Similarly, in groups, the personal can be hidden behind roles and social facades. The emphasis is then on how a person fits into a particular group rather than who the person really is. Groups can encourage "performances" by the members at the expense of abdicating important aspects of self.

Global Transferences

At the end of the 1940s, Foulkes and Anthony placed therapeutic value in the exchange between the group members themselves. They emphasized the dynamics and the interactional rhythms that "develop" when the group is given freedom and a here-and-now horizontal orientation. They presented interpretations only to the group as a whole. Their view of transference as a global phenomenon in the group is based on the intense relationships that develop between the members. They recognized that the group therapy situation introduced "powerful" and completely new parameters of its own."[28]

The relationships in the group were seen as complex, mutual interactions that enable the individual member to gain a greater sense of freedom. The most significant therapeutic process was identified as the interaction between the individual and the group—"a two-way process operating on many levels." The greater freedom is associated with the increased spontaneity that develops in the members and the therapist.[29] The group looks at the "social unconscious" and not the deep layers of the psyche. This means that social relationships not usually revealed are examined.[30] The individual is then seen as dependent on a group reference point. Foulkes and Anthony have observed that the nurturing network of the group can even provide the media for the exploration of paranoid reactions, which are usually intractable to treatment. In fact, paranoid and other psychotic responses that come up in the group can serve as indicators of "hidden currents in the group, and can function as a kind of psychological seismography." This helps the social network in the therapy group focus on eliminating communication barriers that short-circuit people's quest for contact, support, and reciprocal caring.[31]

Analysis in the group is seen as horizontal because it deals with the "social unconscious" as it is evident in the reactions of the members to each other and to the group as a whole. This is in distinction to the psychoanalytic process, which is vertical since it examines the psyche of the individual searching out the contents of the unconscious mind.[32] This makes it sound as though the past has an existence by itself, buried there in the deep unconscious, and that it has no place in the group. As with the approach to the client's past that emphasizes its relationship with the present, it would be useful to perceive the layered psyche as operating in a highly selective fashion as the past comes to bear its impact on the group. The release of deeply repressed experiences does occur in the group and contributes in a highly significant way to sharing in the present. It is the basis of the personalized exchange that encourages greater closeness.

Focal Conflict and Solidarity

Whitaker and Lieberman developed their focal-conflict theory in groups in the early 1960s. It bears some relationship to Bion's group cultures which also are based on the assumption that focal group conflicts will develop. In contrast to him, however, they advocate active participation by the therapist in the group process. They did not think it was necessary for the therapist to remain passive and indifferent in order that the typical early struggle between dependence and independence develop as a common focal conflict. The absence of clear-cut instructions and directions forces groups to struggle to get more direction from the therapist, and, when this is not forthcoming, they eventually have to rely on their own resources.[33]

Group members usually enact habitual ways of dealing with problems. Although they are based on earlier experiences, Whitaker and Lieberman emphasized the experience of the conflict itself in the present. Occasionally, the conflict may simulate past experiences and sometimes it may not. In either case, an essential part of the treatment is the experience of conflicts held in common with the other members, the attempt to handle them in typical ways that are usually unsatisfactory, and the group's reaction to this. An important feature of the group work is the "shared affect experience."[34]

Group resistance and denial are inadequate solutions to a nuclear group conflict. For example, the members may temporarily siphon off their feelings of discomfort and apprehension by maintaining only friendly feelings in the group. Such an early cohesiveness is not uncommon and protects the members from confrontation with underlying feelings of hostility, envy, and competitiveness, which are reactions that can lead to rejection and isolation in the group. Thus, a generally nurturing climate may take a pseudoform of mutual support and caring lacking authenticity and preventing experimentation with the give-and-take that are the curative aspects of group therapy. Usually, early cohesiveness does not become crystallized, but rather acts as the means for further group growth with its attendant periods of disequilibrium and eventual development of more intense cohesiveness based on shared struggle and acceptance at a more fundamental level. The members' cooperation and struggle through conflict resolution build genuine feelings of support and solidarity.

Some focal group conflicts experienced in four treatment groups were:

1. the desire to be nurtured and protected by the therapist and fear this will be denied;
2. the wish to be accepted by the group and fear of rejection;
3. the wish to share emotional reactions and fear of losing control; and
4. the desire for a close relationship with therapist but fear of rejection.

One early solution attempted in one group was avoidance of the areas of conflict and eventually acting this out by singing songs and having parties. These apparent avoidance tactics however, became the vehicles for solving the group conflicts by developing intense reaching out and greater intimacy. The other three groups, after considerable denial, attempted to discuss directly how to control behavior that alienated them.

Another group developed conflict between wishing to express anger toward family and group members and fear that doing so would make them less desirable group members. The attempt to resolve these conflicts was dealt with in four stages:

1. denial of anger;
2. trying to get the therapist to control anger in the group;
3. acting crazy and out of control; and
4. recognition that the group was a source of acceptance and nurturance.[35]

Reciprocating Perceptions

The principle of reciprocity between persons is central to Sullivan's theory of interpersonal relations. He believed that excess anxiety and its consequent destructive influence on behavior were based on primordial experiences with the mother. He saw "the need for tenderness" being replaced by "malevolent behavior" under "the impact of anxiety."[36] The mothering that relieves the infant is experienced as tenderness. Hence, this pleasant feeling becomes associated with the activity of another and takes on the "characters of a generalized need for tenderness."[37] The complex self-system we develop is aimed at building ways of providing ourselves with internal sources of support and self-caring. In severe forms, the system does not depend on objective others at all, but rather on fantasy. The search for sources of nurturance leads to distortions or "fantastic personifications" and "parataxic distortions" that are not quite the same as transference, since they can be based totally on fantasy.[37,38] Sullivan's position that the therapist should be a participant observer[39] raised the question of how much participation and at what level.

Peplau, a Sullivanian, has maintained the importance of sustaining "a one-way view focused on the concerns of the patients" and applying "a matrix of theory for making sense" out of what is being presented or enacted.[40] In keeping with this position of therapeutic detachment, Sullivan warned that the therapist can be "a compendium of unwitting security operations" because he or she is vulnerable to anxiety. There is a realistic need to prevent the therapist from becoming involved with the group members in such a way than an "unending, unrecognized, contest of security operations" prevents the therapeutic interactions from developing.[41] In other words, the countertransference of the group therapist, although it can be the source of the highest form of therapeutic exchange, can also, when out of control, move the therapist to engage in a personal struggle for freedom from anxiety in the group. Regardless of the hazards involved in the use of countertransference, the restriction of the group therapist to an impersonal, detached stance is questionable. Sullivan did, in fact, prescribe that the therapist express his or her "real feelings and thoughts" and exploit these reactions in the therapeutic enterprise.[42]

The method of studying interpersonal perception presented by Laing, Phillipson and Lee, has some implication for the complexities of interpersonal relations in groups. Their system of direct meta and meta–meta perspectives goes beyond the usual sociometric methods that seek to establish the relationships and sentiments group members have toward one another. They used direct inquiry and paper and pencil responses to assess the dyadic relationship. They measured people's views of themselves in dyads, their views of the other person in the dyad (the meta), and their view of the other person's view of them (the meta–meta).[43] This "spiral of reciprocal perceptions" highlights the complexities of interrelationships in a group in which the spiral is compounded by as many people as are present. In a group of seven members there are 126 perceptions of the self and the other affecting the group interaction.

Exchange of Strokes

Berne's contention that we have a biological need for social contact is consistent with the position that a core of innate nurturance needs fuels our adaptive mechanisms.[44] Berne's transactional analysis model depicts three specific forms of reciprocal nurturance in which "strokes" support and nurture. These patterns are based on ego states that come to the fore at different times. Portions of the ego appear as either emphasizing conscience and authoritative ways of behaving, or early childhood ways of being, or realistic approaches to appraising what is going on. These are respectively the parent, child, and adult ego states.[45]

The transactions occur when our propensity to act according to one of these ego states is prompted by the presence of another behaving in behalf of the dictates of their ego states of the moment. The potential for spontaneous interactions resides in the childhood ego, since it is not burdened with conscience, conformity, or objectivity. The authority or parent-ego part is helpful in building learned responses, since interacting with others cannot depend simply on spontaneity. The realistic or adult-ego part functions when we objectively examine what is going on. It plays a prominent role when we are trying to determine what is happening and what the outcome might be and is, therefore, "research oriented."[46] The portion of the child in one person asks for help and support, while the adult part of another renders this. Or, for instance, a situation requiring the removal of a heavy object blocking the road stimulates the adult-ego portions of two or more persons to work cooperatively in removing the obstruction by complementary action. It can be a superficial form of reciprocal interaction, or it can be part of a more complex interrelational pattern. Typically, conflicts that befall us daily are based on others playing parental roles by issuing directives and bringing out a discomforting, childlike conformity in us.

Psychological strokes, which are experienced when someone is gratified in an interaction with another, is an essential reaction in all forms of reciprocal nurturance. The parent-ego state has the potential to harbor a positively or a negatively nurturing state. A positively nurturing state is permissive and stimulates growth in the recipient; the negatively nurturing state is smothering and may inhibit growth, for the recipient may be incapacitated by the one-way excess giving by the other. The negative form can also be outrightly punitive. Whether the negative parental behaviors have nurturing components depends partly on the recipient's view and reaction. It is important to understand that ideal or pure states are not implied by these ego modes and that they really are applicable to limited instances in time. The states do not exist continuously without interruption or change except in extremely fixated individuals. If confined to studying the moment, this schema may be helpful in pinpointing interferences to the establishment of mutually rewarding reciprocity.

> The progress of two treatment groups was enhanced by parent-child stroking exchanges. In one group, the parent role was played by one woman who helped stabilize group activities and orient the others to reality, especially two members who were troubled by threatening hallucinations and bizarre delusions. They came to depend on her support and encouragement. When she was no longer able to attend the group, another member took on this role. The nurturance experienced enabled the more troubled members to begin to give support and share impressions that were helpful to the others in later sessions.
>
> In the other group, the early dominance of one female member was completely eclipsed when three male members began to assert themselves and give direction to the group. It appeared that parent ego states in the males may have precipitated a child ego state in the female. Periods of disruption were caused by one member who on occasion was quite delusional. In this group the member was supported and nurtured by most of the other group members. Given this support she was able to make significant positive contributions consistent, at times, with an adult ego state.[47]

Social Exchange Model

The social exchange model is based on the norm of reciprocity. It has been primarily applied to two-person primary groups that are comprised of friends, lovers, spouses, siblings, and coworkers. Davis noted that social exchange can be divided into preparatory and true reciprocal interactions in the group process. Preparatory factors include recognizing positive things in others, relating to others over a period of time, and the creation of a warm climate. This sets the stage for exchanges, by which people are helping one another and developing a sense of solidarity.[48]

Reciprocal needs, propinquity, and similiarity of attitudes encourage attraction of one person to another. The reciprocal sense of liking is the key to a mutual friendship. This is, however, not enough. There needs to be some free give-and-take that is not always so accepting. When there is some exchange of annoyances, complaints, and grievances, close relationships may be enhanced, for there they are constantly being renewed and stagnation and satiation is prevented from setting in.[49] When we develop sufficient liking for each other, we seek out ways that we can agree and try to reduce areas in which we differ. The closer we come to another, the more similiarities found, and the more pressure there is to discover new areas of agreement so that the equilibrium established may be maintained.[50] Whereas some of this also occurs in the group, it is the understanding and appreciation of differences that is the more powerful interaction. Differences may also play an important part in dynamic friendships, provided a solid base of acceptance is present.

Homans' social exchange theory is essentially a reinforcement theory maintaining that we expect to be rewarded for what we do. He postulated that social behavior is stamped in by the presence of reward and the absence or minimization of cost.[51] For instance, a person without any obvious admirable traits or status is rewarded with acceptance, in exchange for not competing for high status. Generally, our interactional exchanges are governed by rules and formal roles. It is unlikely that close personal exchanges will occur between persons whose power status is markedly different. This approach has explanatory power for the behavior that occurs in treatment groups before the therapeutic climate and norms have been established.

Thibaut and Kelly described interpersonal reactions as a give-and-take phenomenon. When a need is fulfilled or a drive reduced, a reward is experienced; if an individual must struggle with his or her inhibitions and conflicts in order to participate, it is a cost that decreases the "reward value" of the relationship. People tend to repeat the interactions that are rewarding and to drop those that are not. Therefore, successful relationships are probably based on the predominance of interactions that are rewarding to both.[52]

It is possible to consider relationships in terms of the "comparison levels for alternatives" that help determine whether it is worthwhile to seek relationships elsewhere.[53] In voluntary relationships, persons may experience deprivation emotionally as well as physically, for instance, when deprived of sufficient space. A great deal depends, however, on the expectations in the situation. Occasionally, a limited interaction is necessary to accomplish the purpose at hand, and dropping expectations can limit the frustration incurred. Alliances between individuals who feel deprived and poorly supported can be effective in changing the situation. If, however, the chances for change are low, such an alliance can increase frustration.[54]

Blau extended the social exchange explanation of behavior to include the social processes that are "set in motion as every member of the group seeks to become or remain attractive to the others."[55] Ordinarily when a person enters a new group, he or she tries to find out the values of the other group members in order to decide how to make a favorable impression on them. On the other hand, we are hesitant to be friendly to a more attractive person, for he or she makes us seem less attractive and subject to rejection. Besides, friendship is withheld because everyone is trying to make a good first impression. Acknowledging the attractiveness of another gives that person a lead over everybody else. As a matter of fact, group members may conspicuously refuse to recognize the obvious attractiveness of a particular member for this very reason. When the attractive person shows vulnerability and self depreciation, others feel more safe in relating to him or her and, in fact, may be drawn toward such a person.

In the dependent relationship, we give and support, while the other, on occasion, may actively give support in return. A more egalitarian interaction occurs when each member equally meets the dependency needs of the other alternatively, and sometimes at the same time. The revolt stage in the group is heralded by the buildup of an interdependence between members. They give up their individuality to build solidarity. This enables the members to gain greater control and to pave the way for one or more of them to assume leadership. It is remarkable to observe generally compliant and passive people caught up in this action.[56]

Reciprocity in Experiential Groups

Reciprocity is the cornerstone of experiential groups, such as encounter, sensitivity training, and T-groups. They concentrate on (1) facilitating emotional expressiveness; (2) building feelings of belongingness; (3) fostering a norm of self-disclosure; (4) studying personal behavior; (5) making comparisons; and (6) sharing responsibility for leadership and direction with the appointed leader.[57] These groups were at the forefront of the human potential movement of the 1960s and 1970s. Shaffer observed that "This movement and the vast amount of publicity attending it, helped to consolidate into a distinctive school of humanistic psychology the various strands of existential–phenomenological thought that had already existed in American psychology for roughly 25 years."[58] In psychiatry, Szasz proclaimed that mental illness was a myth and concentrated on the society as a causative agent.[59] Leininger gave caring high priority as an area of study and work and gathered together nurse scholars interested in this pursuit.[60] In sociology, Sorokin formed an organization to study caring and altruism.[61]

These efforts attempted to free people from the dehumanizing effects of the prevailing culture. Consistent with this aim, humanistic psychology, viewed by its followers as a third force in contemporary psychology, espoused no particular therapy methods and concerned itself primarily with

> . . . topics having little place in existing theories and systems: e.g., love, creativity, self, growth, organism, basic need gratification, self-actualization, higher values, being, becoming, spontaneity, play, humor, affection, naturalness, warmth, ego-transcendence, objectivity, autonomy, responsibility, meaning, fair play, transcendental experience, peak experience, courage, and related concepts.[62]

The adherents of humanistic psychology frequently emphasize an existential approach to treatment. This entails consideration of the "self-as-subject" and "self-as-object," the dialectical relationship between subject and object, the concept of intentionality, and the importance of the authentic experience.[63]

The T-group places less emphasis on reciprocity and more on learning. There is a concentration on exploring and experimenting with behavior. The theme is learning how to discover ourselves. Participants learn about causes, the nature and implications of their behavior by expanding social and personal awareness, inquisitiveness, and desire to participate in decisions affecting them. The focus is on learning from the here-and-now or the experiences of the present moment.[64]

The encounter group is an experiment in direct confrontation with others, uncovering some of the positive and negative aspects of reciprocity. Members are encouraged to participate in a free and open manner, giving their perceptions and feelings about each other. Emotional outbursts, personal revelations, and intense interpersonal encounters lead to enactment of reciprocal exchanges at a superficial level that for some individuals may lead to some degree of insight, understanding, or occasionally, in the other direction, to heightened anxiety.[65] The emphasis on the uses of the body in contact with others is a short-cut to a precipitous, spontaneous (but lacking in substance) type of reciprocal nurturance. Moreover, the use of psychological and physical techniques may be intrusive and controlling and obfuscate genuine development of reciprocal acceptance based on the uniqueness of each group member. Conformity to the prescribed methods can overshadow completely who the individual members are. Malcohm's *The Tyranny of the Group* brought this out very well.[66]

The sensitivity group tries predominantly to increase awareness of self and others. Participants develop heightened awarenesses of each other and their environments. Consciousness raising for women, for widows, for single parents, for cancer clients, and for the elderly are usually sensitivity groups helping individuals enlarge their perceptions and perspective of their life situation. Some leaders may find encounter tactics can help them use limited time frames more effectively. Such abrupt intrusions are more acceptable when group members know that time is limited and that interactions have to be accelerated for something to happen. Allen's *Free Space* describes how a consciousness raising group structured its time and dealt with the personal and political aspects of feminism.[67]

Therapy groups have generally incorporated much that has been learned from these three types of groups. The sensitivity group is closest to most therapy groups. The encounter has some similarities with behavior therapy, in that specific behavior is enacted and rewarded, and with such therapies as gestalt and rational–emotive approaches, in that there is an abrupt and precipitous push toward eliciting intense reactions.

The existential model, which is distinguished by concentration on ways of being in relation to the past and the anticipated future, is likely to come to the fore in any experimental group because the past and the future continuously interact in groups.[68] The need of the moment stimulates selective perception and memory, affecting how we react to others in the group. The technique of free association, basic to psychoanalytic practice, contributes to the existential mode since it creates a sense of "simultaneity of sentiments and ideas."[69] The use of time in this way enables us to confront our experiences as givers and receivers of nurturance from different times in our lives. The group members help each other by enacting parts of themselves in their exchanges with each other.

CONCLUSIONS

All therapy groups develop some forms of reciprocal nurturance, but some therapists encourage greater symmetrical involvements of all participants, including the therapist, with each other. Some analysts consider the group merely an extension of individual psychoanalysis, but most recognize that new phenomena develop in the group. Freud saw the "father–therapist" as the authority figure who held the group together and the relationships between the members as based on their common relationships to him. The competition between the members for the love of the therapist was seen by Slavson as intensifying transference in the group. The analysts tended to accept the exchange of nurturance in the group as instrumental to the probing, which was seen as central to therapy.

Models placing greater emphasis on reciprocity and mutual aid prevail among group therapists, but most do not identify this as a curative or central force. Open communication is associated with the ability to empathize, have rapport, the capacity to be altruistic and to develop self awareness. The therapeutic dialogue is the essence of a personal exchange theory that emphasizes experiencing fully another's world. Whitaker and Lieberman explain how the group's struggles with conflicts contribute to group solidarity, whereas Berne's "strokes" represent forms of nurturance that support and reinforce. Countertransference reactions in the reciprocating perceptions of the group are significant and require study and direction. The social exchange theory helps explain nurturance in its function as a reward and determinant of behavior.

Experiential group work with catharsis, acting out, and increased self-awareness have contributed considerably to reciprocity in group therapy. Reciprocity is the cornerstone of most experiential groups, but the nurturance phenomenon may be minimal, for the emphasis is often placed on limited aspects of the person.

NOTES

1. Anthony, E. J. (1972). The history of group psychotherapy. In H. I. Kaplan & B. J. Sadlock (Eds.), *The evolution of group therapy* (Vol. 2). New York: Jason Aronson, p. 25.

2. Ibid.
3. Kadis, A. (1963). Coordinated meetings in group psychotherapy. In M. Rosenbaum & M. Berger (Eds.), *Group psychotherapy and group function.* New York: Basic Books, pp. 437–47.
4. Shostrom, E. L. (1976). *Actualizing therapy: Foundations for a scientific ethic.* San Diego, Cal.: Edits.
5. Bach, G. *Intensive group therapy.* New York: Ronald Press, pp. 3–4.
6. Starr, A. (1977). *Rehearsal for living: Psychodrama* Chicago: Nelson Hall, pp. 1,15.
7. Moreno, J. L. (1953). *Who shall survive?* Beacon, N.Y.: Beacon House, p. 42.
8. Ibid., pp. 43,44.
9. Ibid., p. 47
10. Freud, S. (1940/1922). *Group psychology and the analysis of the ego,* London: Hogarth Press, p. 82.
11. Ibid., p. 83.
12. Ibid., p. 93.
13. Ibid., pp. 99–100.
14. Slater, P. E. (1966). *Microcosm.* New York: John Wiley. Scheidlinger, S. (1974). On the concept of the "Mother Group." *International Journal of Group Psychotherapy,* 24:417–28.
15. Slavson, S. R. (1947). *The practice of group psychotherapy.* New York: International Universities Press, p. 9.
16. Ibid., p. 28.
17. Ibid., p. 80.
18. Slavson, S. R. (1956). *The fields of group psychotherapy.* New York: International Universities Press, p. 3.
19. Ibid., p. 26.
20. Burrow, T. (1927 July). The group method of analysis. *The Psychoanalytic Review* 14: pp. 268–280.
21. Rabkin, R. (1970). *Inner and outer space.* New York: W. W. Norton & Co., Inc., pp. 180,182.
22. Ibid., p. 189.
23. Shainberg, D. (1973). *The transforming self.* New York: Intercontinental Medical Book, p. 135.
24. Ibid., p. 138.
25. Leavy, S. A. (1980). *The psychoanalytic dialogue.* New Haven, Conn.: Yale University Press, p.xv.
26. Ibid., p. 31.
27. Ibid., p. 32.
28. Foulkes, S. H., & Anthony, E. J. (1965). *Group psychotherapy* (2nd ed.). Baltimore, Md.: Penguin, pp. 23, 27.
29. Ibid., p. 30.
30. Ibid., p. 56.
31. Ibid., pp. 257–258.
32. Ibid., p. 42.
33. Whitaker, D. S., & Lieberman, M., (1964). *Psychotherapy through group process.* New York: Atherton Press.
34. Ibid., pp. 265–66.

35. Groups led by Susan M. Egan, Sue Kujalowicz, Concetta McPeak, Harriet Muir, and Jan Weitz, graduate nursing students at Rutgers, the State University.
36. Sullivan, H. S. (1953). *The interpersonal theory of psychiatry.* New York: W. W. Norton & Co., Inc., p. xv.
37. Ibid., p. 40.
38. Thompson, C. (1950). *Psychoanalysis: Evolution and development.* New York: Hermitage House, p.216.
39. Ibid., p. 219.
40. Peplau, H. E. (1969). Professional closeness. *Nursing Forum,* 8:346.
41. Sullivan, H.S. (1949). Notes on investigation, therapy, and education in psychiatry and their relations to schizophrenia. In P. Mullahy (Ed.), *A study of interpersonal relations.* New York: Grover Press, pp. 199–200.
42. Millon, T. (1969). *Modern psychopathology.* Philadelphia: Saunders, p. 615.
43. Laing, R. D., Phillipson, H., and Lee, A. R. (1956). *Interpersonal perception: A theory and a method of research.* New York: Springer, pp. 23–36.
44. Berne, E. (1963). *The structure and dynamics of organizations and groups.* New York: Ballantine Books, p. 215.
45. Berne, E. (1964). *Games people play.* New York: Grove Press, p. 23.
46. Ibid., p. 24.
47. Groups led by Susan M. Egan and Harriet Muir, graduate nursing students, Rutgers, the State University.
48. Davis, M. S. (1973) *Intimate relations.* New York: Macmillan.
49. Nixon, H. L. (1979). *The small group.* Englewood Cliffs, N.J.: Prentice-Hall, p. 88.
50. Ibid., p. 99.
51. Homans, G. C. (1974). *Social behavior: Its elemental forms* (Rev. ed.). New York: Harcourt, Brace, Jovanovich.
52. Thibaut, J. W., & Kelly, H. H. (1959). *The social psychology of groups.* New York: Wiley, p. 63.
53. Ibid., p. 21.
54. Ibid., p. 187.
55. Blau, P. M. (1960 May). A theory of social integration. *American Journal of Sociology* 65:545–46.
56. See discussion of Bion's group theory in Chapter 8.
57. Shaw, M. E. (1976). *Psychology of small group behavior* (2nd ed.). New York: McGraw-Hill, p. 323.
58. Shaffer, J. B. P. (1978). *Humanistic psychology.* Englewood Cliffs, N. J.: Prentice-Hall, p. 124.
59. Szasz, T. S. (1961). *The myth of mental illness.* New York: Dell.
60. Slack, C. B. (1981). Caring: An essential human need. *Proceedings of three National Caring Conferences.* Thorofare, N.J.
61. Sorokin, P. A. (Ed.) (1971). *Forms and techniques of altruistic and spiritual growth: a symposium,* Boston, Mass.: Beacon Press.
62. Schaffer, J. B. P., op. cit., pp. 1–2.
63. Ibid., pp. 19–31.
64. Golembiewski, R., & Blumberg, A. (Eds.). (1970). *Sensitivity training and the laboratory approach.* Chicago: University of Chicago Press.
65. Nixon, H. L. (1979). *The small group.* Englewood Cliffs, N.J.: Prentice-Hall, p. 103.

66. Malcohm, A. (1975). *The tyranny of the group*. Totawa, N.J.: Littlefield, Adams.
67. Allen, P. (1970). *Free space: A perspective on the small group in women's liberation*. New York: Times Change Press.
68. Weisman, A. S. (1965). *The existential core of psychoanalysis*. Boston, Mass.: Little, Brown, p. 91.
69. Ibid., p. 93.

5

Use of the Nurturance Model in Forming a Treatment Group

The premise that nurturance is the essence of the therapeutic group process has implications for how clients are selected and how contracts are formed. The building of pathways into each other's lives and experiencing the individuality and humanness of others follows a concentrated effort to establish norms of mutual aid and respect. In the absence of some altruistic tendencies, this aim is almost impossible to achieve. This chapter is concerned with methods of evaluating clients for groups with special reference to the capacity to engage in some form of reciprocal behavior. Clinical syndromes are reviewed in terms of their implications for nurturance needs.

CRITERIA FOR GROUP MEMBERSHIP

Estimations of suitability for group membership are made through interviews, use of projective measures, and trial periods of group attendance.[1] The most important questions to be asked are whether the prospective group member has altruistic tendencies, tolerance for struggles that may be encountered in achieving mutual reciprocity, and readiness to begin to participate in give-and-take relationships. Other member characteristics recognized as contributing to effective group therapy include the ability to work with authority figures, to disclose aspects of self before a peer group, to express aggressiveness, and to tolerate tension.[2] Members drop out of groups when they feel unable to fit in, feel rejected by the group, or have difficulty in expressing themselves. They also leave the group prematurely when they are unable to share, have disclosed themselves too soon, or are upset by subgroupings that occur. A very important reason given by some is inadequate preparation for the group experience.[3]

People who generally will do poorly in a group, and who sometimes make it impossible for a therapeutic climate to develop, include those whose contact with reality is limited or who are unpredictable. The significant factor is how pervasive these characteristics are. Most people will not constantly present such behaviors, but rather will exhibit these antisocial tendencies episodically. In looking at behavior that suggests the individual is unsuitable for group work, the observer needs to consider the deviance "in terms of degree, variation, and circumstance, rather than in simplistic 'either-or' classification."[4] A paranoid reaction is only relevant when it is pervasive and colors most reactions, leaving no behavior free of this distortion.

The selection of an individual client for an ongoing group is based on his or her capacity to adjust to the level of reciprocity anticipated for the particular group.[5] The expediency of setting up groups in clinics, hospitals, and private practice has frequently limited the therapist's opportunity to interview and prepare clients properly. The "unique group ambiance" is derived from the network of relationships that develop, and the selection process needs to concentrate on supplying the essential ingredients to create a warm, caring, and stimulating ambiance.[6] In the psychiatric institution, the members in therapy groups may be from the same unit and share common living conditions and daily happenings. Their exchanges may center on the shared living problems with authority figures in the setting. The types of therapeutic reciprocal nurturance that can develop in such a "captive group", whose freedom has been curtailed, is almost entirely dependent on the climate in the institution. Occasionally, the building of greater reciprocal nurturance among the staff members may have more of an effect on those housed in these places than direct group work with the clients.

A particularly well-developed group with well established norms and an effective working climate can absorb behaviors that a less advanced group could not. In an ongoing group, group members decide whether they want to welcome a particular candidate. The prospective member's ability to recognize his or her problem area and the presence of a conscious desire to develop reciprocal relations with others need be considered. A member may be only minimally disruptive and tolerated by the group when he or she brings other traits that the group values, such as a general caring or sensitivity. A highly suspicious person, however, who accuses the other members of suspected aggressions and plots may destroy a group that is not already highly cohesive. The possiblity of mutual aid between other members and such a member is very low, although certainly not zero. Moreover, when an individual is preoccupied with a crisis situation, he or she may not be able to tune in to the problems facing others. Yet, some people may gain a new perspective of their crisis situation through group attendance, if they have the patience to stay and listen to the others, without constantly monopolizing the group.

Some believe that the group members should come from different social strata and educational backgrounds, and represent different ages, both sexes, and different symptoms. Nevertheless, a withdrawn woman might do better in a group of all women close to her own age. An elderly client might achieve more mutual reciprocity in a group of elderly persons. Although there is greater stimulation in a group in which the individuals differ, this can be carried to an extreme when the members may have difficulty establishing a common language. Even when group members are alike in many basic characteristics, such as the nature of the problem and life style, they will most certainly differ in how they express themselves and in their capacity to interact with others.[7]

THE INITIAL INTERVIEW

The initial interview is really the beginning of the therapy group, for what transpires there gives the therapist and the potential group member an opportunity to observe each other and estimate if participation together in the group would be desirable and fruitful. In the interview, the therapist does not focus on symptoms, but rather on the nature of the exchange that takes place. The interview is used to ascertain the major way the client deals with people. In doing this, the therapist and client together examine what daily life is like and what some of the difficulties may be.

Information that may be obtained in the interview includes the nature of the client's primary groups, especially who the family members are, and what sort of people are the father, mother, siblings, spouse, and children. The interview itself is an excursion into a mutual exchange of expectations, getting to know one another, and experiencing each other as persons with unique interests and concerns. Without reciprocity in the interview, it is doubtful that the client will get the notion that the "desired" changes in awareness, behavior, and basic relationships are up to him or her. Moreover, it is questionable that any relevant client perceptions will be forthcoming.

The therapist determines with the prospective member his or her characteristic behavior pattern, current capacity to give and receive nurturance, and what can be gained from participation in the therapy group. The interview itself helps establish the levels of exchange that the member is able to achieve. Taken into account is the functioning level and mode of expressing, caring, and loving that is typical for the social setting from which the member comes. A person from a background that is culturally different from that of all the other members will suffer loss of self under the influence of the cultural norms the others bring. A primary form of support and reinforcement can be provided by selecting at least one other person culturally similar. When this cannot be done, the therapist will have to offer the additional support, at least at first. The therapist hypothesizes what the interactions will be like between each potential dyad among the planned group members.[8] The person who has a history of destructive relationships with peers or has been unable to establish any peer contact may need one-to-one therapy first, or group work concurrent with individual sessions.

The therapist demonstrates caring, interest, and concern and ensures that the interview fulfills some of the client's needs for support. As Sullivan noted, as long as the client receives support, "the communication situation improves, and the interviewer comes finally to have data" on which a formulation of some values can be made. Both the therapist and prospective group member gain from the interchange that takes place in the interview. The therapist concludes the interview by telling the client what he or she heard, asking the client to correct those things that have been misunderstood and to point out any important things that may have been omitted.[9] The therapist also shares something about him or herself as an individual and exchanges notions with the client about the nature of group therapy itself.

Projective methods may be helpful in the initial contact, since they may enable the therapist to get much more understanding of the client's level of functioning in a shorter period of time. They are standardized presentations of relatively ambiguous stimuli to which the client responds by using his or her own behavioral style, perceptions, emotions, and ability to organize. The use of "tests," however, does contribute to making the relationship even more asymmetrical than it already is, for the therapist is put in the position of being an administrator of specific tasks to be performed. An accepting and caring climate can counteract this effect. The interaction between the therapist and client, during the administration of the projective test, provides a behavioral sample of what the client might bring to the group setting. The responses to the stimuli presented may be especially helpful in eliciting evidence of nurturance styles and needs that might not be readily forthcoming in the interview. This is particularly so because the reactions of the client are indirect and not specific. The more ambiguous the stimuli are, the more the client has to use his or her unique way of structuring situations.

A projective test suggested by Bach for group screening is the Schneiderman's MAPS Figure Grouping that requires the client to place human figures, made of cardboard, into groups.[10] How this is done can reveal attitudes toward the opposite sex, parent and authority figures, capacity to form meaningful groupings, and the range of persons with whom the client is potentially ready to interact. Particularly important may be how the client carries out the task.

The Thematic Apperception Test, or versions of it, in which the client tells stories about pictures, may also be used to evoke thematic data. This gives the client the chance to show, in an indirect way, areas of concern and how he or she handles problems. The person is asked to tell stories about each picture, telling who the people are, what they are doing, and how it all ends. When administered and recorded in a standardized way, the responses can be scored for levels of nurturance, negative interactions, content of themes, type of characters portrayed, moods presented, and the nature and number of resolutions achieved. Particularly, levels of nurturance expressed can be examined by identifying the types of interactions portrayed, the lack of or presence of reciprocal behaviors, the status relationships of the people interrelating, and the amount and nature of give and take. It is important that the stimulus material used not be threatening. Brightly colored abstract paintings can precipitate increased disruption and frightening delusions in clients with schizophrenic patterns.

The Life Space Drawing (LSD) can be a clue to the client's world of significant others.[11] Moreno observed that the emotional potential of the others may be perceived as agreeing, disagreeing, different, or unknown.[12] A circle, containing the initials of the client, is drawn at the center of an ordinary sheet of typing paper. The therapist asks the client to think of the circle drawn in the center as representing the client. The individual is then asked to draw circles to represent each important person in his or her social world and to place each circle in relation to the client's circle, based on the closeness of each relationship.[13] In this way, clients can show their current primary group, how close they feel toward each person, and who they are. It may be found that images of the significant others are sometimes not based on current circumstances, but rather that they exist at a fantasy level.[14] During the course of therapy, the therapist may use the LSD in the group at different times to get a view of changes taking palce in the client's perception of his or her world and the place of group members in it.

Using a modified version of the LSD, two graduate students asked each prospective group member (hospitalized male) how he sees himself in a five-member therapy group for which he was being considered. Only one client presented himself as out of the circle of other clients and close to a door, which he drew. When in the group, he related poorly to the other group members and was primarily preoccupied with trying to get the cotherapists to intercede on his behalf with various hospital personnel. Such a performance on the LSD may suggest lack of readiness for membership in a group.

Establishing the Nurturance Level

An assessment of members before, during, and after the completion of the therapy sessions provides some basis for studying and evaluating the treatment. Ordinarily, behavior is labeled by someone who is applying some group rule. Behavioral variations are not, however, static entities. Rather, all behavior can be seen as a "continuously shaped and reshaped *outcome* of dynamic processes of social interaction."[15]

One of the aims of the assessment is to determine the way nurturance needs are currently being met. For instance, hoarding may be seen as an attempt to nurture the self. This does not contradict Freud's view of this as part of the anal character complex. Freud's position is consistent with an effort to prevent the loss of nurturance. He characterized "greed" as "largely an extension of an unresolved conflict from the supposedly anal stage in personality development" when the resistance to toilet training is prompted by the denial of the previous freedom and total acceptance experienced. In other words, the pressure of toilet training turns a loving, caring nurturance into a conditioned nurturance in which it is withheld, pending compliance to a demand. The requirement that the expulsion of feces occur in the proper place at the proper time becomes symbolic of the deprivation of a more freely given nurturance. Greed and retention of feces become part of the mechanism used to prevent loss of unconditioned nurturance.[16] On the other hand, Binswanger sees greed as being prompted by a person attempting to store up supplies. This is then an active quest for nurturance and support. It takes the form of hoarding money or "taking hold" of people by impressing, seducing, or selling them something they do not need.[17] Freud's "greed" then is a way of preventing loss of nurturance and Biswanger's is a way of storing up reserves of nurturance.

One way of assessing nurturance potential would be to examine how "fantasies, attitudes, and expectations about interpersonal relationships"[18] are used to seek and give nurturance. In the interview, it may be possible to identify impaired capacities and to examine evidence of distortions in the nurturance experience by using, as a standard, the American Association's Psychiatric Diagnostic and Statistical Manual (DSM-III). The syndromes may be used as guides for what to look for in certain clients. The following discussion of nurturance needs associated with specific clinical syndromes is based on descriptions of the syndromes as they appear in the DSM-III.

Clinical Syndromes

Schizophrenic Reactions. Persons with schizophrenic disorders are usually experiencing disrupted or insufficient nurturing relationships. They may doubt they exist at all for there is "a loss of ego boundaries and . . . extreme perplexity about one's own identity and the meaning of existence."[19] A feature that usually accompanies the negation of self is "a tendency to withdraw from involvement with the external world and to become preoccupied with egocentric and illogical ideas and fantasies in which objective facts are obscured, distorted, or excluded."[20]

For individuals thus bewildered, the group experience is productive if it becomes a source of the most elementary forms of nurturance. This can occur in a group in which most of the members are struggling with the development of more advanced forms of reciprocal nurturance if the members are tolerant of lesser functioning members and can offer them support and assistance. Mutual benefit may then be accrued by all at some level.

Paranoid Thoughts.

> A person may have persecutory delusions which involve a single theme or series of connected themes, such as being conspired against, cheated, spied upon, followed, poisoned or drugged, maliciously maligned, harassed or obstructed in the pursuit of long-term goals . . . Impairment in daiy functioning is rare. Intellectual and occupational functioning are usually preserved, even when the disorder is chronic. Social and marital functioning, on the other hand, are often severely impaired.[21]

Generally, when a person's orientation to the world is predominantly filled with paranoid thoughts, it is extremely difficult for him or her to participate in a group that focuses on establishing reciprocity. When delusional thoughts are compartmentalized, i.e., limited to certain topics or relationships, there is a sphere of flexibility that will permit therapeutic exchanges and contribute to group development in activities not touching on the sore points. Often, it is possible to spot the compartmentalized paranoid thoughts in the initial interview, although such a mode of thinking is unlikely to be associated with seeking out therapy. Nurturant exchanges may be reachable if the delusions can be bypassed.

In the schizophrenic form, delusions are "more likely to be fragmented and multiple rather than systematized"[22] and therefore more invasive. The possibility for reciprocity may be limited to periods when delusions are less prominent and may vary from day to day. Intermittent participation in a group may provide the experience for a more sustained involvement later on.

Manic Behavior. In the manic episode,

> the hyperactivity often involves excessive planning and participation in multiple activities . . . Almost invariably there is increased sociability, which includes efforts to renew old acquaintances and calling friends at all hours of the night. The intrusive, domineering, and demanding nature of these interactions is not recognized by the individual. Frequently expansiveness, unwarranted optimism, grandiosity, and lack of judgment lead to such activities as buying sprees, reckless driving, foolish business investments, and sexual behavior unusual for the individual.[23]

The pressure to associate with others appears to be fired by an intense need to extend and get nurturance. The aggressive struggle for contact with almost anybody is an example of a nurturance need that is so extreme it leads to violating the other by bombardment. Under the burden of these patterns of behavior, it is most likely that a person will completely disrupt any group, but when the hyperactivity has been controlled by medication, the flow of ideas can contribute to the group's effectiveness. The potential for disorganization can then be cut down and the group can assist in the redirection of some of these energies toward caring and supporting others in a more moderate and considered way.

Depression. In a major depressive episode, the mood is,

> depressed, sad, hopeless, discouraged, down in the dumps . . . Sometimes, however, the mood disturbance may not be expressed as a synonym for depressive mood but rather as a complaint of 'not caring anymore' or as a painful inability to experience pleasure . . . The sense of worthlessness varies from feelings of inadequacy to completely unrealistic negative evaluations of one's worth. The individual may reproach himself or herself for minor failings that are exaggerated and search the environment for cues confirming the negative self-evaluation. Guilt may be expressed as an excessive reaction to either current or past failings or as exaggerated responsibility for some untoward or tragic event. The sense of worthlessness or guilt may be of delusional proportions . . . Thoughts of death or suicide are common. There may be fear of dying, the belief that the individual or others would be better off dead, wishes to die, or suicidal plans or attempts.[24]

Depressive disorders respond dramatically to pharmacological agents. There is general agreement that therapy should be directed toward diminishing environmental stress and the client's vulnerability to react to such stress in a self-destructive way.[25] Toward this aim then, the nurturing atmosphere experienced in an effective therapy group may serve as a buffer of support. Attachment to a caring group of people may provide some element of basic security needed to endure uncontrollable pressures from the environment or from within. Moreover, the reestablishment of patterns of reciprocity through the group experience may eventually help to alter the way others are perceived and reacted to and, in effect, change the nature of the environmental pressures and the experience of self.

Phobic Reactions. Other clinical syndromes described in DSM-III are anxiety, phobic, somatoform, dissociative, and psychosexual problems. Behavior modification, which is a task-oriented approach in groups, has been considered the treatment of choice for some of these conditions.[26] An examination of these problems suggests that nurturance needs may also predominate here. People with various phobias tend to be hypersensitive to social rejection and being left alone, or to situations in which they are subject to the control of others.[27] Phobic reactions tend to elicit support and sympathy from others. For instance, a phobic person may get friends or family members to be with him or her to avoid facing a feared situation. This is usually recognized as a way of fulfilling dependency needs. More specifically, however, it is a way of obtaining support and nurturance. The phobic reaction is a quest for nurturance that can become, when properly handled, the first step toward a more mature interchange. Similarly, the dissociative response, in which a person unconsciously assumes a new identity, provides the advantages of a " 'new life,' an escape from boredom, the attraction of attention, affection, and nurture."[28]

Obsessive–Compulsive Pattern. Obsessions are

> recurrent, persistent ideas, thoughts, images, or impulses that are egodystonic, that is, they are not experienced as voluntarily produced, but rather as thoughts that invade consciousness and are experienced as senseless or repugnant . . . [The] compulsions are repetitive and seemingly purposeful behaviors that are performed according to certain rules or in a sterotyped fashion.[29]

The Freudian explanation for these patterns has been that the preoccupation with ritual diminishes the oppressive buildup of guilt feelings for having had forbidden impulses. Ritualized emphasis on order and cleanliness may be quite rewarding since they often bring forth approval and acceptance from others.[30]

There is a possibility that a nurturing, supportive therapy group just might provide an alternative source of reward and satisfaction that could overshadow, at least in some cases, the rewards achieved from meaningless rituals, particularly since the seeds for planting more authentic relationships may be present in the group. Usually, however, the compulsive–obsessive adaptations are firm structures that are very difficult to modify.

Personality Patterns

The DSM-III describes personality patterns that may be differentiated in the way nurturance and reciprocity are handled. In the schizoid pattern, "the essential feature is . . . a defect in the capacity to form social relationships, evidenced by the absence of warm, tender feelings for others and indifference to praise, criticism, and the feelings of others."[31] The adaptation usually includes withdrawal, seclusion, and usually pursuit of solitary interests or hobbies. Help or treatment is not sought when living conditions and the job do not require much involvement with people. This mode of living can result from the absence of basic experiences in caring and sharing at the most elementary level, or difficulty in internalizing such experiences if they do occur. Occasionally, such personality development can be traced to an early separation that was never resolved.

It is possible to achieve a relatively satisfactory adjustment by avoiding close relationships. Despite social withdrawal, there can be a high awareness of other people and sensitivity to what others are saying and feeling. This often takes the form of being on the alert for potential rejection and humiliation. Anxiety about the possible outcome of attempting to interact with others can be very high and may lead to further detachment from others as a protection. This is compounded by the fact that such individuals tend to be isolated and lonely and have a very strong need to be accepted, a need of which they either are not fully aware, or, if they are, do not fully acknowledge.

Behavioral problems almost always signify sufferings that result from deficient experiences in the exchange of nurturance. For instance, one pattern consists of making constant demands for reassurance to remedy feelings of helplessness and dependence (the histrionic personality pattern). Another pattern consists of a constant need to demonstrate importance and competence, and especially to achieve acclaim for "performances" (narcissistic personality pattern). These personality patterns provide superficial sources of nurturance. They are usually the result of early childhood rearing practices in which reciprocally nurturing relationships were never attained. Often, there is simply inadequate contact with parental figures in childhood. Sometimes, there is outright rejection and hostility from significant adults, and little if any nurturance. In the other direction, an overprotected child, excessively nurtured, may develop an inadequate personality because total and complete unconditional acceptance beyond infancy can impede the ability to experience mutual reciprocity. Also, confusion in reaching some functional sense of self occurs because there is no regularity or predictability as to when acceptance and love will be forthcoming.

CONTRACT FORMATION

The social contract is the basis of the treatment alliance. Social contracts are determined between individuals rather than by tradition, although some standards or norms by necessity enter into contracts. The conditions under which certain accepted standards will be carried out can vary and are controlled by the participants. The contract itself sets the nature of the relationship: who will do what, and how time will be used to fulfill the obligations being entered into.

In some ways, the therapy group is like an intentional community in which members band together to work and live in their own unique, chosen way.[32] Similarly to those in collectives, members also hope to gain personal growth and increased satisfaction in living. Although group therapy time is very limited, usually one 90-minute period per week, the intensified exchange between members during the session affects them constantly. During this time they think about what happened and have further reactions that can be shared with the group in the following session.

Precontract Reciprocity

One of the first "group events" is an exchange of information about therapy: what the prospective member knows and expects from group therapy, and what the therapist has to tell about the nature and possibilities of group therapy. The prospective member examines and clarifies his or her notions of group therapy, particularly in reference to the specific group for which he or she is being considered. The therapist learns what the person thinks about groups, what he or she might wish the group to be like, in which groups the client already participates, what his or her reactions are to these groups, and how the proposed group would fit into the client's schedule.

The differences between group and individual therapy and between nonstructured and more structured forms of group treatment need to be considered in terms of the presenting needs of the prospective member. It is important for the therapist to be aware of the treatment modalities available and to consider the level of nurturance required by the client. Some discussion of the various emphases is in order. The potential group member or his or her advocates need to know the options available. For instance, whereas the objective of all group methods is improving communication, developing some insight, and expanded consciousness, behavior modification more specifically is directed at ridding clients of particular symptoms; psychoanalytically oriented groups focus on the corrective emotional experience; and institutionalized groups usually directly handle the need to increase social behavior.

Persons relatively intact might be able to handle a number of different groups in addition to the therapy group, such as clubs, occupational and art therapy groups, and instructional groups. Others might find membership in more than one or two groups confusing and disruptive.

Behavior modification groups are particularly appropriate for persons who have identified a specific behavior problem and want to modify or change it. It is usually a short-term treatment and may include assertiveness training, relaxation methods, and desensitization. Nondirective methods are applied differently by therapists, depending on their theoretical frameworks. These may include rational, gestalt, actualizing, and primal therapies. Some therapists may be considerably more directing, and concentrate on the use of very specific techniques. It is helpful to be aware of what they are before entering therapy, since some methods are not palatable to all people.

Persons who have general problems in living and would like to modify their overall orientation are likely to find nondirective groups helpful. Family therapy is best for persons having difficulty in establishing reciprocity with family members. It often includes working with subgroups of the family, and may use techniques such as sculpting (recreation of family scenes) and genograms (diagrammatic construction of generations in the family). The traditional pschoanalytic treatment would appeal to persons concerned with evaluating what happened in the past, its meaning and implications, and its contribution to insight. It applies a specific theory of human psychosexual development and concentrates on the analysis of the client's symbolic reactions to the therapist (transference) and his or her efforts to avoid dealing with fundamental problems (resistance). Minimally educated persons, or those not comfortable dealing with concepts, tend not to respond to this model.

There are also training sessions, usually set up for neophyte therapists, to guide them in their work with client groups. They usually place emphasis on the study and use of the countertransference. In the community, among a wide range of self-help groups there are consciousness raising groups that focus on a specific point of view, the members' perception of it, and its relationship to their personal lives. They may concentrate on exposing the exploitation of women or focus on racism or the class struggle.

Some group members may need very elementary experience in relating and establishing living patterns. They may fit into some of the above, but they may require some preliminary experience in a support group first. Support groups are geared toward helping members manage daily routines and elementary social relations. They offer continuous support and protection and may include a variety of structured formats, including the viewing and discussion of films emphasizing the establishment of behavior patterns and schedules. Structured reality orientation sessions for persons who are relatively isolated and functioning minimally are used to assist people in keeping in contact with the world about them.

The host of self-help groups would appear to be common knowledge, but this cannot be assumed. Some of these groups may be suitable if the ideology of the particular group is compatible with the client's general views. Although self-help groups tend to place some emphasis on reciprocal nurturance, they may function within a relatively authoritarian atmosphere and foster dependency or specific ideological commitments. Being with other people with similar problems may be the most crucial factor in helping the client establish therapeutic relationships. Some of the groups are Alcholics Anonymous, Weight Watchers, Overeaters Anonymous, Widow-to-Widow, Parents without Partners, Re-Evaluation Counseling, groups for child abusers, and groups for persons with specific physical or mental disabilities (mastectomy, oncological conditions, etc.). People need to know, if they do not already, that there are crisis centers for rape victims, drug addiction, potential suicides, pregnancy and abortion counseling, and shelters for abused wives. They need to know that training groups exist for parents, preparation for marriage, learning assertiveness, and other types of help, such as vocational counseling, legal assistance, health care, pastoral counseling, and general assistance from social welfare agencies.

Interchange between members is the therapeutic force, even in groups with an authoritarian climate. Among some groups, specific ideologies give direction to the mutual aid offered. For instance, the language used in Alcoholics Anonymous (AA) has a distinctly religious tone. The moral commitment becomes the therapeutic agent, partly because it helps reestablish a meaningful relationship between the person and his or her world. The philosophy behind Recovery, Inc. (RI) is based on the notion that doctors are always right, that will power is of the utmost importance, and that emotional reactions are meaningless. Synanon (S) emhasizes catharsis, i.e., "emptying your gut," "dumping garbage," and "emotional bathroom" work in the words of some of the participants. A member is part of a residential community that permits discharge of stress and offers acceptance and support on a 24-hour basis.[33] The "Game" is an essential activity in S. Activities called "contract breaking" challenge agreements made with oneself as well as with others. The assumptions behind S activities are "that contracts of any kind pose serious dangers [and that] they rob the individual of energy and impose an increasing burden of anxiety, guilt, and depression."[34] AA and RI place prime emphasis on a nurturing environment in which the support of others encourages "good" behavior. AA has most effectively used the nurturing peer member who is always ready to help a new member become abstinent.

The Contract

The written contract is not generally used. Group members usually enter into a verbal contract that is flexible and adjustable as the sessions continue. When written contracts are used, there is more apt to be a uniform understanding among the group members about the nature of the group. Such a contract-orienting sheet, which has been used by Shostrom and others, deals with criteria for admission, prohibition of extra office sessions, confidentiality, and the importance of sharing experiences.[35] A written introduction, prepared by De Schill, orients clients to psychoanalytic group therapy by discussing how to behave in the group and the relationships to the analyst and the other group members. Some of the most useful parts deal with advising the client that becoming accustomed to the therapy group takes some time, that members talk about experiences and reactions that are important to them when they are ready, and that the exchanges and interactions between the members are a major source of increased understanding and growth.[36]

When the contract is signed by the client, he or she indicates that the conditions of therapy have been read and that he or she agrees to cooperate fully. A contract that helps to establish reciprocity among members more readily would require all group members to sign the same agreement. The signatures of all group members and of the therapist appear on the same contract, and each participant receives a copy. The contract is then an agreement between all participants. A helpful addition to the contract is the listing of each individual member's personal goals. The reciprocal agreement is ratified at the first or second group meeting. This method is suitable to therapy that is limited to a specific number of sessions. Arrangements that do not have a termination date leave the members subject to the vagaries of the therapist and are generally discordant with the objective of establishing a dynamic reciprocity in the group. Under these circumstances, the reproduction of the traditional family unit is unavoidable. Whether the therapy should take place in a unit similar to the family unit, where it all happened in the first place, is not entirely certain, although it is commonly thought to be. It can be argued that, no matter what the setting, the family will be recreated in some way; that the prototypical relationships reappear again and again. They are never, however, the original ones, and the layers of experiences are always there to alter them, sometimes in major ways.

The Shostrom contract and the De Schill orientation leaflet exemplify some of the commonalities between experiential and psychoanalytic groups. They both inform the clients of the importance of their part in making the therapy work. Neither goes far enough in encouraging a full mutual aid and reciprocal nurturance in the group. On the contrary, De Schill clearly informs the new member that he or she is not able to judge when the treatment should be concluded; the therapist unilaterally makes this decision. It is interesting that, in an informal survey of 15 writers, who identify themselves as feminist therapists, I found none used written contracts, and a few simply said they had never thought of it. It is possible that it is viewed as "too binding" and as apt to elicit some apprehension about too much structure.

From the very beginning, the members need to be aware that the quest for meaning is of paramount importance, for it is the meaning we attach to our lives that determines how we see ourselves and others, how we feel about what is happening to us, and what we actually do. Members need to know that exchange and sharing with others, the resultant altered perceptions, and the experience of helping, understanding, and viewing other social worlds have the possibility of enriching daily existence, providing alternate modes of being, and adding new meaning to our lives.

THE GROUP

Techniques used to promote group interactions are used during the early sessions when the members need to get acquainted and can use some assistance in breaking through the customary social norms that prevail. Some of these techniques are more conducive to the initiation of beginning nurturing approaches than others. One technique that can stimulate a dramatic interaction between members and a marked arousal of interest in each other is the Depth Unfolding Experience described by Otto. This method shortens the time needed for the getting acquainted phase. Each person is given 5 minutes to describe the experiences believed to be central to the formation of who he or she is. The sharing is concluded with each member relating one of the happiest experiences he or she has had.[37]

The visiting approach may be used when new members are being considered for an ongoing group. In ongoing groups, Bach suggested that one or two members may meet with the prospective member, or the entire group may meet to chat with the person before or after a group session.[38] This permits the prospective member and the group to consider whether they wish to establish relationships. Moreover, the initial interview and the initial group session or trial group session are used to orient the new member to the ways of the group. The airing of expectations and the discussion of what happens in such groups can help the new member become familiar with the norms of reciprocity, thus setting the climate for group interaction. In the formation of new groups, members may meet for two preliminary sessions before they decide if they wish to establish or remain in this group. A temporary two- or three-session contract is then used. This affords the members the opportunity to share and explore their concerns about joining a group.

The orientation phase for all groups is the time when the contractual arrangements are reviewed with the members, this time as they sit together. It is the time when the therapist reaffirms what he or she wants to happen, and the members, as a group, indicate what they want to happen. This is when the therapist with a psychoanalytic frame of reference again informs the members that he or she would use the Freudian paradigm that concentrates on the analysis of the transference between the members and the therapist and the resistances of the members. Or the therapist, using the Ellis's rational approach, will explain that his or her approach to treatment is based on the assumption that irrational ideas and "the many corollaries to which they normally lead are the basic causes of most emotional disturbances."[39] In the process of doing this, the therapist establishes with the group a common understanding that the therapist will adhere to certain views of behavior.

A group uses therapeutic nurturance, whatever the therapeutic orientation of the therapist. A therapist could stress its importance while still emphasizing specialized concepts relevant to a particular theory. For instance, in psychoanalytically oriented groups, the therapist can note the exchange of nurturance and support that takes place in the "transference relationship" when the client reacts to the therapist or members of the group as if they were a particular person in the client's life. The exchange of mutual reactions can be seen as partly prompted by "countertransference responses" when the therapist responds to the client in terms of his or her own needs. Rather then emphasizing the technical terminology or the psychoanalytic concepts of tranference and countertransference, the therapist could point out the stages of the transference exchange that move progressively to higher levels of reciprocity.

When the therapist is the prime decision maker, agreements with clients are asymmetrical and the nurturance exchange takes the form of a teacher to a pupil, or a parent to a child. Under these circumstances, the contract is an asymmetrical one. The therapist attains gratification when the clients cooperate and support what is being done. It is doubtful whether a therapist bent on giving interpretations, or the opposite, one who is passive, can stimulate the development of mutual aid, interperceptual discovery, and the exploration of explanatory theories formulated by the members.

As mentioned previously, groups are sometimes established to help people learn behavior patterns by following models. For instance, Goldstein and colleagues controlled group learning by admitting a confederate of the therapist as a member of the group.[40] In this way, the desired behavioral goals may be demonstrated and supported by a group member. This approach works when the group members are regressed and have difficulty carrying out the most elementary social acts. Films may be used to demonstrate how people talk to each other in social settings and to encourage the members to try some of the methods shown. Psychiatric institutions have established classes for learning how to maintain oneself in the community. These methods stress asymmetrical and nonreciprocal relationships. Such an approach could lead to interactions between the group members; ultimately higher forms of reciprocal sharing, support, and aid can occur particularly if postsocialization groups are set up for this purpose and a new contract, with relevant goals, is set up.

In educational settings, a group may be comprised of therapists (usually student therapists and their teacher) and one client. This is most likely to occur in an institution where the activity is planned to give students some group experience with a client present and where a particular client is able to deal with such a setting. What actually happens can vary widely from a didactic interchange to the reciprocal nurturance characteristic of a therapy group. In the didactic situation, the client shares his or her difficulties with the "therapists" and they offer some support, advice, and sometimes analysis. Such a group could in fact become therapeutic. This would require adequate preparation of the students and the client; it would ultimately result in the breaking down of the barriers between who is the client and who is the student or therapist. Eventually, there would be no identifiable client. At best, such a group would be limited to a short series of sessions, probably not more than four. This approach is more likely to be used in a general health care setting where the participants are a client who has an organic illness and health professionals. The support and nurturance offered is usually superficial, but the sharing of information and emotional experiences may have an impact on the participants. This type of arrangement is also used in psychiatric institutions where the intake or progress interview takes place in a group conference. There is free interaction between the client and the staff members and input by the client in the discussion of diagnosis and treatment. It is an enlightened form of the old staff conference in which the client was interrogated by a group of professionals and then left the room while the staff discussed diagnosis and disposition.

At Rutgers Medical School, B. Cohen has lead treatment sessions and seminars pairing medical students with clients as partners. In this way, the students can offer support and guidance to their client-partner and thus people who might not otherwise be able to function in groups are able to do so. The students themselves participate in the group and the clients may occasionally attend the students' classes. I have found that four weekly sessions at a psychiatric institution with nursing students and their individual clients as members can be effective. Clients have experienced a surge of self-importance and responsibility for helping others, while the students gained a greater awareness of the similiarities between some of the clients' perceptions and their own and an appreciation for alternate concepts and extraordinary thoughts and logic. A year after one such series, two clients, still hospitalized, spoke of "the group" as a memorable experience, referred to it when speaking to other residents and hospital personnel, and asked when another group like that would be established.

CONCLUSIONS

The selection of clients inevitably involves labeling if the therapist examines the client's behavioral patterns and estimates the possible outcomes of participation in a particular group. Each client is considered in terms of capacity to participate in giving and receiving at some level. Estimations of suitability for a group membership are made through interviews, sociometric methods, and trial group attendance. Characteristics that have been considered reasons for exclusions are (1) poor reality contact, (2) culturally deviant behavior, (3) evidence of being a chronic monopolist, (4) psychopathic defenses dominant, and (5) impulsiveness. Those unable to relate at a simple level and those without some altruistic concern for others will impede the development of the group.

Because the DSM-III is a descriptive approach to behavior based on an attempt to assist in determining what is needed, it can be a helpful guide in evaluating the potential candidate for group therapy. It provides a possibility of examining clinical syndromes and personality patterns for styles of interacting and nurturance experiences and needs.

The initial interview with the prospective group member is crucial in establishing an atmosphere of mutual reciprocity between therapist and client and setting the climate for building reciprocal relationships between group members. Prospective members need to know about the existence of self-help networks and to be cognizant of possible choices in treatment. A group contract between all members and the therapist can facilitate the reciprocal process by stipulating the group objective to achieve mutual aid and reciprocal nurturance.

NOTES

1. Bach, G. (1954). *Intensive group psychotherapy*. New York: Ronald Press, p. 13–27.
2. Powdermaker, F., & Frank, J. D. (1953). *Group psychotherapy*. Cambridge, Mass.: Harvard University Press.
3. Yalom, I. D. (1975). *The theory and practice of psychotherapy* (2nd ed.). New York: Basic Books, pp. 127, 225–41.

4. Schur, E.M. (1971). *Labeling deviant behavior.* New York: Harper & Row, p. 15.
5. Bach, G., op. cit., p. 13.
6. Sadock, B. J., & Kaplan, H. I. (1972). Selection of patients and the dynamic and structural organization of the group. In H.I. Kaplan & B.J. Sadock (Eds.), *The evolution of group therapy* (Vol. 2). New York: Jason Aronson, p. 119.
7. Ibid., p. 127.
8. Ibid., p. 119.
9. Sullivan, H.S. (1954). *The psychiatric interview.* New York: W.W. Norton & Co., Inc.
10. Bach, G., op. cit., pp. 15–16.
11. Moreno, Z. T. (1978). Psychodrama. In H. Mullan & M. Rosenbaum (Eds.), *Group Psychotherapy* (2nd ed). New York: Macmillan, p. 359.
12. Moreno, J.L. (1952). *Who shall survive?* Beacon, N.Y.: Beacon House, p. 334.
13. Bach, G., op. cit., p. 16.
14. Moreno, J., op. cit.
15. Schur, E.M., op. cit., p. 8.
16. Freud, S. (1953). *The standard edition of the complete psychological works of Sigmund Freud.* London: Hogarth Press, Vol. 17, p. 132.
17. Binswanger, L. (1975). *Being-in-the-world.* London: Souvenir Press, pp. 63–4.
18. *Diagnostic and statistical manual of mental disorders* (3rd ed.). (III). Washington, D.C.: American Psychiatric Association, p. 11.
19. Ibid., p. 183.
20. Ibid., pp. 183–4.
21. Ibid., p. 195.
22. Ibid., p. 196.
23. Ibid., p. 206.
24. Ibid., pp. 210–11.
25. Gregory, I. (1968). *Fundamentals of psychiatry* (2nd ed.). Philadelphia: Saunders, p. 424.
26. Millon, T. (1969). *Modern psychopathology.* Philadelphia: Saunders, p. 416.
27. Ibid., p. 396.
28. Millon, op. cit., p. 403.
29. DSM III, op. cit., p. 234.
30. Millon, op. cit., p. 407.
31. DSM-III, op. cit., p. 310.
32. See Chapter 9 for a discussion of the intentional community.
33. Lieberman, M.A., Borman, L. D. and Associates. (1979). *Self-help groups for coping with crisis.* San Francisco, Cal.: Jossey-Bass, pp. 285–89.
34. Ibid., pp. 296–97.
35. Shostrom, E. L. (1976). *Actualizing therapy.* San Diego, Calif.: Edits.
36. De Schill, S. (1974). Introduction to psychoanalytic group psychotherapy. In S. De Schill, (Ed.), *The challenge for group psychotherapy.* New York: International Universities Press, pp. xxi–xxviii.
37. Otto, H. (1970). *Group methods to actualize human potential: A handbook.* Beverly Hills, Calif.: Holistic Press, pp. 25–36.
38. Bach, G., op. cit., pp. 16–17.
39. Ellis, A. (1963). *Reason and emotion in psychotherapy.* New York: Lyle Stuart, p. 89.
40. Goldstein, A. (1973). *Structured learning therapy.* New York: Academic.

6

Nurturance Between Therapist and Group Members

The personality and attitudes of the therapist are central to the establishment and utilization of a therapeutic exchange of nurturance. The therapist's knowledge of his or her own life experiences and adaptations is used therapeutically in the group. How this is done will have an effect on the group's activities and developments. A therapist needs to have a full commitment to an egalitarian group climate if in-depth reciprocal nurturance is to be achieved.

THE THERAPIST AS NURTURER

To be ourselves fully is not at all easy, since we do not always know how to do this. As group therapists, we have to be able to be precisely that, and to face others directly. We need to be unafraid of living and experiencing to the full what is going on. In some sense, the life of the therapy group is removed from "real" life, since it is an intense experience that has no real functional value in the organizational structure of society. Nevertheless, the question of real life and artificiality really begs the point, for so-called real life is filled with pseudo and uncaring relationships, whereas the therapy group may be the source of compassion and genuine feeling.

The norm of reciprocity is prominent in effective therapy groups. If we establish a group in which nonreciprocal exchanges prevail, our personality remains an unknown and the members are supposed to reveal theirs, it is questionable that the group members themselves can get very far in knowing each other. The most that is possible under such circumstances are object relationships in which members understand some generalities about each other. The double standard, one for the members and another for ourselves, retains the traditional professional dominance and presents a nonreciprocal, nonnurturing and inegalitarian relationship as a desirable model.

Dependence on the therapist and parallel expressions, with no interactions or relationships between what people are saying, is expected to predominate only in the beginning sessions. The leader nourishes at an elementary level by simply being there. If he or she remains aloof personally but works hard at giving meaning to what is happening, then a level of parental involvement, concern, support, and caring is conveyed. While interpretations can be personal gifts from the therapist to the group, possibly initiating similiar gift giving between the members, they can seriously interefere with the development of a cohesive group when rendered too early. If the therapist brings the richness of his or her personality and life experiences to the group, then caring and support is much greater and reciprocity that is beyond intellectualized interpretations and analyses becomes possible. When there is an intense interaction between leader and members at the fantasy level, the way is paved for peak experiences that unify the participants in a transforming awareness of themselves in relation to the universe. If the leader does not participate actively and emotionally in the group happenings, the openness and self-disclosure encouraged in the group often can become a meaningless and empty format permitting much play-acting and little real participation by each member and the leader in each other's lives.

There is often a fetish made of the importance of being independent and autonomous. The glorification however, of one person not being dependent on the other contradicts the central importance of nurturance exchange in our lives. To proclaim that we do not exist to please each other, because this would compromise our individuality, violates the essentially social nature of being human. The intent of the proclamation of independence is to free individuals from enslavement to the dictates of others, but independence from others is never fully possible nor desirable. Most of the time we are working out unequal relationships, handling entanglements, and changing perceptions of ourselves and others in the process. There is no question that we need each other, for we live in order to be a someone to another person. To deny this is to turn our backs on the essence of what it means to be human. The real question is how relationships are developed and whether they are democratic and reciprocal, or hierarchal and status-ridden. Defective and stunted growth are often the aftermath of a destructive, restricting relationship with a significant other who is controlling and domineering. This is one compelling reason why it is imperative that the therapist dispense with the shackles of the authority role as much as possible. Although the therapist will be perceived in many different ways, he or she cannot be a person who enjoys holding power and controlling others.

Rosenbaum noted that it was unfortunate that therapists are often enticed to fulfill society's need for a secular priest. The reification of a treatment theory, assigning it a life of its own, is sometimes a way of taking on such a role. Instead of dealing with life as a coparticipant, therapists sometimes become primarily authorities on uncovering the unconscious. They then come to believe that the solution to everything resides in the unconscious. The therapist cannot, however, compromise his or her integrity as a genuine person because the client has a need to believe in his or her infallibility. "What we are doing, if we are honest, is to share with the client the fact that we are all engaged in a struggle to understand and live in the wilderness."[1] Perhaps even more important is the recognition that the therapist also receives nurturance and support from the group members. At the minimum, it is forthcoming when the members are active and show their caring for the therapist by being responsive and giving of themselves. Group psychotherapy can, however, be much more.

In his plea for genuineness and authenticity in the group psychotherapy situation, Rosenbaum warned therapists against presenting therapy as a means of making life easier to live, for there is a danger that therapy can become just another manipulation, another technique for avoiding life. Rather, he entreated therapists to boldly face the absurdities of life, to relish "the anxiety of creation," and to face the human condition squarely and directly.[2] This position stands in danger of being an extension of the view that we need to accept our condition and situation because much of it cannot be changed. Certainly, however, paradoxes, contradictions, and the unity of opposites are central to the way we think, develop ideas, and create new understandings. The beauty of creative relationships hinges on the inherent paradoxes and absurdities in new and challenging events. To become more free to control our own lives may mean to laugh in the face of confusing and disruptive paradoxes and to have the courage to change the human condition in spite of these humorous but disquieting observations.

The paradoxes created by family therapists to get clients to break rigid behavior patterns bring into startling relief the vulnerability of fixed positions. Instead of working directly at helping the client change undesirable patterns, the therapist takes the client's absurd position in exaggerated form and insists that he or she intensify the rigid pattern of behavior under consideration. In group psychotherapy, this would be a violation of the unity and solidarity between group members and therapist. It is more like a hoax than a sharing, a controlling of the other rather than appreciating the unique individual. For instance, the therapist requests that the mother needs to be far more concerned about her adolescent son cleaning his room when, in fact, the mother's total preoccupation with haranguing the son to clean up his room has created a household that is in a constant uproar. The use of paradox is the application of an authoritarian approach that bypasses the building of a reciprocal and egalitarian relationship. It can be considered a behavior modification approach to get movement in a situation in which a stalemate has been reached. For instance, the mother begins to react against the intense pressure that she harangue her son even more to be clean. Soon she stops. Once a disruptive behavior pattern has been stopped in this way, it may free the client to move on to more reciprocally rewarding relationships, but this is far from inevitable.

Therapists bring with them the patterns of exchange that they have learned in their personal and professional experiences. The therapeutic venture is essentially the application of professional clinical modes of exchanging to personal exchange patterns. No matter what the professional training, it tends to compromise the life patterns of the therapist. A clinical supervisor may help enhance the nurturing qualities that the student therapist has already developed in the process of living, growing, and adapting. On the other hand, the supervisor may attempt to so change the student's way of being with others that the main source of his or her humanity and value to others is squelched. It is as important for the supervisor to recognize and appreciate the uniqueness of each individual that happens to be a student as it is for the student to do so with clients.

A common expectation is that the therapist will be like a nurturing parent who provides love, wisdom, and relief from pain. Occasionally, the therapist is seen as someone who can be converted, "who will see the world in the way we do."[3] In the early sessions a group member tries to gain some understanding and support for what he or she is, a person obsessed with certain ideas or whatever. The therapist's recognition of this is at least confirmation of that member's existence as a special individual. Linton's description of his total involvement with a client's "trips to outer space" brings out the precarious borderline between being a therapist and being a client.[4] Yet, without such involvement by the therapist, the group members are left to be the subordinates in a world divided into the bad and the good, the sick and the healthy.

Group members help enormously in correcting distortions by the therapist. When the therapist becomes enthralled with a member's fantasies and is having trouble keeping one foot solidly planted in reality, there will be, almost always, another group member who will be, at any particular stage in group development, more solidly rooted in reality. It could even be a group member who is not consistently conscious of his or her self boundaries. It is remarkable to observe that clients with chronic schizophrenic patterns can play this stabilizing role. An individual, primarily withdrawn and inactive in the group, can rise to the occasion and deliver an astute perception that others are unable to make at the time. This is facilitated by a sharp selective process, sometimes present in such members, which enables them to highlight a point everybody else has forgotten or missed.

The group members need assistance in taking on and shifting between the new roles of being cotherapists and clients. In the earlier sessions, the therapist may demonstrate client and therapist roles. He or she may show how to engage in an internal, intrapsychic monologue and follow it up with what another person might say to express interest, acceptance, or need for clarification. Members who follow this lead will need support in their efforts. In other words, we verbalize the internal dialogue that takes place as we try to handle personal issues and concerns. This helps members recognize similiar processes in themselves and gives them the courage to engage in both objective exchanges with other members and the therapist and in subjective excursions within themselves.

Occasionally, the group members may have considerable difficulty sharing and helping. The inability of the group to move forward can be the result of too much diversity between the selected members resulting in a limited basis for communication. The most elementary means of talking to each other has to be established. The group may also have difficulty getting off the ground when too many members are passive or withdrawn. On the other hand, superficial exchanges or nonresponsiveness may merely represent a social mask. By the third or fourth session, there should be evidence that the members are beginning to reach out.

THERAPEUTIC EMPATHY

Empathic understanding is fundamental to the living together with others in a caring atmosphere. Schafer compared the empathic experience with the aesthetic illusion of the observer of a work of art, since in both situations a certain amount of distance is retained. The empathetic process in the therapy group, however, is much more involved than the simple appreciation of someone else. It becomes part of an interaction whose outcome is not clearly predictable. Generative empathy is the inner experience of "sharing in comprehending the psychological state of another person."[5] It is the basis of altruistic behavior, but it is much more than that. It is an attitude that leads inevitably to helping someone grow. The generative empathic process is based on relating our own experiences to those that someone else is having and assuming their feelings are similar to those we have had. Observing a client's life at any one point, "we tentatively project onto him the feelings we once felt under similiar circumstances, and then test this projection by further observation."[6] Therapeutic empathy is the use of generative empathy in trying to understand someone.

Schafer differentiated between a primarily passive empathic experience and a deeper sense of thinking. The latter is exemplified when we say, "I know what you feel because I know that I once felt something like it and I know how you make me feel."[7] The primary experience is aligning with the other in some way, such as repudiating something together, or simply sharing an emotional experience, view, or grievance. To develop a deeper empathy, we introject that aspect of the person we think we understand and then react to it. This reaction calls into play our beliefs, defenses, and norms. The image of the other thus undergoes change because of our reaction, which is determined by our unique ways of seeing and thinking. Thus, we see the person through our own images. We now see them differently as a result of reacting to the aspects of them that we have managed to absorb. Schafer believed that the empathizer's personality remains intact and untouched by this process. If, however, change is *not* taking place in the therapist, it is probable that the empathy developed is not the result of an interactive process, but a superficial acceptance of a known entity. The former requires involvement; the latter does not.

Oscillation between observing and experiencing is an important component of empathy. It has its beginnings when a person is able to share some aspect of the self with which the other or others can identify in some way. It has a fantasied component that may have little to do with the content of the exchange. This process involves countertransference, since the therapist brings the self to interact with the group within the context of his or her own world. Barriers in this process are compounded by the difficulties members have in presenting themselves. Their feelings and reactions may have to be extricated from their projections and other distortions. Therapists may also have resistance in empathizing with certain members whose behavior may represent some unresolved conflicts of their own. In an empathic institutional setting, the group therapist, who may be a nurse specialist, psychiatrist, psychologist, social worker, the milieu mangager (who is usually a nurse), and the client are predominantly altruistic toward each other. "Altruistic surrender" occurs when empathic understanding centers on a particular behavior. The client may feel that he or she will lose support if the behavior is abandoned. This tends to keep the client frozen in the same state in order to retain the empathy gained because he or she is afraid of losing the continued interest of others.[8] Such a reaction stands out as limited and potentially paralytic, like the broken record when the needle cannot move out of the groove in which it is stuck.

Clients living together have many opportunities to develop empathic understandings. Nurse–therapists often arrange group experiences that provide for close contacts between clients and nurses. Parental type support that is marked by nonreciprocal nurturance is sometimes necessary before a client is able to begin to experiment with a more advanced relationship. The milieu manager emphasizes the essential importance of mutual relations in the residential setting; the usual goal is to help the person to achieve some end. Concentration on specific objectives, like the achievement of greater self-control, however, usually interferes with the development of a true dialogue.

The unilateral nurturer is a problem. So long as one person remains in greater control, the relationship is not equal and therefore limited in possibilities. Schafer saw empathic understanding as undirectional; he did not see the client empathizing with the therapist. Without this happening, there is insufficient reciprocity of activity to term the empathy anything other than the reaction of the therapist to a predominantly "I–It" relationship as described by Buber. In the I–It situation, the other is an external object that the therapist has fit to his or her own personal training, beliefs, and favorite theories.

The therapist has been seen as moving from being a nurturer, in the dependent stage, to a facilitator in the independent stage;[9] however, the nurturer and facilitator roles are not separate and apart. It is reasonable to consider various forms of reciprocal nurturance as occurring throughout the group sessions with more advanced forms emerging as authentic and genuine therapeutic experiences occur more regularly.[10] For instance, total acceptance and support is a never-ending process and continues throughout the therapy sessions. The facilitator role belongs to all group members, who are encouraged to assume it from the very first session. The therapist demonstrates from the very beginning how to develop reciprocal nurturance by showing caring and concern, trying to discover the other, presenting the self so that it is discoverable and appreciated, and reacting to the influence of mutual exchange and perceptual challenge.

The "Shut-Up" Person

Entering the world of the group members is essential, yet this may be very difficult to do. Some have closed themselves up and only a dramatic *unfreezing* could make them available to another. Buber remarked that we can talk to a person with schizophrenic features but usually such a person is inclined to "shut" him or herself and we "cannot go in." He said, "I can talk to a schizophrenic as far as he is willing to let me into his particular world . . . in general he does not want to have you come in. But the moment when he *shut himself,* I cannot go in."[11] This is true, not only for those with overt schizophrenic disorders, but for some of us who are "shut up" on many occasions when we are utterly unavailable to anyone. The question is whether we can be opened up and what it will take to do so. People who do not have outstanding behavioral problems also can shut themselves. It is the opening up of the shut-up person and the shut-up parts of ourselves that is at the heart of the therapeutic encounter.

The psychotic condition is the outcome of an effort to resolve the inconsistencies of existence.[12] In some way, the psychosis is a revolutionary quest for an ideal to fill in the gaps of experiences that appear everywhere. The adaptation to this dilemma is, however, in the form of what Binswanger called a "deficient existential mode," because a foreign value system is brought to bear on events. The person renounces the natural dualistic nature of human thought altogether and usually fills in the experiental gap with fantasy.[13] It is a struggle to make things more clear and ideal. In this respect, it is not totally different from our pursuit of the ideal and our continuous encounter with the discovery that it exists nowhere. Ordinarily, however, we do not develop a system of thought that will make things fit more coherently into an ideal state, nor do we create a substitute world that has a greater potential of being ideal. It is not so much a loss of reality, but the development of a different value system that makes it difficult for others to appreciate the schizophrenic experience.

Empathic understanding is within the province of severely disturbed persons who have "shut themselves up" if they are provided with a nurturing group setting that meets regularly.

A group of four withdrawn and delusional men in their forties and fifties, hospitalized in a state hospital, met once a week with two nurse cotherapists for 8 months. In the early sessions, the members were frequently occupied with repetitious, unorganized, and sometimes rather prolonged monologues that the therapists tried to intercept by selecting out specific content for further development. Only gradually did some give-and-take develop between the clients and the therapists. This moved from discussion of general topics such as sleeping problems, behavior of other clients, and idealistic hopes to concern with the reliability and feelings of the therapists. There were some beginings then made in filling in the gaps. The cotherapists were primarily and foremost nurturing, and provided the members with support and caring as well as models of effective behaviors. The group managed to achieve some level of elementary reciprocal nurturance by the end of the fifth month by beginning to focus on group focal conflicts. They advanced to handling ambivalence toward the therapists and conflict over perceived alliances with one or the other of the therapists. This was facilitated by other members who joined the group for several sessions. Eventually the members advanced to sharing their ambivalence and affection for the therapists. The beginnings of some empathy for each other and the therapists were evident sporadically as they began to interact directly with each other and the therapist. When the sessions ended, three of the members had begun meeting by themselves, showed interest in continuing their relationships, and were cooperating in the purchase of food for each other. A social reciprocity had been established in persons who had been predominantly isolated and almost exclusively preoccupied with delusional material.[14]

The potential of the hospitalized, psychotic client to respond to a group was demonstrated in an experimental group that lasted three sessions.

A grossly delusional 26-year-old man was asked to participate in the three group sessions held for undergraduate nursing students and their clients: the sessions took place in the conference room on his unit. He had periodically confided to the students and myself his ideas of being controlled by monsters and his notion that his organs were floating outside him. He was so eager to join our group that we decided to accept him. He was doing nothing on the unit, participating in none of the programs offered, and generally was almost totally preoccupied with his delusions. In the first two sessions, he sat next to me and responded immediately to my encouragment when he added to the group theme and my discouragement when he talked about his "floating organs." The students and other members were responsive to his comments and he demonstrated a remarkable capacity to care about what the others were saying, even making keen observations about the differences between his own world and his father's, when during a planned group activity, he responded to a picture he had selected of a boy shown with a valentine he had made that said "I love dad." Reassurance was sustained by my placing my hand on his arm as I offered direct guidance. He also placed his hand on my arm when he followed my direction. At one point, when he felt particularly comforted after an exchange, he placed his head momentarily on my shoulder. At the end of the second session, when we had discussed the names we prefer to be called, he loudly called across the room to me as I was leaving the unit, "Good-bye Ruthie!" using the name I had said I liked for myself. He came late to the third session and was unable to sit next to me for everyone was already seated. He left after a few minutes mumbling something about a murderer.

DEVELOPMENT OF THE GROUP

The therapist is central to building a climate in which the highest form of the therapeutic enterprise can occur. This happens when there is an organic merging of the participants' experiences and uniqueness. The individuality of the participants is momentarily lost in the peak experience of unity with each other. The therapist must be consciously aware of this potential and encourage the building of solidarity that leads to it. It does not occur when the working climate is foremost. Rather it follows as an aftermath and periodic sign that the group is experiencing more intense forms of mutual nurturance. There is no higher form of relatedness and unity; the process is fired by an exchange of nurturance that has a strongly cognitive component because the experience includes an awareness that there is a generalized meaning to life and that all our experiences are of the same fabric. This sense of unity with one another grows out of complete acceptance, shared experiences, caring for each person, and the recognition of the great value of each person. Such peak experiences are associated with the experience of the uncanny; they seem to transcend the limits of the objective situation. They are confined to those moments when therapist and all the members together experience a strong surge of solidarity. This often means that there is an active exchange at the unconscious level as well as an intense interaction at the symbolic–cognitive level.

Two therapists jointly leading a group bring their relationships into the group. How they feel about each other will affect the level of reciprocal nurturance fostered in the group. The entrance of a cotherapist into the group, after it has been meeting for some time, is not simply explained as the therapist's decision to bring in a colleague to work with him or her. When a democratic climate and cotherapeutic functions of the members are stressed, the members are consulted about such a change. Their discussions and possible objections are aired, and, if they are not convinced that it would be beneficial, the move is not made. Sexual stereotypes may initially affect the members' expectations of the leader. When the female therapist is brought in to support the male therapist, there is a tendency for unilateral nurturing support to be expected from her. The male therapist may even expect this for himself. When there is actually greater power held by one therapist, as in the case of student–supervisor or psychiatrist–nurse teams, the model for reciprocal nurturance becomes difficult to demonstrate, unless the member of the professionally dominant group totally embraces a democratized version of the therapeutic encounter and the supervisory process as well.[15]

When working with a cotherapist, it is easier to demonstrate how to establish a beginning helping relationship, for the cotherapists will be showing how they cooperate in helping the group get started. Cotherapists usually work out their cooperative therapeutic roles before the group starts and then examine them continuously as the group sessions develop. At some point, when the group is ready, this becomes part of the group work. In the early formation of the group, a third therapist may monitor the conferences between the cotherapists to give a "third ear" to the working out of their relationship as cotherapists. The establishment of a "subordinate" group therapist controlled by a "dominant" one needs to be avoided for this will then become the model that the group will emulate. Cotherapists sometimes tend to think they must agree on everything. This approach curtails the potency of having cotherapists, especially in an advanced group where disagreement between cotherapists can demonstrate that it is safe to bring conflict into the group and that this can be a means of attaining greater understanding of each other.

Any group recordings are agreed upon by all participants. Specific uses and disposition of recordings are clearly established and accepted by the members. It is best to discuss recordings that may be used during the sessions at the very onset of the group. Joint efforts, written and verbal, contribute directly to emotional and cognitive reciprocity, that is, analytic and evaluative efforts can evoke a sharing of feelings or ideas that increase closeness and understanding of each other. Members may summarize their group session experiences and exchange these expressions with each other verbally or in writing. Such activities may be used to focus on some aspect of the group. Members might be asked to point out the most important event that occurred during the session. A record may be kept on filing cards of such events and reviewed periodically by the group. A comparison of different events chosen can be used to gain greater understanding of the relative importance of different values and meanings for particular individuals. Most importantly, however, this can contribute to knowing what each member is like and each one knowing him or herself better.

The viewing of videotapes, motion pictures, and photographs by the members has been considered a confrontation technique. It has helped psychotic persons redirect their concerns outward and has accelerated the process of change.[16] There is general agreement that videotape confrontation can heighten insight. It facilitates members seeing their own behavior through the eyes of the camera, which may represent how others see them.

This is one way of increasing awareness of aspects of self, especially examining behavior that eludes us or that we generally ignore. It is also a way of exploring with the other members the variations in individual perceptions of self and others that exist in the group. This permits the taking in of behavioral cues that are ordinarily not available, for the tapes pick up reactions and expressions not easily seen in the group.

> At their fifth training session graduate nursing student therapists were asked to do a Life Space Drawing to describe how they saw themselves in relation to the others in the group.[17] Six members placed all group members in the center forming a grape-like cluster; the other five spread out the members in a universe of isolated stars with varying degrees of closeness between them. It appeared that the cohesiveness that seemed high during group sessions was only experienced by about half the members. None of the members wanted to know the overall group results at the next session. Reacting differently, a 12 member undergraduate training group of liberal arts majors was able to use such results to facilitate understanding and to grow closer. The projective test, however, needs to be used with caution with an ongoing group. It may facilitate the development of interactions between members when the group is beginning or has reached an impasse. It may have a negative effect on a group that is actively working on achieving an accepting and supportive climate by bearing critical and negative connotations as interpretations and analyses might. In addition to the stress and anxiety caused by expecting to hear the worst about how others see us, this method may be seen by some as producing an inaccurate momentary "photograph" of interactions in progress.

A simple, generally nonthreatening tool that may be used is a very short member-generated adjective list done pre- and post-session, by which the members describe how they are feeling or thinking by listing relevant adjectives. The group results may be reviewed at the end of the session or at the beginning of the next session and contribute to the understanding of the group process. Check lists used at the end of each session can focus the members on specific observations to be made or suggest aspects of group behavior to which they might pay attention. They might include lists for identifying emotions felt, themes expressed, interactions observed, focal conflicts that developed, resolutions of conflicts, and reactions to the therapist. Occasionally, such forms are seen only by the therapist and are therefore underutilized in terms of their potential therapeutic value if shared with the group members. The overall group responses to the items may be presented as an additional measurement of the group process. Often, however, such data will reveal reactions that have not come to the fore in the group. In such instances, they will tend to appear alien and inconsequential to the group but may assist in determining undercurrents.

In two training groups of graduate nursing students run concurrently for six sessions, the results of check lists prepared at the end of each session by each member indicated that the 15-member group experienced the second session as much more meaningful and intimate than any of the others. It is interesting to note that during this session, there was a structured sharing of significant events in each member's life. It is probable that in time-limited sessions with larger groups, structured exercises foster greater sharing. The other group, which consisted of five members, evaluated all six sessions as outstanding in these areas.

TERMINATION

The termination of a group is the physical end of a usually meaningful exchange of nurturance. It is extremely important that this be accomplished in a manner appropriate to the ending of significant relationships. The life of the group comes to an end because either (1) the members have achieved a high level of reciprocal nurturance and concommitantly have experienced a release of creative and innovative ideas; (2) the length of time for the group was predetermined by contract; (3) group members are lacking in sufficient altruism to develop beginning levels of mutual aid and caring; or (4) excess anxiety and conflict have prevented the group from reaching a workable exchange.[18]

Although the therapist builds and maintains cohesiveness during initial and middle stages of treatment, he or she needs to work toward diminishing cohesiveness as the group draws to an end.[19] A new form of cohesiveness may be created to substitute for the one associated with the continuation of the group. This means that intensive reciprocity is replaced by altruism and shared warm memories for the events that the group has lived through. There is a need to evaluate the success or failure of the members, which, by inference, is an evaluation of the success or failure of the therapist. Because of the desire to avoid this, the therapist may sometimes unconsciously delay consideration of termination and therefore not give the members sufficient time to deal with it. Even if termination has not been discussed, the members may give signs that they are ready for termination. They may talk of the gains they have made and express more confidence in the future. The weakening of group cohesiveness can be detected when members start to attend irregularly, break interpersonal ties, and create reciprocally nurturing relationships outside the group.

The expectation of termination can elicit reactions of anxiety and fear because close, caring relationships are going to end. It is not completely different from losing a dear one. The anxiety may also come from an awareness of the lack of sufficient personal progress or change and the fear that the conclusion of the sessions means all is hopeless. Termination is often seen as rejection, just as divorce or death may be experienced this way. These are some of the reasons that discussions or anticipation of termination brings forth reactions of panic, rage, and a sense of worthlessness. When the group remains ongoing and the therapist decides that one member is ready to terminate, the group may have strong reactions to not having been consulted, and experience jealousy or feelings of unworthiness. It can damage the group's experience of solidarity and the meaning and significance of the group experience. Ongoing groups that have no end, with members coming and going, also have a birth, a life, and a death. When a member leaves, or a new one enters, the group begins again starting anew building a "new life." There may be some value associated with this, since it recreates what, in fact, happens in ongoing groups in our lives.

In the last two or three sessions there is usually a gradual return to customary norms, along with the lessening of intense relationships and caring. Communication may become more free and easy and increasingly less serious and involved. There is a lessening of group controls and a strengthening of the members' sense of independence and separateness from one another and the therapist. Occasionally the group has the need to deny that the end is drawing near and so it totally disregards it. Earlier patterns of behavior may return, and renewed dependence may appear. Members may express a desire to begin all over again or proclaim that "We still need the group." This may go along with expressions of uncertainty about being able to function on their own.

There may be anger when the members realize that separation is impending. It is important that the anger be expressed. However, it is difficult to express this anger toward people to whom we are saying farewell. It may precipitate out-and-out conflict on irrelevant issues or a temporary state of depression in which the members become altogether inactive. Members are likely to feel ambivalent about leaving the group, although pleased at goals achieved. They are apt to fear the loss of close relationships with the therapist and group members. Some members may feel rejected by the therapist and react to this by rejecting the therapist and the group. This is usually accompanied by a denial of the group's worth and the meaning it has had. It is hard on the therapist when the group pushes him or her out prematurely as part of the struggle with the pain of termination. The therapist may also have to struggle with an inclination to assume a unilaterally nurturing parental role as the members disengage from involvement in the group, and an impulse to hold "the children at home" surfaces.

The ending of the group is a significant part of the therapy. If there has been a vibrant group experience with extensive interaction and sharing of close and intense experiences, the ending is the cessation of these experiences, for there is no means for them to continue. The members will never again meet in this group, thus ending the aura and intensity of these relationships forever. It is inevitable that there should be a sense of loss or rejection, and at this time *debriefing* becomes essential. Debriefing usually refers to the explanations that experimenters give to their subjects upon the completion of their experiments so that the subjects will understand how they were directed or manipulated into giving certain reactions. Obviously, here it has a different meaning, for it means clarifying what has happened in the group and the nature of the relationships that developed. The members and therapist engage in a final experiment in living as they experience the full impact of the departure. Placing great emphasis on the final stage as a significant part of the group's life together may prevent some members from leaving precipitously in order to avoid the ending of a relationship and, possibly, a sense of abandonment.

The therapist shares the sadness he or she is experiencing as the group draws to an end. The group concentrates on positive reactions and reminiscences about what happened in the group. Some evaluation of progress is made by the members as they talk about new, mature nurturing relationships that they will pursue outside the group. The members need to talk about their ties to the group and their experiences of each other and what it has meant to them. Most of all, however, this is a farewell and, like all separations, the very last session is handled best by a social ritual celebrating the group's end. For example, a farewell celebration could consist of sitting down to a group-prepared dinner and perhaps even exchanging small gifts among all the participants.

CONCLUSIONS

There has been an increasingly greater emphasis on therapist participation in the group as a genuine person and in the democratic climate as therapeutic in itself, especially among the humanists who are represented in all helping professions. Therapists bring with them the patterns of exchange that they have learned in their personal and professional lives. Therapeutic empathy goes beyond the passive empathic experiences in which a person takes the same position as another. It must involve countertransference, since the therapist brings the self to interact with group members within the context of his or her own world. So long as one person remains in greater control, the relationship is limited in therapeutic possibilities. Levine has noted that leaders are "nurturers" or "facilitators." This merely means that nurturance takes on different forms as leadership and relationships change and undergo permutations. The facilitating leader encourages progress toward a more egalitarian exchange of nurturance.

In the early sessions, members tend to be dependent and look to the therapist for direction and cure. The next stage tends to be marked by struggle, rebellion, and efforts to form alliances. There then usually follows a period during which a high level of cohesiveness and solidarity and an advanced form of reciprocity of nurturance predominates. When working with a cotherapist, it is easier to demonstrate how to initiate helping relationships. Any recording and review of group activities, written or taped, is a joint effort of the group and contributes directly to the increase in emotional and cognitive reciprocity, both of which fall under the rubric of nurturance.

The expectation of termination of the group can elicit reactions of anxiety and fear because close, caring relationships are coming to an end. In the last two or three sessions, there is usually a gradual return to customary norms and intense relationships diminish.

NOTES

1. Rosenbaum, M. (1978). Toward an ethic and philosophy of group psychotherapy. In H. Mullan & M. Rosenbaum (Eds.), *Group psychotherapy* (2nd ed.). New York: The Free Press, pp. 35–6.
2. Ibid., pp. 39–40.
3. Kelly, G. A. (1955). *The psychology of personal constructs.* New York: W. W. Norton & Co., Inc., pp. 575–608.
4. Linton, R. (1979). *The fifty-minute hour.* New York: Bantom Books.
5. Schafer, R. (1959). Generative empathy in the treatment situation. *The Pschoanalytic Quarterly* 28:342–73, p. 345.
6. Ibid., p. 347.
7. Ibid., p. 349.
8. Ibid., p. 355.
9. Levine, B. (1979). *Group psychotherapy: Practice and development.* Englewood Cliffs, N.J.: Prentice-Hall, p. 282.
10. Ibid., p. 283.
11. Buber, M. (1965). *The knowledge of man.* (M. Friedman & D. G. Smith, Trans.). New York: Harper Torchbooks, pp. 175–76.
12. Binswanger, L. (1963) *Being-in-the-world.* (J. Needleman, Trans.). New York: Harper & Row, p. 253.
13. Ibid., pp. 257–58, 264.
14. Group led by Barbara Robinson and Agnes Roelens, graduate nursing students, Rutgers, the State University.
15. Mullan, H., & Rosenbaum, M. (1978). Transference and countertransference. In H. Mullan & M. Rosenbaum (Eds.). *Group psychotherapy* (2nd ed.). New York: The Free Press, p. 188.
16. Berger, M. M. (1978). Confrontation through videotape. In M. M. Berger (Ed.), *Videotape techniques in psychiatric training and treatment.* New York: Brunner/Mazel, pp. 19–36.
17. See Chapter 5 for a description of the Life Space Drawing.
18. Sarri, R. C., & Galinsky, M. J. (1974). A conceptual framework for group development. In P. Glasser, R. Sarri, & R. Vinter (Eds.), *Individual change through small groups.* New York: The Free Press, pp. 77–8.
19. Johnson, C. (1974). Planning for termination of the group. In P. Glasser, R. Sarri, & R. Vinter (Eds.), *Individual change through small groups.* New York: The Free Press, pp. 258–65.

7

Nurturance in Group Structures

This chapter examines the underlying structures forming the basis for nurturance in the group. The structured elements in groups, such as norms, conformity, cohesiveness, personalities of the members, and communication networks are barometers of the levels of nurturance that can be achieved at any specific time. The group processes to be discussed in the next chapter are the activities emerging from the structure. They define the way nurturance will be transmitted. Although structure and process inevitably interact, sometimes making them indistinguishable, it is helpful to consider roles, goals, tasks, specific social exchanges, and the group phases, as processes dependent on the structural properties.[1] The separation of group structure from process is arbitrary, since both emerge from the functioning of the group. The components of the group structure develop from the group interaction, and it is the interaction that determines both the structure and the process. It is helpful, however, to think in terms of those features of the small group that give the group its form and mode and those that are group events. The structural elements persist over a longer period of time and comprise the climate and framework within which the process emerges.

Some of the small group research bears directly on how mutual aid is propagated and used. Other research that concentrates on competition and the exploits of the individual at the expense of others contributes to understanding the factors preventing or cutting off the human capacity for reciprocal nurturance. The small group work of Golembiewski, Hare, McGrath, and Altman[2] appeared concurrently with the proliferation of therapeutic small groups on campuses and communities in the 1960s. Encounter groups, new-left formations, self-help groups, and therapy groups arose to challenge traditional forms of leadership. Simultaneously, participatory groups in industry continued to grow and there was an increase of autonomous small workgroups. The study of the small group reached its height during this period.

The group has a life and reality of its own and therefore needs to be considered as an entity quite above and beyond its membership. The members of a small group that persists long enough develop emotional attachments and a unique way of interacting that establishes the group as an entity. The helping, exchange, and attacking behaviors in any particular group build up to a total entity for a specific session that, in terms of content and quality of group climate, will never occur in quite the same way again. Each group session is a complete whole, similar to a finished painting, and transcends the individual members in it. Allport refuted this concept by stating that group behavior is based on the simple additive effect of stimuli transmitted from individual to individual.[3] In other words, he perceived small groups as collections of individuals, somewhat as Slavson, at first, perceived therapy groups as simply a series of individual interviews. The group has, however, also been reified as almost a living organism with a life and mind of its own. An extreme example is Jung's assignment of group patterns to the collective unconscious inherited from the past.[4]

PRIMARY GROUPS

Primary groups provide a nurturant and supportive climate and emotional intimacy. The primary group can also, however, "restrict, inhibit, or even smother . . . in its close embrace." We all have ambivalent feelings, wishing to belong to and yet wishing to be free of a particular group. This is typical of the adolescent who, having outgrown the need for the protective haven of the family, rebels against it. This revolt is made easier by the availability of an alternate group comprised of peers. "In other words, one primary group . . . helps to break the emotional hold of another primary group. . . ."[5]

Primordial, Personal, and Ideological Forms
The prototype of the primordial primary group is the original group into which we are born or come to live as an infant or very young child. It is the training ground for our humanness and where we learn who we are and how to be. The dawning awareness of self is derived from the early perception that we are separate beings from our caretakers. The initial family stamps into existence our very being and gives us the gift of who we are.

In contrast to the primordial group, the personal group is actively chosen because the members like each other and enjoy being together. The ideological primary group is also voluntary, but its main raison d'être is an intense devotion to a specific cause or belief.[6] There are also ideological elements in the primordial group. Olmsted spoke of the "sacred" quality of the primordial experience that is not dissimilar from what happens later in the ideological groups we form. It is the traditional order that holds together the primordial group and inspires awe and respect on the part of the group members, whereas the ideological group has the appeal of a new order, the cause that is "holy." Both these types stand in contrast to the more casual and noncharismatic personal primary group.[7]

Loss of contact with any primary groups is strongly felt and often leads to an intense struggle to find ways to replace the emptiness felt. Occasionally, the solution is to give up independence and fuse with any group offering substitute bonds for those lost.[8] The bonds may be realized through submission–domination or masochistic–sadistic relationships because a strong feeling of powerlessness propels us to seek power by submitting or controlling another.[9] This is an example of asymmetrical reciprocal nurturance, since one person gains a sense of relevancy and significance by controlling another, while the other equally gains a sense of relevancy and significance by being controlled. It is an unhealthy state of affairs when it becomes the dominant mode of being rather than a transient state.

The Therapy Group as Primary Group

The therapy group is a combination of primordial, personal, and ideological groups. It is a special type of primary group with a history, an identity, and shared memories. It resembles the ideological group when the solidarity developed becomes the cause célèbre, placing the group in a significant position in the lives of the members. Usually, the members hope to gain greater understanding of themselves and to change certain behavior patterns they find uncomfortable or troublesome. It is through exchanges of nurturance of the most intimate type that their objectives can be achieved. One of the assumptions of a treatment group is that, since it is through closeness and warmth of a primary group that we have become what we are, it is through a similiar group that we shall acquire the ability to change and become the way we want to be.

Treatment groups, similarly to natural groups, place limitations on behavior. This is particularly apparent when the prevailing norms and standards take precedence over the rights and uniqueness of individuals. Some groups will place the interests and welfare of the group as a whole above those of any one member. In contrast, another group may seek to find a happy meeting ground between individual and group interests. When the control of the group, its functions and outcomes, are vested in the members, it is more likely that a more accepting and flexible primary group will be created in which members have the opportunity to break undesirable ways of seeking and giving nurturance. They develop their own norms and support systems and methods of experimenting with ways of exchanging nurturance. Although self-management is more or less appropriate to many therapy groups, it does not account for the role of the therapist who is in the group by virtue of his or her expertise and therefore is in the group for different reasons than the other members. It may be helpful to see the therapist as the instrument of the group, ready to help it do whatever it needs to do. Two factors differentiating a therapy group from all other groups are (1) the required norms of acceptance, support, sharing, helping, and nonjudgmental attitudes, and (2) the individual member's responsibility for his or her own personal goals.

Primary and Secondary Groups

Secondary groups are collectivities that usually are formally organized. There is lack of face-to-face contact, a narrow range of roles possible, extremely limited reciprocity and spontaneity, and impersonal, cold interactions.[10] Primary groups may arise within the secondary group to meet the need for informality, warmth, and reciprocity. A beginning therapy group may have some of the characteristics of a secondary group that will eventually give rise to the therapeutic primary group.

Lipset and colleagues observed that, "A high frequency of interaction among men on the job or in a residential neighborhood . . . serves to increase the likelihood that friendly relations will develop among them," and that group norms and solidarity will develop, "especially if the participants are on the same status level." To what extent relations approximate primary groups will be affected by the choices available to find those who share the same values. Large shops seem particularly to give rise to primary groups, perhaps because of the unbearable isolation felt.[11] Members of work groups that have specific task goals may become more interested in associating with each other personally rather than adhering to the job objectives. Conversely, family primary groups may concentrate on business at the expense of personal objectives.[12]

The effectiveness of the primary group outside the family-type group has been questioned, because some believe spontaneity and warm feelings interfere with organizational objectives.[13] Basic to such reasoning is the premise that primary groups exist in pure form and that, once a group comes into being, it continues on an unwavering course. The fact is that most groups enjoy mixed functions, albeit emphasizing one at the expense of another, and a group that exists for any length of time will undergo some variation and modification of functions and even purposes.

The primary group within the larger organization may increase productivity, but it can also do the opposite by fostering group sabotage, buck-passing, and gold-bricking. This has been referred to as "familyness" in the Soviet Union! The relationship between the closely knit primary group and the larger organization, of which it is a part, is always problematic. When the importance of society or the collective is foremost, familial groups are usually downgraded. It is believed that individualism suffers in such social orders.[14] Nisbet decried the diminution of protection afforded by primary groups, because it forces people to look for the lost group in religions, psychotherapy, and other available means.[15]

In 1954, Stanton and Schwartz said that the hospital would be wrecked if it emphasized primary groups because, among other things, such groups serve different goals than those of the total institution.[16] Yet, this is precisely what many institutions have attempted ever since Jones tried to establish the therapeutic milieu in a psychiatric institution in England just after World War II.[17] Usually institutions are hemmed in by regulations that are centrally determined and are able to foster primary groups only in a very limited way. Nevertheless, the efforts of many psychiatric institutions to establish a therapeutic milieu or "healing community" have been experiments in creating organizations based on the principle of the primary group. These efforts have often created havoc with the personnel, including the professional staff. Professionals often feel that their rights are being violated when (1) primary, self-governing patient groups do in fact make real decisions that affect the timing and direction of treatment sessions, (2) the professionals are required to assist groups of paraprofessionals to assume responsibility for therapy, and (3) decisions about the running of the unit are made by a team in which paraprofessionals and patients are the majority. On the other hand, the professionals tend to dominate such groups anyway. The apprehension over potential disruptive influences of the primary group in organizations has some validity, and to dispel this would require considering how the small group might be used most effectively in protecting minorities from majorities, in providing for the participation of less powerful groups in decisions affecting their lives, and in protecting clients from control by professionals.

The concept of the therapeutic community, popularized by M. Jones, has been generally accepted, for most psychiatric institutions attempt to follow Jones' dictum, "the whole of a patient's time spent in hospital is thought of as treatment."[18] Almond described the initial great importance of the charisma of the psychiatric director in establishing a therapeutic community, suggesting that faith, confidence, and inspiration in a leader and authority figure was a crucial element. He then quickly toned this down, however, by referring to the importance of "routinizing" charisma with the desired outcome being the sharing of the charismatic excitement, furor, and drive for creative change.[19] This explains efforts at the blurring of professional and nonprofessional roles when therapeutic communities are developed. Regardless of these efforts, the restrictive, hierarchal structure of a psychiatric institution remains and prevents the full development of truly democratic treatment groups. The efforts at a therapeutic milieu are similiar, in some respects, to the pseudoparticipatory and "therapeutic" models found in industry.[20]

It is probable that in a large group the forms of mutual exchange do not go beyond elementary or socially prescribed reciprocity, and when they do, a primary group is emerging as a subgroup of the larger. Under commune living conditions, however, it is possible for the total group to function as a very large primary group. The Israeli kibbutzim and some of the collectives that have flourished in Europe and the United States are examples of nurturing, cooperative, and radically democratic societies that are organized, and function like primary groups.[21]

NORMS

Norms are simply the rules, given or covert, that determine how the group members will behave. How people act toward each other in a small group is generally predetermined by their previous experiences in groups. A knowledge of what is expected in small groups comes from the established code of behavior in the larger society and from our own personal experience. These may be respect for others, waiting our turn, listening attentively to the leader, following directions, not being either overly aggressive or overly passive, not speaking unless asked to speak, not allowing others to get the better of us, and not saying too much lest we appear foolish, etc. Giving and receiving nurturance is not ordinarily a generally accepted norm. It has to be deliberately built into the therapy group.

The establishment of norms in a therapy group rests with the therapist. In this sense, the ordinary therapy group is not free to establish its own norms. The therapeutic climate is created through norms of nurturance that support complete acceptance of each member, nonjudgmental attitudes, concern for the individual, responsibility to try to understand what the other is saying, and helping clarify statements that are ambiguous or unclear. This may be conveyed to the members during their first meeting directly, demonstrated to the members by the therapist, and formally described as rules of the sessions in some written introductory material that all members receive. How these norms evolve and develop will depend on the group members. The leader usually helps the group establish the appropriate rules of procedure that fit the goals of the specific group. The group norms are so basic to the groups functioning, that adherence to them becomes the elementary conditions of membership. A viable small group will build its norms on behavior that is acceptable to the members. The norm of reciprocal self-disclosure that has been a taboo in the family and the community has to be developed. It is most desirable that adequate orientation to group norms be given to prospective members.

Norms within the small group are affected by those of the larger organization of which it is a part. When they are violated, it is usually with some express goal that requires the deviation; for example, women in consciousness-raising groups may talk about their personal relationships with men in order to study the patterns of their lives as women. Ordinarily, such conversation is considered beyond the domain of "polite" social group discussion. Adhering to group norms that deviate from general norms in the community can bring the members to a state of cognitive dissonance, a concept developed by

Festinger.[22] It asserts that we experience conflict when we are required to engage in behavior that is not consistent with our beliefs. Confronted with this conflict, we can either rationalize the unacceptable behavior, refuse to conform and therefore become a deviant, or simply leave the group and escape the struggle altogether. Attempts to establish the norm of self-disclosure, a behavior that is not considered "normal" in most groups, evokes dissonance in the group at first. The conflicts that arise when new modes of behaving are expected are often handled by linking them to worthy goals. For instance, the worthy group goal of developing the ability to handle personal problems makes the heretofore "anti-social" self-exposure norms fostered in the therapy group acceptable. Superficial positive mutual reciprocity is a norm common to many groups and is therefore, easier to establish. It is difficult for new group members to give feedback to others. Hence, this norm is not easily established. The pressure to conform to this prescribed norm often produces superficial reactions to others. The results may be we feel even less understood and cared for then before we received the feedback; the therapist can assist by pointing out the positive intent of the responder.

When one group member is the only one not conforming to expectations, such as someone who constantly interrupts others or does not pay attention to what others are saying, there may be considerable pressure from the other members to obtain compliance. The presence of at least one other nonconforming person is sometimes enough to support the two to continue their deviance. Two dominating individuals, united in their efforts to get everybody to reveal themselves too early in the sessions, can have catastrophic effects on the group. In the early life of the group, when norms have not yet been fully established, the group is wide open to such influence. One person alone trying to do this would find it difficult to influence the group, although a person viewed as prestigious could do so. It is easier to build up workable group norms when the members have had similiar experiences because they are the same sex, have the same attitudes, or are the same age.

A fundamental norm put forth by the therapist and accepted by group members is that whatever a member says is acceptable and that each member will be accepted as he or she is. This makes it easier to express unique views and perceptions. It becomes difficult to maintain this norm when members are truly upset with what is being said and it is impossible for them to accept it. The way this is handled distinguishes a social group from a therapy group. The group is carefully and persistently led by the therapist to accept and to appreciate the individual who, in an ordinary social group, would be ignored, rejected, or roundly condemned.

It is inevitable that members will interpret the norms differently. As the group continues to meet, this usually is resolved, but occasionally, the behavior is so extreme it cannot be incorporated into the group norms. The member then, usualy voluntarily, leaves the group, because it becomes very clear that the group is unsuitable for him or her. The member might also be asked to leave. This is a situation the therapist handles with great care and consideration, for there is always the possibility that the individual and the group might be able to work out their differences. Prevention of this type of development is best handled prophylactically by fully assessing candidates and making careful selections.[23]

One of the group norms that eventually becomes effective as the group grows, is its capacity to review and interpret what is happening to it. Some group therapists view this as the purpose of the group and other activities as simply contributing toward making this possible. Others consider the analysis of behavior simply one of the interactive processes, along with other such behaviors as supporting, caring, and accepting. Analysis then ceases to be the chief purpose of group therapy and takes its place, along with other therapeutic events, as a mutual aid endeavor.

Adaptation of a group to a deviant member may produce solidarity among the members as they unite around their support and protection of one member and act, in many respects, as "parents-of-the-whole." This achievement may also help them develop higher levels of reciprocal caring between all members. Such a development can have negative repercussions: the deviant may become victimized and not allowed to change and develop more conforming behavior because this would interfere with group solidarity in support of his or her deviance.

Some group norms permit greater tolerance of deviants. For instance, of ten Quaker work projects, those most successful in achieving their objectives also had the highest proportion of isolates and deviants. Other group members worked hard to understand the deviants and went out of their way to do things to make them feel accepted. It seems that the deviants became more committed to the group because the others accepted them and worked on making them more like themselves.[24]

Basic training squad members also were observed to develop a tolerance and place for deviant members—the deviants often being referred to as "our teddy bear," "our pet," "mascot," "little brother," or "toy." The deviant's duties were usually performed by others and they became very protective of him. When the deviant was finally removed and hospitalized as a schizophrenic, squad members were disturbed and angry, insisting that it was alright for him to be in the squad, that he was not ill, and should not be hospitalized. Tolerance for the deviant means that such members can remain in the group and learn and experience in a much slower and perhaps even entirely different way than do the others.[25]

CONFORMITY

The level of conformity in the group is determined by the degree to which norms are adhered. Clearly, without some degree of conformity, a small group cannot continue to exist. The elementary, superficial giving and receiving contribute to its development. Resistance to conforming at certain stages in the group development, may be signs the group is getting ready to move on to new norms and a higher level of reciprocal nurturance.

Conformity has a generally negative connotation, in that it suggests circumvention of the individual, restriction of creativity, and reduction of all group members to some common denominator of behavior that is "average" and represents no one. Nevertheless, adherence to group norms is essential to the viability of the group. Without this, there is no group, for the most elementary feature of a group is that the members agree to conform to certain rules. Conforming behavior becomes the evidence that members have decided to abdicate their individuality in order to form a group.[26]

In general, it might be expected that the more informed and knowledgeable the individual, the less likely he or she is to conform. On the other hand, a group that contains a majority or a considerable number with authoritarian viewpoints is more apt to strive for conformity by seeking direction from the leader and trying to lay down rules that keep the nurturance level at a superficial and unegalitarian level. When the requirements are not clearly defined, members attempt to identify with and copy the behavior of others, especially those who take the initiative in propelling the group forward. Also, the more threatened we are, the more likely we are to conform to whatever example is available. If, at the first meeting of the group, each member is asked to tell how he or she feels about being in it, and the first person reports that he or she is full of anticipation and hope about what will happen in the group, it is likely that most of those who follow will give similiar responses. Not fully knowing what is expected, conformity is comfortable and quite reasonable. Once one person breaks the pattern, others will also be encouraged to do so.

It is difficult to express feelings when no one else is doing so. Moreover, the desire to be accepted by the others induces caution. A typical mood that is shared early in the group's life is the expectation that the group will be productive. Expression of pessimism at this time is usually not welcomed by the other members, although the pessimistic person occasionally gives the others the opportunity to nurture and guide him or her toward a more postive view of the group's potential. This in itself contributes to reaffirming or establishing norms that contribute to hope.

Extensive self-disclosure by one person before everyone has become acquainted can be disquieting enough to interfere with the struggles to establish the group. Conformity to the self-disclosure norm early in the group's life is often tempered with careful screening of what is said. It is helpful for members to present themselves in a relatively positive light in the beginning, for this points out assets while also giving something of the self to the group. This is suitable to establishing early forms of nurturance giving.

Whereas conformity is present in effective groups, when it predominates, it can stifle development of higher forms of nurturance exchange and prevent achievement of group goals. This is the reason that the member willing to risk nonconformance is vital to the elimination of norms which have become nonproductive or fixated. For instance, in early group sessions, a love-in atmosphere can develop in which the norm is to be loving and accepting of everyone. This is helpful and necessary initially, but if it persists, the group will not move beyond this superficial acceptance. This level of acceptance is based merely on the fact that everyone is a member of the group and has little or nothing to do with the members' special problems, perceptual prerogatives, and uniqueness as people.

COHESIVENESS

Cohesiveness is the pull of the group that binds members together to an established network of nurturance exchanges. It has been described by Golembiewski as the essential small group characteristic. Members of cohesive groups "hang together," engage in group activities energetically, do not miss group meetings, and are very reponsive to the group's successes and failures.[27] The "sum of the feelings of attraction to the group of each of the individual members" contributes to the group cohesiveness.[28] In this sense, it is a barometer of how the members as a whole are attracted to each other. Other notions of cohesiveness tend to be imprecise and blurred.[29] Early group cohesiveness often comes from placing high value on the group experiences, ignoring the goals of the members, and avoiding conflict.

Yalom noted that cohesiveness was not a curative factor per se, but instead a "necessary precondition for effective therapy." Just as cohesion in this framework is a prerequisite for group therapy proper to take place, so "loving acceptance" is only the precondition necessary for "self-disclosure, intra- and interpersonal testing and exploration."[30] In this formulation "loving acceptance" is not the healing process but only a "precondition" for the healing stage in which testing takes place. Authentic loving, which is something quite different from the acceptance that develops early in the life of the group, comes about as a result of a successful group experience that usually includes the traditional activities of self-disclosure and exploration.

In other words, there are levels of acceptance and caring and, at the highest level, cohesiveness is based on the reciprocal nurturance by which we give and receive from the very core of ourselves. In the first stage, it is the unconditional and generalized caring that helps form a cohesive group. At the end, this has become "me knowing you as you know yourself," and "you knowing me as I know myself," and "our seeing ourselves and the world differently because of this." The use of analytic concepts, that were helpful at an earlier stage in opening up some areas of common understanding can interfere with the development of advanced cohesiveness. It places prime emphasis on established theories rather than permitting a free reintegration of events and experiences and the dawn of new theories that emerge from the experiences in the group, an approach that Freud himself used when he violated the prevalent ideas of his day by refusing to place his observations into established paradigms that neither explained his observations nor gave any possibility of predicting them.

The most concrete way of determining group cohesiveness is to ask each member to write who they would prefer as associates for various activities. The more often group members actually select members of the group, the more cohesive the group. Furthermore, cohesiveness can be estimated via the relative frequency by which the group members use "we" and "I" in their discussion, by the regularity of attendance at meetings, and by members' comments about how they feel about the group. A group cannot continue to exist if there is not some cohesiveness. The degree of cohesiveness present will affect the nature of the interaction, the influence of the group on the members, group productivity, and general satisfaction with being a member of the group. Although it makes social order possible, in the early life of the group it is also a source of social control, which can sometimes become coercive for individuals struggling against the tide of the group pressures.

Early cohesiveness is affected, not only by the attraction of the members for the group, but by the members' commitment to carrying on the group's work. It is an indicator of overall group climate. Groups that become highly cohesive at an elementary or social level of exchange tend to be less tolerant of deviants since their nonconformity threatens the established network of nurturance exchanges.[31]

Such groups are friendlier, more cooperative, and more inclined toward achieving group integration, although such cohesiveness may not mean a high level of therapeutic exchanges. In fact, the group may be less therapeutic because its integrity as a group has high value regardless what is accomplished.[32]

Cohesiveness and the amount of consensus among group members are not equivalent. Direct questions about reactions to the group as a whole do not correlate significantly with attractions to individual members.[33] The affinity felt toward individual members is the usual basis of cohesiveness; it is possible, however, that some members are attracted to the group as a whole but do not see any of the members as special. However, the greater the interchange between each and every member, the greater the group's cohesiveness. Some of the factors attracting a member to a group include (1) possibility of obtaining and evaluating information, (2) the group creation of some aspects of reality that are relevant to the individual, (3) satisfaction of needs for affiliation and self-expression, and (4) support and defense against a threatening and non-nurturant environment.[34]

NETWORKS

By regularly communicating with other members of a group, we develop a sense of order and an awareness of an interactional matrix in which we play vital roles. The process requires learning what others think, adjusting our own views, and trying to understand the views of others. When our attraction to the group is high, we are more open to this process.[35] However, accomodating to fit in and fully accepting differences are not the same. The establishment of a network based on accomodation has to be guarded against in the therapy group: Although it is necessary in early sessions, if it persists, it can destroy the possibilities of therapeutic encounters by simply adding suitable protective layers that enable people to be civil to each other without getting to know each other at all.

Yalom's curative factor called, "imparting of information," is one of the activities that expand and develop the communication network. It can include a wide range of topics, from members sharing a particular newspaper item to a comprehensive presentation on the theory of the mechanisms of defense by the therapist or a member. Most often, as Yalom noted, the imparting information is implicit, although some groups may include planned formal instruction. It can function as a binding force as well as a method of explanation and clarification. The advice-giving characteristic of early sessions is a type of information giving that demonstrates the intent of the member to help and explain; the actual content of the advice is secondary and often not important at all.[36] Catharsis also is an ingredient in the communication network[37];releasing emotions that have been pent up is a way of imparting knowledge and stands as an important aspect of the sharing of information and self.

Bales' Interaction Process Analysis can be used to construct interaction matrices showing the cycles of requests for information and emotional reactions and the responses occurring in reaction to these requests.[38] It can account for the number of responses a person received and identify who is making the most requests for information or seeking emotional reactions. Such communication does not mean, however, that members are gaining awareness of each other as unique individuals. Rather it is evidence that they are exchanging messages and information and building connecting links that may or may not open people up to one another.

We tend to seat and position ourselves in ways that communicate what is happening to us in the group. Ordinarily, preference for a particular chair is respected; we tend to sit in the same location from session to session. The distance between ourselves and others we find comfortable varies and often is related to how ready we are to give nurturance to others at some level. We may avoid sitting next to a "high status" person, but on another occasion we may deliberately sit next to that individual. These reactions have to do with expectations of rejection or the forthcoming of nurturance. Most of us tend to avoid sitting next to someone who is seen as cold or unfriendly.[39] Someone sitting "too close" can at times be threatening and seem like an intrusion into our very existence. This is especially so when we are not ready for closer relationships with the particular individual.

PERSONALITY

Group characteristics may be marked by the distinctive personality traits of particular members.[40] Which aspects of our personality come to the fore are influenced by group norms, the distribution of power, and the general group climate. Often potential behavior, kept in the background, is activated and brought into the foreground in new circumstances. Traits of dominance tend to be related to high participation and leadership, whereas submissiveness may lead to supporting, modifying, qualifying, or rejecting behavior. Warm, personal, and cooperative behavior is associated with positive traits.[41] The dominant type tends to offer a parental nurturance and controls others by encouraging childlike behavior in them; cooperative types tend to be the antithesis of the dominant type, encouraging peer level exchanges and group decision making.

Dominant and submissive persons complement each other and, therefore, in relation to each other, represent a common form of reciprocal nurturance, often found in a hierarchic society. The person who gets pleasure from dominating needs submissive people in order to carry out this activity. Conjointly, the submissive person has learned to accept and expect dominance and, therefore, to need it in order to feel comfortable. Breaking of reverberating circuits that create such behavior patterns is dependent on being able to see in a full mirror what is happening.

The possibility of predicting group behavior from personality data have been considered. For instance, "persons who like close personal relations with others would be expected to be imcompatible with persons who wish to keep everyone at a distance, and therefore [would be expected to be] less productive" in a work group.[42] In a therapy group, such differences would enrich the potentialities for such persons getting to know and understand one another. It was found that "persons who tend toward values of egalitarianism and integrity of subjective experience tend to form alliances with rebellious, alienated persons and to protect them as long as they are in the position of underdogs and are under attack by group members."[42] It has been shown earlier that this kind of support can enable more disturbed individuals to remain in a group. Dominance together with aggression, as well as high self-esteem, tend to be positively correlated with high participation in the group; conversely, depression, anxiety, and low self-esteem correlate positively with low participation. Warm, cooperative behavior in the group is associated with persons high on extroversion, trusting, and affiliative responses.[43] The combination of these behavior constellations provides a facsimile of the real world in the group.

Whereas the array of characteristics among group members affects the group, it is not possible to predict behavior in the group, because "combinations" of behaviors develop to meet group needs. For example, people high on affiliation who were afraid of rejection by the other members tended to compete with them, probably as a way of warding off rejection. Ironically, in certain groups, highly affiliative people who would ordinarily be expected to be highly cooperative were found to do better on competitive tasks and not as well on tasks requiring cooperation. Although high intelligence tends to be related to dominant behavior in the group, and high anxiety with submissive behavior, when an individual is high on intelligence and anxiety as well, the person tends to be very task oriented and serious.[44] Using the Breer Personality Test, which measured how personality affected reactions to others with given characteristics, Hare found that, "in general, dominant behavior pulls submissive behavior (and vice versa), positive pulls positive, and negative pulls negative."[45]

Schutz found that in mixed groups containing persons preferring closeness as well as those preferring distance, the functioning of the group on given tasks was impeded. On the other hand, in two other type groups, in which the members either all preferred closeness or all preferred distance, the functioning was equally high, so that it was not the characteristic per se that was important, but the fact that the members in the group were alike in their preferences.[46]

When a group is primarily focused on dealing with problems of affection or control, members who have excessive internal conflict will not function well and probably will limit the group's progress. Moreover, individuals who require more than average time to adapt to small changes may keep the group at an early stage longer than it ordinarily would remain there. Personality characteristics tend to have more influence upon the pattern of group interaction in newly formed groups than in groups that have developed a stable group culture.[47]

CONCLUSIONS

Mutual aid and the exchange of nurturance are established through group structures. When a group is formed, something unique happens that transcends the sum of the individuals present. It has a life of its own with a beginning and end, and for every member, the mutual exchanges of nurturance in a specific group are special and different from that of any other group. Although it is in personalized peer groups and in ideologically committed groups that we live out the exciting and creative aspects of our lives, a therapy group can at times take on the characteristics of these groups. The range of nurturance exchanges possible in a treatment group, contribute to it appearing, at different times, as a peer, ideological, or family group. It is through the primary group that we have become what we are, it is through a similiar group that we can acquire the ability to change and become the way we want to be.

Elements differentiating a therapy group from all other groups are nurturance exchanges that are transmitted through norms of acceptance, support, sharing, nonjudgmental attitudes, and helping. Although therapy groups have greater tolerance for deviance from norms, there reaches a point when such deviance may be too disruptive and may jeopardize the existence of the group. A therapy group may at first be very much like a secondary group that is formal, nonspontaneous, and rational. Relationships may be viewed as means rather than ends in themselves. Since hierarchic vertical structures predominate in the larger society, it is probable that they permeate primary and secondary groups unless deliberate efforts are made to create other norms.

The structure of the group is based on norms of nurturance exchanged and the group's conformity to them. This gives rise to other structural elements which include cohesiveness, communication networks, and use of personality. Cohesive groups sometimes come to value group experience to such a degree that they ignore group goals. In a therapy group, this can mean that the group has come to value the group experience as a goal in itself and therfore begins to deemphasize or perhaps ignore the goals that members had when they joined the group. Ultimately, all relationships are built on the willingness of people to accept therapeutic norms and to give and take different amounts and types of information. In the beginning, group activity may center on establishing and challenging the rules of the group. Eventually, a group may establish some norms that are unique to it, which may include tolerance for extremely deviant behavior. Cohesiveness develops when the group becomes attractive to the members and is based on elementary and socially sanctioned reciprocal behaviors. The nature of the cohesiveness changes qualitatively when therapeutic exchanges become more dominant.

The interactions between the group members and the leader tend to move in the direction of mutual accommodation. In a therapy group, it is efficacious to have some congruence or hetereogeneity between members and leader to facilitate building the preliminary cohesive climate. Personality factors do affect the directions and processes that develop, and some consideration of this, before setting up the group, can make the difference between having a group that is effective or one that is hamstrung from the very onset.

NOTES

1. Golembiewski, R. T. (1962). *The small group.* Chicago: The University of Chicago Press.
2. Golembiewski, R. T. op. cit.; Hare, A. P. (1976). *Handbook of small group research* (2nd ed.). New York: The Free Press (1st ed., 1962). McGrath, J. D. & Altman, I. (1966). *Small group research.* New York: Holt, Rinehart & Winston.
3. Allpoit, F. H. (1924). *Social psychology.* New York: Houghton Mifflin, p. 4.
4. Jung, C. G. (1956). *The collected works of C. G. Jung* (Vol. 9). (R. F. C. Hall, Trans.). New York: Pantheon Books.

5. Olmstead, M. S. (1959). *The small group.* New York: Random House, pp. 48–9.
6. Ibid., pp. 58–9; Shils, E. A. (1951). The study of the primary group. In D. Lerner & H. Lasswell (Eds.), *The policy sciences.* Stanford, Calif.: Stanford University Press.
7. Ibid.
8. Fromm, E. (1942). *The fear of freedom.* London: Routledge & Kegan Paul, p. 122.
9. Ibid., pp. 52.
10. Nixon, H. L. (1974). *The small group.* Englewood Cliffs, N.J.: Prentice-Hall, p. 14–15.
11. Lipset, S. M., Trow, M. A., & Coleman, J. C. (1956). *Union democracy.* Glencoe, Ill.: The Free Press, pp. 156–58.
12. Nixon, H. L., op. cit., p. 18.
13. Olmsted, M. D., op. cit., p. 63.
14. Ibid., p. 55; Russeau, J. J. (1962). The social contract. In E. Barker (Ed.), *Essays by Locke, Hume, and Rousseau.* New York: Oxford University Press. pp. 169–309.
15. Ibid., p. 57; Nisbet, R. (1953) *The quest for community.* New York: Oxford University Press, p. 47.
16. Ibid., p. 64; Stanton, A. H., & Schwartz, M. S. (1954). *The mental hospital.* New York: Basic Books.
17. Jones, M. (1953). *The therapeutic community.* New York: Basic Books.
18. Ibid., p. 53.
19. Almond, R. (1974). *The healing community.* New York: Jason Aronson, p. 40.
20. For further discussion of this, see Chapter 9.
21. Ibid.
22. Festinger, L. (1957). *A theory of cognitive dissonance.* Stanford, Calif.: Stanford University Press.
23. Discussed earlier in Chapter 5.
24. Dentler, R. A., & Erikson, K. T. (1959). The functions of deviance in groups. *Social Problems,* 7:98–107.
25. Ibid.; Artiss, K. L. (Ed.) (1959). *The symptom as communication in schizophrenia.* New York: Grune & Stratton.
26. Shaw, M. E. (1976). *Group dynamics: The psychology of small group behavior.* New York: McGraw-Hill, p. 261.
27. Golembiewski, R. T. (1962). *The small group: an analysis of research concepts and operations.* Chicago: University of Chicago Press, p. 149.
28. Nixon, H. L., op. cit., p. 76.
29. Golembiewski, R. T., op. cit., p. 152.
30. Yalom, I. D. (1975). *The theory and practice of group psychotherapy* (2nd ed.). New York: Basic Books, p. 47.
31. Schacter, S. (1951). Deviation, rejection, and communication. *Journal of abnormal and social psychology* 46:190–207.
32. Nixon, H. L., op. cit., p. 80.
33. Nixon, H. L., op. cit., p. 77.
34. Golembiewski, R. T., op. cit., p. 164.
35. Festinger, L. (1955). A theory of social comparison processes. In A. P. Hare, E. F. Borgatta, & R. F. Bales (Eds.), *Small groups: Studies in social interaction.* New York: Alfred A. Knopf, p. 185.

36. Yalom, I. D., op. cit., p. 12.
37. Ibid., pp. 83–84.
38. Bale, R. F. (1950). *Interaction process analysis*. Reading, Mass.: Addison-Wesley.
39. Shaw, M. E., op. cit., pp. 119–120.
40. Haythorn, W. The Influence of individual members on the characteristics of small groups. In A. P. Hare, E. F. Borgatta, & R. F. Bales, op. cit., p. 338.
41. Hare, A. P., et al., op. cit., p. 199.
42. Ibid., p. 182.
43. Ibid., p. 184.
44. Ibid., p. 185.
45. Ibid., pp. 188–189.
46. Schutz, W. C. (1958). *Firo: A three-dimensional theory of interpersonal behavior.* New York: Rinehart.
47. Hare, A. P., et al., op. cit., p. 334.

8

Nurturance in Group Processes

When speaking of group processes, we must include the way leadership and roles emerge, the phases of development, the impact of subgrouping, constellations, and the formulation of goals. Greater versatility among the members in taking roles and a more tumultuous passage through the early stages of role taking and the later stages of personalized and therapeutic exchanges are apt to occur in democratic groups. This is reflected in the way goals are formulated and reformulated and the way specific group goals are approached and carried out. The longer the life of the group, the more movement there is back and forth between stages of dependence and independence. Not all groups are vehicles of change as curative groups generally are expected to be. They can perpetuate or reestablish old patterns so that, when members are threatened with overwhelming changes in their lives, they can simply reaffirm who they are.

INTRODUCTION

The way authority is distributed will affect the group's potential for nurturance exchanges. The direction may be imposed by the therapist or it may emanate from the interactions among the members. The therapist may structure the leadership by encouraging specific members to take on co-leadership roles and executive functions. In the absence of this, group members may confer greater power and status on some members and less on others. This is such a pervasive tendency in the larger society that, a group may permanently "install" one member as leader or co-leader. If this is to be avoided, very deliberate steps must be taken to do so.

A therapist may be appointed by the authorities, as may happen in some institutions, or he or she may be chosen by common consensus of the members. The members' perception of the relatively autocratic functions of the therapist may not necessarily be based on how the leader was actually selected.[1] It may have more to do with how accepting and caring the leader appears. The nurturant process may be established and maintained by executive functions that are shared by the group members,[2] and the power of the appointed-from-outside leader is almost always modified by group action. To some extent, every leader symbolizes authority and control and, when nurturance exchanges begin to develop between the members, the tendency to reject the leader is very strong. It is common for the therapy group to reject the given leader, yet demonstrate ambivalence toward authority by conferring on one or two members decision-making prerogatives.[3] This represents the pervasive conflicts in our society, the struggle between the yearning for unilateral nurturance from a parenting figure and the need for a more independent egalitarian relationship with peers.

ROLE ENACTMENT

Roles are part of personality for they are the means by which relatively structured and established ways of coping are enacted. They are adapted to the needs of the group, and are the means by which the group carries on its functions.[4] The status of a member in a therapy group is not necessarily related to his or her private popularity, e.g., standing with each member. Public popularity, sometimes referred to as socio-group status, occurs when a member is openly recognized as liked by most members. He or she usually has a marked influence on the group climate.[5,6] Those high in group status but low in private popularity, however, tend to leave the group prematurely.[7] This suggests that a person who assumes important group roles, but who does not engage in personal exchanges of caring, tends to feel alienated and alone regardless of his or her public involvement.

Global judgments of each other, usually based on stereotypes, are made by the members, although not always openly in the early sessions. Ultimately, a specific status for an individual is attained when the members agree on this. This contributes to a status structure that affects how the group goes about initiating activities and making judgments.[8] If a highly hierarchic group is established, it will be extremely difficult, if not impossible, to move it into therapeutic phases. Hierarchic behavior occurs when one member acknowledges the superior status of another by giving compliments and agreeing readily with what that person says. This increases the likelihood that the person upon whom this status has been conferred will

attempt to maintain a position of superiority by giving directions and imposing his or her opinion. Such inegalitarian reciprocity, natural to most social
groups, becomes a key to understanding how the group members deal with
people who dominate and control and what leads people to take on such
roles. If it persists over many sessions, and members are unable to take up
the therapist's efforts to understand what is happening, the group may
sometimes have to be disbanded.

Members of cooperative groups and natural groups tend to take on
specific roles. Sometimes they play more than one role in order to help the
discussion. Occasionally, they play self-oriented roles that seem to have
little to do with the purposes of the group. When members are not prepared
to expect that one of them has been given more information, they tend to
reject that person. It is more likely that the knowledgeable person will be
accepted in that role when the members have not been ignored and instead
have been informed that someone in the group may have more
information.[9] To be treated with respect, concern, and as an intelligent
decision maker is greatly nurturing. Conversely, if someone has been singled
out for such treatment, leaving the rest of the members in the dark, they will
tend to feel uncared for and abandoned.

The idea person and the emotional stimulant tend to be liked by the
other group members. A more passive person may also be well liked. This is
usually due to his or her tendency to respond to the emotional needs of the
group, recognizing when others feel uncomfortable or need support. Occasionally another role emerges: that of the talker who is probably expressing
or reflecting the anxiety of the group members. Although performing an
important function, he or she tends to be liked less than others and rated
lower on task ability. Also the person who tries to get the group to concentrate on the goal of building intense interactions and to build the base for
therapeutic encounters may not be very popular, for the group may feel
pressured and not ready. It can only do this in its own good time. The
passive person who helps restrain the group may be best-liked precisely
because he or she helps maintain some balance in a group that might have a
tendency to move too fast for the comfort of most.[10]

The specific roles are sources of nurturance to the role player who
receives approval and recognition from the group, and to the group members who may receive support, guidance, or direction from him or her.
When the roles become dominating and controlling, the oppression and
subjugation of group members may jeopardize the life of the group. Talland
believed that some of the role distinctions are not apparent in therapy
groups since their "task" broadly deals with personal feelings and new
awarenesses.[11] The distinctions may more often occur between those wanting to relate more closely and others wanting to adhere to sociable interactions. This can lead to a division of roles: a member–leader who strives for
greater communication and deeper interactions, while another member–
leader attempts to maintain an accepting and comfortable climate free of

conflict and therapeutic encounters. This is fairly typical of the dichotomization of group forces that occurs periodically.

Role conflict may result from role incompatibility when one person assumes the role of task leader as well as socio-emotional leader. This is frequently the role of the group therapist, who is pulled between the members' needs to be totally accepted as they are and their needs to move on to discover new perceptions and ways of exchanging nurturance.

The active participant is a basic therapeutic group role, that may be played by only one or two persons at first, but it will be a role accepted by all members eventually. The role of idea person, who helps formulate goals and give direction to the activities, is usually limited to one or two individuals. The emotional stimulant, readily demonstrating likes, dislikes, and strong reactions, tends to be taken on by a specific individual.[12]

We take on or discard roles based on how they fit into our self image.[13] Roles are often not clear-cut and seldom are they pure. They tend to vary from time to time as may be required by each situation and our state of mind. Role collision, incompatibility, or confusion are not always experienced as stressful although they often are the outcome of inconsistencies. Role collision may occur when there is a struggle for leadership. It may occur between two members, the appointed leader and member, or two appointed coleaders. Resolving these difficulties can help establish therapeutic group norms of sharing, exchanging, and understanding.

Systematic taking on of specific roles in the group increases the danger of role reification: roles then appear permanent and immutable. Frequently the concept of role becomes expendable when we are doing something specific in a particular group at a specific time that is not generalizable without distorting the personal event.

Role stabilization arises out of the need to be able to predict what will happen in a given social situation. This leads to relationships based on established scripts that are difficult to relinquish. We are, however, constantly faced with new situations and the need to change these very roles. Group roles are often offshoots of roles played in the larger society. The more a member performs in a unique way, the more likely that a personal way of behaving is being disclosed. Parts played never remain quite the same because the group never stands still. It is always transitory and in the process of becoming something else.

LEADERSHIP AND GROUP PARTICIPATION

The variations in the vast literature on leadership over the years demonstrates vividly that the concept of leadership has changed. The "person approach" that predominated in the early years of leadership research placed importance on the leader as someone qualified to direct others. Personality traits were emphasized and the social unit and the interrelationship between the leader and the followers were ignored.[14] Some may still think that in large institutions this is an appropriate approach. The differences, however, between leaders in larger organizations and those in small groups are not as extreme as it might appear. In a truly democratic larger organization, leadership would also continuously develop and be shared by all. Certainly, elitist leadership types also can and do appear in small groups as well as in larger organizations. The therapist is constantly on the alert to his or her own tendency to dispense nurturance asymmetrically and to influence the group direction based on personal or organizational needs.

Leaders tend to exhibit certain traits such as intelligence, enthusiasm, dominance, self-confidence, social participation, and egalitarianism.[15] The leadership role cannot, however, be considered apart from the role and the characteristics of the followers. As a central figure in the group, the leader may play the role of the patriarchal sovereign, the idol, or somewhat more mundanely, the organizer. Although the therapist may be perceived as playing any of these roles, it is important that, in fact, none of these roles are enacted.

Leaders emerge in accordance with the group's expectations, i.e., groups with members who are low in authoritarianism are more apt to have a more egalitarian leader. Groups with either an authoritarian leader or a predominance of authoritarian members, do in fact show authoriarian behavior.[16] Psychoanalytic theory has placed emphasis on the central role of the group leader in organizations and in small groups. For instance, Redl described the "group love" of children for their male teachers, basing his interpretations on Freud's analysis of group behavior.[17] This was associated with feeling secure in the leader's "trusting presence" or controlling dominance. The "group love" and the "trusting presence" represent levels of nurturance in an early stage of development. They also contribute to identification with the teacher and solidarity in the group.[18] These reactions are, however, clearly inegalitarian and make the teacher a parent figure. In therapy groups, this would be a transitory or preparatory stage to more reciprocal and egalitarian interactions.

A central figure may emerge from among the group members and serve as a leader with the same impact as that of the designated professional leader. This member–leader may furnish the group with a model of caring and supportive behavior that they can envision themselves carrying out. This person often represents a unique combination of behaviors beyond the therapist's repertoire. The member–leader is more like the other members in having difficulty in caring and loving, yet he or she has made a significant start in developing the capacity to nurture in many ways. Such a member presents, therefore, a model of behavior that is understandable, and within reach.

A number of years ago, I was leading a six-person activity group of 9- and 10-year-old boys, when the group sessions became progressively more chaotic because of rampant acting-out behavior. This changed precipitously when Ed, a new member, was introduced to the group. Ed was singularly set on building a bench and immediately set about to do this. Moreover, he informed everybody that he was not going to keep this bench but give it to his class (from which he had been removed temporarily for disruptive behavior). Ed did not assume a leadership role, but his behavior stunned the members. The peer leadership from Peter, who seemed to have personal relationships with most of the others, was as important as the behavior model presented by Ed. It was he who led the group back to working on projects and talking about themselves when Ed joined the group.

The combination of a caring cotherapist with one who is a model of how to make significant contacts with others is almost an unbeatable therapeutic method. Actually, groups do tend to preserve themselves, and in this instance it is almost certain that the group would have returned to more constructive activities and further sharing of themselves without the entry of a new member, but it may not have been as effectively accomplished.

Occasionally, the anger against a nonsupportive leader is directed toward a member of the group making him or her a scapegoat for the anger group members cannot or will not express directly. In Lewin and colleague's classic experiment with leadership styles it was demonstrated that there was more scapegoating in autocratic leader groups than in democratic or laissez-faire leader groups.[19] Scapegoating may be one way leadership is shared in an autocratic setting. In one group, a member was made the target of attacks and hostility by the others until that person was compelled to leave the group altogether. The autocratic atmosphere prevented them from interacting with each other and exchanging suport, and they certainly were not free to vent their frustration on the leader. Consequently they struck out at someone whom it was safe to attack. This left the equilibrium of the autocratic group structure intact and the members relatively safe from punishment by the leader. This is not the only way to look at this development; a member may seek out this kind of "attention" to gain at least some interchange from others in a sterile situation drained of possibilities for reciprocity. It can also be used as an excuse to leave a very unpleasant situation in which there is diminution of self and relationships with others.

Leadership style affects the morale of the group, i.e., how hopeful the members feel and to what extent they identify with the group. High morale could represent the members' sense of "having come home," in that they feel recognized, accepted and genuinely part of the group. This is especially so when the group has assisted them in "greeting" parts of themselves not fully encountered before. Whether this happens or not may rest on the compatibility of the individual's value system with the type of leadership offered.

In a democratic therapy group there is more verbal interaction, greater permissiveness on the part of the therapist, and more group decision making and goal setting.[20] Dramatic change is more apt to occur in a group that is group centered. This style also encourages emotional ties and involvement, cohesiveness, and the attainment of satisfaction by the members.[21] Although this is the preferred group mode for the attainment of reciprocal nurturance, it is possible that for certain groups located within the folds of a larger organization that is highly autocratic, a modified form of member participation is more satisfactory.

GOALS AND TASKS

Any small group combines concrete tasks with some degree of emotional involvement.[22] The family group demonstrates par excellence the combination of these goals. Family members exchange love, help each other, and share a religion and ideals. They also carry out many concrete tasks that are necessary to maintain a home, send children to school, and earn a living.[23]

Task-oriented groups are involved in activities and roles that are more oriented toward explicit and tangible goals than ones having a socioemotional orientation. Generally, tasks are carried out with an exchange of nurturance that is either superficial or unilateral; emotional involvement is minimal. The technical skill is far more important than the relationships.[24] A task-oriented group comes together for the purpose of doing a job. Despite its apparent close focus on a narrow objective, members often do become subjectively involved when establishing rules and redefining the task. This can, however, impair the functioning of such a group. A study of 72 decision-making conferences showed that the more often self-oriented needs were expressed, the more often were decisions made unacceptable to the participants and the more intensely were the chairperson and the meeting considered to be unsatisfactory. The meetings were also less productive and lasted for longer periods of time.[25]

Group goals may be commonly shared by all or a composite of separate, personal goals that have no apparent common thread. Golembiewski called attention to the complexity and importance of the interaction between personal and group goals.[26] Bion's group assumptions (see the discussion under Stages) are goals based on the acceptance of a group mentality and a group purpose. When the personal goal is consistent with group goals, the member feels comfortable in the group and finds it easier to internalize the group's goals. Occasionally, the group's goals may be too ambitious for a particular member. Whereas most of the members seem unified in wanting to know each other as deeply as possible, one member may need to experience the most elementary acceptance and understanding. The idea of gaining full awareness of the others and they of him or her is far removed from the needs of this member. This may be because the member has great doubts about his or her own identity and a strong need not to look below the surface. When personal goals cannot be integrated into those of the group, members may withdraw, become disruptive, or leave the group altogether. An effective therapy group amalgamates personal goals of the members with the general group goal. This becomes easier if members are not at very different levels of self-awareness.

Lewin demonstrated that tension states accompany personal goals and that achievement of the goal relieves these states.[27] In the 1920s Zeigarnik experimentally showed that when goal achievement is interrupted the resultant tension state exerts such force that people tended to recall incompleted tasks much more readily than completed tasks (known as the Zeigarnik effect). In terms of her formula, the tension level could be determined for each person by dividing the number of unfinished tasks remembered by the number of finished tasks remembered.[28] When goals are shared by the members, the tension around the unachieved group goal is also shared by the members; a "group Zeigarnik" effect[29] would occur in a group that had coalesced sufficiently to have built some unity.

In general, the more frequently the group has to produce something for others, as does the workplace group, the more likely the emphasis on superficial contact and surface cooperation. The more often the group focuses on the individual, the more intense the contact and reciprocity will develop. Probably, no group is purely therapeutic or task oriented, unless forced into either mold by supervisors, forepersons, or therapists who are narrowly focused on what they want the group to do or not do. A therapist may ignore the possibility of group members keeping group records or other tabulations because of his or her conviction that this will deter a spontaneous group process or because he or she rejects the sharing of the analytic role with members. Similarly, a supervisor at the workplace may discourage subordinates from relating to each other on a personal level at work because of the fear that this will diminish his or her ability to control them.

Additive tasks dominate the beginning session; the comments of individuals are not related to each other, and the emphasis is more on participation rather than meaningful connecting up with the other members. Disjunctive tasks tend to make artificial barriers to achieving reciprocity; for instance, when each member is given five minutes to present a problem, the separateness of each presentation is emphasized. The conjunctive method usually develops in later sessions, since it is the achievement of a high level of cooperation with everyone working together in unison. The divisible method refers to the division of roles. All of these methods can be functional at different times; in the successful therapy or task-oriented group the method is adapted to suit the issue, problem, or type of task. Complex and enduring groups employ a range of goals, tasks, and methods.[30]

The problems associated with the place of the small group within the larger organization is exemplified by the classic Western Electric (Hawthorne) Studies that initiated the participatory era in industry in the early 1930s. They were interpreted as showing that production would increase and continue to increase if the work group was small and cohesive.[31] It is, however, never possible to eliminate the effects of other factors such as physical and economic conditions and conscious or unconscious selection of compliant group members. It is probable that members of small groups, wherever they are and no matter how apparently effective in some ways, are subject to great pressure from within the group to conform particularly if there are no risk takers among them. This is in fact, a "side effect" of participation in small groups and demands serious study for potentially negative after-effects.[32]

There can be considerable confusion in groups that mix primary with task-oriented associations since each of these is linked to different norms. Too great an emphasis on primary group norms of closeness and caring can interfere with the completion of concrete tasks and bring the group into a state of disorganization and inability to complete required tasks. Time and again small T-type groups, formed in conjunction with the teaching of group dynamics, interfere with the coverage of reading assignments that are part of the course goals. Surgical teams in the operating room would be courting disaster if the norms of primary groups based on intimate relations prevailed over those of the task-oriented group.[33]

> Children, ages 9 to 11, had varied reactions to therapy groups and goal-oriented remedial sessions when they participated in both type groups during the same school year. In multiple-choice questions administered at the end of the school year, the children showed considerable variation in perception of these two groups. Most compared the therapy group to a family and the remedial group to a class. Nevertheless, some had difficulty differentiating between the groups, and children with more severe behavior problems were particularly unable to make distinctions.[34] Confused persons in hospitals and rehabilitation programs in the community sometimes also have difficulty adapting to the variety of different groups in which they are members, because of the differences in norms, purposes, and levels of reciprocity expected.

The characteristics comprising a group, no matter what kind of a group, depend on the give-and-take between the members who may offer a considerable amount of support and reassurance in a task-oriented group, as well as in a more personalized group. In every functioning group, there is some form of nurturance taking place. In some, it is merely the help and support that is expressed in accordance with the rules and regulations of the group. In others, the nurturance occurs in an emotionally laden context and becomes part and parcel of the meaning of who we are and what we are becoming.

STAGES

The group stages represent the progressive maturation of the group as a complex social entity. It is possible for one stage of the development to be so different from another that an observer might have difficulty recognizing that it is the same group. These stages include:

Stage 1   Elementary nurturance exchange including seeking out orientation, response to leader as parental figure, and testing what is possible;

Stage 2   Prescribed social roles including acceptance, involvement, and responsibility;

Stage 3   Negative reciprocity including questioning the leader's authority, disapproval and rejection of each other, and conflict about one's place in the group;

Stage 4   Therapeutic reciprocal nurturance with shared leadership and flexible role assumption periodically interrupted by personalized disapproval or rejection;

Stage 5   Some in-depth exchanges accompanied by unity and solidarity with periodic evidence of disharmony and conflict.[35, 36]

These stages reappear again and again. In an advanced group, they may occur alongside each other in one session. As the group progresses, negative reciprocity contributes to group focal problems that are handled differently at each stage. Groups of hospitalized members tend to criticize the institution fairly early in the sessions. For them, this is the means of beginning to relate to each other. It is also a testing of what is permissible in the group. In contrast, the critical positions taken in later stages are focused, personalized, and reflect the members' way of perceiving the world.

Structured aspects of the group, such as norms, leadership, and cohesiveness will depend on the stage in which the group is. If the particular stage is not taken into account, some misconceptions may arise as to what is going on. For instance, cohesiveness established in the earlier stages is quite different from that which appears later on. The first cohesive climate grows out of the hope and expectation of the members. The later one is more intense and fraught with conflict and the electric atmosphere of discovery and altered perceptions. To an uninformed observer, the group, in the later stages, would appear much less warm and caring than it was earlier. It is, in fact, dealing with far more complex forms of the nurturance exchange and has gone well beyond the initial nurturing atmosphere of joining together in a common enterprise.

Whitaker and Lieberman noted that the same issues continue to recur in the group. These issues have to do with handling anger, emotions and maintaining some sense of self in close relationships.[37] In the early sessions, the members try to induce the therapist to provide the solution. They demand a guarantee that therapy will be worth the trouble. They want the therapist to provide direction, to control things, and especially to make rulings about deviant clients. The formative stage closes when the group begins to take on some of the responsibility for establishing its own nurturing system and begins to rid itself of the need for unilateral nurturance from a parental figure. At times, the close of the formative stage is clear, at times vague. Some of these beginning behaviors occur in later stages, sometimes as a stabilizing effort, other times as an accommodation to the needs of individuals. For instance, when members begin to get close to and depend on each other, they may become frightened and look to the therapist to take over and control the situation.

Bion's Formulation

Bion's insightful formulation of the stages of development in therapy groups has had considerable influence. These were briefly mentioned earlier in respect to group goals or assumptions and include (1) dependency, (2) fight–flight, and (3) pairing.[38] There is a correspondence between Bion's stages and human development. The dependent child (dependent stage) learns to be assertive (fight stage) and eventually becomes an adult ready to birth a child (pairing stage). Bion believed that none of these stages are really working stages but rather that they represent interference with the work of the group. Nevertheless, the pairing and move to create a new leader is an advance over the dependency and fighting stages: it is the group's effort to bring order to the group despite the leader's refusal to do so. Bion believed that the creation of a leader in the group has its limitations. It is as if the group has produced a Messiah and consequently there is nothing else as magnificent as this to strive for.[39] A group may become fixed at one stage of development because to move on thrusts it once more into uncertain waters.

Bion invoked psychoanalytic concepts of the British school to explain group assumptions. He postulated that members face the complexities of the group by regressing to the use of mechanisms typical of early stages of development. In the process, members experience a sense of loss of individuality and possibly depersonalization as well.[40] The therapist is at the receiving end of the members' projections of these reactions. He assumed that the group symbolizes the mother and elicits early childhood projective identification mechanisms described particularly well by M. Klein.[41] Some of the group's reactions are considered vestiges of "very primitive phantasies about the contents of the mother's body."[42]

The effort to identify in-depth processes of the emerging self in relation to the other, and the splitting off of parts of the self and the other in the process is a brilliant excursion into the world of the unconscious. It is possible that these types of processes occur throughout life within the context of close relationships. The crucial factor is, however, the real and imagined nature of the relationship and the type of nurturance exchange taking place.

The projection onto the leader of felt inadequacies, doubts, and desire to control appears in all groups; however, leaders also project onto the members. The emotional reactions of the leader to what is transpiring, that is countertransference, is an important part of the therapy. If it is not understood and dealt with, the emergence of true knowing between the members is irreparably frozen. The interaction between projections, of members and leader is always a part of the group development. This means that, rather than countertransferring, which has a negative connotation, the therapist is fully in the group as is everyone else, the difference being that he or she is in a position of power and needs to control how the self is handled in the group.

Slater, accepting Bion's formulations, reasserted Freud's theory that the group needs to kill the leader symbolically, in the spirit of the primal horde action against the all powerful father.[43] The declaration "The King is dead, long live the King," proclaimed in monarchies to symbolize the succession to the throne, is represented in the group by the fight–flight stage and the pairing that brings forth the new leader from the group's midst. The group's venting of its unanimous animosity toward the leader frees the members to develop positive reciprocal interactions with each other. The mythical eating of the leader and absorbing of his or her ability, techniques, and power is symbolized in the group by the emergence of leaders from the group, who "replace" the therapist.

Are these behaviors that we observe really dependency, fight, and pairing phenomenon, or might they be more realistically characterized as examples of hope for support, revolt against an ineffective authority, and an attempt to remedy a hopeless situation by creating the means for self-support and self-help? This is a way of describing essentially the same behaviors, but in terms of the adult rather than the child. Although the stages of growth in a group are partly related to maturation, they are heavily influenced by the existing social order. The dependency stage, an inevitable protracted stage of development in early childhood, reappears again and again in different form throughout life. This is partly due to limitations of the lone individual and the ultimate dependency of each of us on a hierarchic social order that, too often, fosters dependency at the workplace, in the schools, and in personal relationships.

SUBGROUPING

Frequently, a subgroup develops within the group. It can become a threat to the group, since members become affiliated with some more closely than with others and, in some real sense, have begun to establish their own group within the group. Subgroups that develop different goals from the group can bring about its dissolution. On the other hand, they can become countervailing forces, eventually affecting the group goals by positively modifying them in some way. This could enable the group to proceed with its work, and the subgroup, having accomplished its objective, could then be reabsorbed into the main group.

A subgroup may be problematic in a behavior modification group that focuses on superficial behavior change.

> One leader in a weight-loss group was confronted with a therapeutic subgroup that upset the functioning of the main group. Four out of eight members had formed a "mutually reinforcing subgroup and began enjoying each other's company outside

the group."[44] Subgroup activities were directed toward the emotional aspects of change associated with weight loss. Conflict in the group broke out between the subgroup's efforts to bring emotional problems before the group and the resistance of the other members who felt this was not the purpose of the group. The leader handled this by establishing two groups, each of which included members of the subgroup and the others: it was arranged that they compete with each other for best weight loss each week.[45] This prevented the subgroup from interferring with the established purpose to remain a task-oriented group with the focus on weight loss. The socioemotional developments were then confined to a subgroup that was not allowed to change the narrowly focused goal. The seat of the socioemotional developments and mutual aid then took place outside the main group.[46] Sometimes, a group can consciously modify its objectives and integrate subgroup activity by modifying the contract that was set up. It depends a great deal on whether the members of the subgroup are seen as positively nurturing and accepting or predominantly threatening or condescending.

The subgroup can be an effective way to help members gain status in the group and handle hostile forces. Members of "cotherapeutic alliances" have strong mutual attraction and influence. Some of the most important therapeutic advances are made through "cotherapeutic pairing".[47]

Postsession meetings between group members may be used to develop closer relationships and to advance the therapeutic process. It is here that the full impact of subgroupings may be observed because the therapist is absent, and blocks to free expression are lowered.[48] The subgroup can provide a safer setting for experimentation with giving and receiving nurturance at personalized and deeper levels long before an individual is able to do this in the group. Subgroupings also occur in member dyads when special forms of reciprocity are central. Occasionally, one client will become a parenting figure to another, protecting and advising him or her. We would look in the group toward the time when this relationship would eventually become a more advanced form of mutual nurturance, with the passive member more active, the active more passive. There can be multiple pairing in the group with one person being a follower in one, a leader in another, and an equal member in still another. Subgroupings that perpetuate a submissive, passive role in one member need to be monitored carefully to prevent a person from becoming a victim to another's aggressive tendencies.[49]

Heterogeneous groups are more likely to form subgroups since the members with like social characteristics tend to band together. This may be a temporary and loose subgrouping that occurs during the early stage of group life. Emphasizing similarities with some other members helps build positive and accepting attitudes toward the group. If it persists at the expense of relating to other members, it becomes a disruptive force in the group, interferring with its cohesiveness and creating barriers between the subgroup members and the others.

Differences in beliefs and life styles can result in conflict about how group members should conduct themselves. Conflict about basic principles is much more serious than disagreement over some concrete matters. A viable group shares some basic principles of how the group members should behave and what is important.[50] Wheaton demonstrated that clashes over basic principles among female roommates influenced their relationships negatively, whereas conflict over living arrangements did not.[51]

The question of subgrouping in therapy groups has some similiarity to subgrouping in any primary group. For instance, one of the most commonly accepted taboos in almost all societies is the incest taboo that forbids sexual subgrouping in the family beyond the accepted subgrouping of the two parents. The parent subgroup sets the prototype of the "clique" that has greater social control over the other members of the group. All other subgrouping in primary groups might be considered versions of this. The basic dyads and triads of the family form the prototypes for some of the subgroupings in the therapy group. Caplow specified three classic forms in which either the father dominates, the mother dominates, or there is equal power between the parents. Two generations are represented in every primary triad and, in that respect, a parental coalition is a coalition of like partners and a parent–child coalition of unlike partners.[52] The primary triad can provide different types of nurturing relationships. Those based on members with unequal power could only achieve a limited type of reciprocal nurturance since the freedom to give or not give, receive or not receive, is uneven. Although similar triangles may develop in groups, they are not apt to be anywhere nearly as intense and crystallized as they are in the family.

Bowen believed that the study of the "family ego mass" and the "emotional process that shifts about within the nuclear family" was crucial and provided more flexibility than the traditional analysis of the Oedipus Complex.[53] Nevertheless the Oedipus myth may still provide a satisfactory explanation of the child's desire to achieve the more egalitarian and reciprocal relationship enjoyed by the parents. It can be explained as the inferior member engaging in a hopeless power struggle with the others, or as that member searching for greater positive reciprocity with one or both parents. It is possible that the quest for a fair and equal amount of nurturance is more fundamental than the struggle for power and control. Some coalitions are democratic part of the time, as when the members have an egalitarian partnership in one area, but in other matters, one dominates.[54] Positive reciprocal nurturance may be an outcome of strongly negative feelings that are shared, as when common hatred builds solidarity.[55] It is not usually the means of knowing the other in the coalition, nor does it usually have any life in the absence of the hated person.

CONCLUSIONS

The exchange of nurturance in the group establishes the base for therapeutic communion. Whereas a therapy group concentrates on socioemotional factors, it is not without explicit tasks that serve as vehicles for building an exchange network. Overt goals and tasks are the most directly observable in the group's activity. Members of groups live through stages together and, in the process, contribute to each other's new awarenesses, altered perceptions, and knowing each other more deeply. Interpersonal reciprocity is manifested in the roles, goals, tasks, and stages that develop in a group. It is based on reciprocal need, the unity of social action, and is observable in social exchanges. Quite often, members may intially practice mutual exchanges in smaller units, or subgroups, of the group.

How the group is organized is probably the one most influential factor determining in which direction the group will go and how it will get there. The leader who plays a central role in the group, offering considerable direction and rewards gives nurturance of the nonreciprocal type. A more democratic leader implicitly accepts others for who they are and gets involved in a nurturance exchange that itself becomes the prized development. How roles evolve among the members will affect whether the group can achieve therapeutic reciprocity. Emphasis on content and its analysis may detract from the development of spontaneous and creative modes of being with others in a group, but it can be the means of expressing mutual concerns and interests. In a democratic and caring group, there is likely to be more versatility among the members in taking roles and a more tumultuous passage through the group stages. This is reflected in the way goals are formulated and reformulated and the way specific group tasks are approached and carried out.

The longer the life of the group, the more movement back and forth between elementary, social, negative, and therapeutic reciprocity. A range of nurturing patterns is experienced, with high levels of reciprocal patterns arising at the end of the group sessions before the termination stage begins. Every group requires the development of new ways of exchanging nurturance and handling anger and aggression. The experiences are sometimes narrowly focused, and other times broad and transcending.

The major goals of a group will affect how nurturance exchange develops and how it is used. The role development and group stages will also vary with the goals. In general, when the group has to produce something for others, as does the workplace group, it is likely that the emphasis is on a superficial exchange of nurturance and surface cooperation. When the group focuses on the individual, it is likely that intense contact and reciprocity between the members will develop. Probably, no group as a whole is purely one type or another. A primarily supportive group that depends much of the time on a parenting-type leader, will develop some reciprocity of support and nurturance among the members. A primarily curative group will almost certainly have to contend with the quest for the parenting figure, but it is likely to go through more distinct stages, engage in painful examination of the self and the other, and develop the kind of intense mutuality and understanding that significantly alters how reality is seen. Subgroupings may be instrumental in moving the group forward in many ways, but they also can destroy cohesion and solidarity. Sometimes, such activity disrupts the equilibrium of the group enough to allow it to move to a new stage of growth.

NOTES

1. Taylor, E. K. (1951, October). Quantitative evaluation of psychosocial phenomena in small groups. *Journal of Mental Science,* 97:698.
2. Mills, T. M. (1967). *The sociology of small groups.* Englewood Cliffs, N.J.: Prentice-Hall, pp. 88–100.
3. Crosbie, P. V. (1975). *Interaction in small groups.* New York: Macmillan, p. 218.
4. Nieman, L. J., & Hughes, J. W. (1951). The problem of the concept of role: A resurvey of the literature. *Social Forces,* 30:149.
5. Taylor, F. K., (1950, October). The therapeutic factors of group-analytical treatment. *Journal of Mental Science,* 96:967–97.
6. Jennings, H. H. (1953). Sociometric structure in personality and group formation. In M. Sherif & M. O. Wilson (Eds.), *Group Relations at the Crossroads.* New York: Harper, pp. 349–50.
7. Taylor, F. K. (1954, November). The three-dimentional basis of emotional interactions in small groups. *Human Relations,* 7:456–57.
8. Crosbie, P. V., op. cit. p. 177.
9. Hare, A. P. (1976). *Handbook of small group research* (2nd ed.). New York: Macmillan, pp. 144–45.
10. Slater, P. E. (1955). Role differentiation in small groups. *American Sociological Review,* 20:300–10.
11. Talland, G. A. (1957). Role and status structure in therapy groups. *Journal of Clinical Psychology,* 13:27–33.
12. Golembiewski, R. T. (1962). *The small group.* Chicago: University of Chicago Press, pp. 104–28.
13. Hare, A. P., op. cit., p. 150.
14. Ibid., pp. 130–31.
15. Ibid., p. 279.
16. Ibid., p. 199.
17. Freud, S. (1940/1922). *Group psychology and the analysis of the ego.* London: Hogarth Press.
18. Redl, F. (1942). Group emotion and leadership. *Psychiatry,* 573–96.
19. Lewin, K., Lippitt, R. & White, R. K. (1939). Patterns of aggressive behavior in experimentally created 'social climates'. *Journal of Social Psychology,* 10:271–99.
20. Golembiewski, R. T., op. cit., p. 214.
21. Ibid.
22. Wolman, B. (1956, February). Leadership and group dynamics. *Journal of Social Psychology,* 93:13–23.
23. Nixon, H. L. (1979). *The small group.* Englewood Cliffs, N.J.: Prentice-Hall, p. 289.
24. Ibid., p. 290.

25. Hare, A. P., op. cit., p. 245; Fouriezos, N. T., Hutt, M. L., & Guetzkow, H. (1950). Measurement of self-oriented needs in discussion groups. *Journal of Abnormal and Social Psychology,* 45:682–90.
26. Golembiewski, R. T., op. cit., p. 182.
27. Lewin, K. (1951). *Field theory in social science.* New York: Harper & Row.
28. Ibid., pp. 6–22; Zeigarnik, B. (1927). Uber das Behalten von Erledigten and Unerledigten Handlunger. *Psychologische Forschung,* 9:1–85.
29. Golembiewski, R. T.. op. cit., p. 185.
30. Steiner, I. D. (1974). *Task-performing groups.* Morristown, N.J.: General Learning Press.
31. Roethlisberger, F. J., & Dickson, W. J. (1939). *Management and the worker.* Cambridge, Mass.: Harvard University Press.
32. See Chapter 9 for further discussion of the group at the workplace.
33. Ibid., p. 113.
34. Greenberg-Edelstein, R. R. (1971, February). Use of group processes in teaching retarded readers. *The Reading Teacher,* 23:318–24.
35. Golembiewski, R. T., op. cit., p. 195; Thelen, H. A. (1954). *Dynamics of groups at work.* Chicago, Ill.: University of Chicago Press, pp. 129–67; Thelen, H. A., & Dickerman, W. (1949, February) Sterotypes and the growth of groups. *Educational Leadership,* 6:309–16; Bennis, W. G., & Shepard, H. A. (1956, November). A theory of group development. *Human Relations,* 9:415–38.
36. Tuckman, B. W. (1965). Developmental sequence in small groups. *Psychological Bulletin,* 63:384–99.
37. Whitaker, D. S., & Lieberman, M. A. (1964). *Psychotherapy through the group process.* New York: Atherton Press, p. 116.
38. Bion, W. R., op. cit., pp. 132–38.
39. Ibid., p. 137.
40. Ibid., p. 128.
41. Klein, M. (1950). *Psychoanalysis of children.* (A. Strachey, Trans.). London: Hogarth, pp. 179–209.
42. Ibid., p. 147.
43. Slater, P. E. (1966). *Microcosm.* New York: John Wiley.
44. Loomis, M. E. (1979). *Group process for nurses.* St. Louis, Mo.: C.V. Mosby, p. 114.
45. Ibid., p. 115.
46. Ibid., p. 114.
47. Bach, G. (1954). *Intensive group psychotherapy.* New York: The Ronald Press, p. 409.
48. Ibid., p. 403.
49. Ibid., p. 409.
50. Nixon, H. L., op. cit., p. 85.
51. Wheaton, B. (1974). Interpersonal conflict and cohesiveness in dyadic relationship. *Sociometry,* 37:328–48.
52. Caplow, T. (1968). *Two against one: Coalitions in triads.* Englewood Cliffs, N.J.: Prentice-Hall, p. 67.
53. Bowen, M. (1966). The use of family theory in clinical practice. *Comprehensive Psychiatry,* 7:345–73, p. 355.
54. Caplow, T., op. cit., pp. 77–8.
55. Ibid., pp. 77–8.

9
Nurturance in Collectives and the Workplace

The therapy group is a product of an industrialized and urbanized society in which the prevailing social stereotypes limit exchange between people and mutual aid is difficult to attain. Throughout history, people have attempted to bypass the pressures of maintaining things as they are by banding together to form their own communities. In this way, they have attempted to establish a caring and nurturing world outside the general stream of society. When people intentionally go about creating their own society within a society, they make a bold move to control their lives, to live in ways that take into account their individuality, and to establish a group culture, norms, and communication networks suitable to their needs.

INTRODUCTION

Some collectives have been relatively temporary, when men, women, and children have set up living arrangements that have lasted only from one to two years. Others have thrived and have become permanent establishments for living and working together. Most carry out some therapy-like activities. The members meet regularly and discuss what is happening to them, how they are feeling, and try to help each other with problems that arise in close living conditions. The School of Living at Heathcote in Maryland consisted of nine members when Loomis wrote about it. She noted, "We have frequent discussions, a kind of T-grouping (probing and sharing of feelings), and have posted a long list of concerns to discuss and work on."[1]

The collective becomes the replacement or substitute for the traditional family. In fact, some intentional communities take strong positions against the traditional family. Often, a painful personality change takes place in order to establish behavior appropriate to the standards of the new group. The relation of the individual to the pressures of the group's goals and rules is pivotal. It is remarkable to what degree voluntary members can become so enmeshed in the group that their voluntary status is lost in the throes of the psychological attraction of the group.

The intentional group is a geographical entity such as a farm, a kibbutz, or a commune. The members usually know each other and have regular contact. These groups have some of the characteristics of a primary group although there may be 200 members or more. The members are also unified around ideas of building a better way of living and generally reject some of the traditional ways that people live in isolated families. Frequently, they have in common a hope for a better life and a truly cooperative society. They also have to handle the governance and economic problems of group living.

INTENTIONAL COMMUNITIES

A very early collective was that of the Essenes, a Jewish brotherhood (2 B.C. to 1 A.D.) that celebrated brotherly love by turning its back on women. The members lived in monastic communities in the region of the Dead Sea and elsewhere. They held property in common and shared unique beliefs affecting how they lived together. They were primarily humanistic and believed that association with women and the care of children deterred from being free and altruistic.[2] It was their belief that the nurturing mother–wife made a man more self-centered, concerned only with his own family, and less able to be nurturing.

The early modern era, which ushered in the Reformation, the Counter-Reformation, and the Radical Reformation saw the proliferation of attempts to live the ideal group life. More, who in the sixteenth century wrote one of the first utopian treatises, envisioned a commonwealth society in which goods were divided among everyone and people performed virtuous deeds because it was gratifying to do so. He tied nurturing to a dictate to do good.[3] In describing the mutual aid communities that existed in Europe during the sixteenth to eighteenth centuries, Kropotkin said, "the masses of people made a formidable attempt at reconstructing society on the old basis of mutual aid and support." Their writings expressed economical and social brotherhood and sisterhood. This movement suffered a severe blow when the state became more powerful, confiscating communal lands and fostering a narrow minded individualism.[4]

Most communes are started with little organization because the partici-pants operate on the premise that group members should make the decisions.[5] Neither the Western utopians nor the Japanese commune leaders did much planning.[6] The utopians were usually discontent with the existing society, believed that all things should be held in common, and were dedicated to work for the group's welfare. Many communes experienced periods of anarchy and chaos. The hope for a higher form of social organization was often strained by much confusion, trial and error, and disenchantment.[7]

People experience the joy of beginning life again when they are free to set up their world as they see fit. In a democratic commune, the members agree about how things will be done. They have to divide the work, set up norms about property, decide which types of relationships will be sanctioned, and determine how to handle problems that develop.[8] The early high spirits are somewhat toned down by the need to develop communal regulations and practices. Group solidarity is enhanced by the presence of an out-group, those who do not belong to the group. The others become in some sense the "unchosen" whereas the group members are the "chosen." This often breeds an "uncanny sense of oneness with the cosmos."[9] Living in the group includes reflections on the nature of the human being and the universe and exercises "for stilling the body and mind and experiencing the Ultimate." It also provides opportunity for dealing with major problems of living.[10]

Utopian communes arose in the last century in reaction to the inhumanities of the industrial revolution. The workers' lives were dreary, empty, and disease-ridden in the rigidly controlled environment of the factory where they were cogs in a wheel and where their potential personalities and abilities were squashed.[11] The Fourier communes in France tried to develop well-rounded personalities and the highest moral, mental, and physical growth. Everyone was in one great family that provided social workshops, cooperatives, and trade unions.[12] Thirty-four collectives in the United States attempted to follow this model. The best known was the Brook Farm commune in Massachusetts[13] that published a weekly magazine devoted to social and political problems.[14] In England, Owen established communities based on the belief that the aim of human society was the greatest happiness for the greatest number.[15]

Members of many religious communes were united in their intense emotional commitment to a charismatic person who had been proclaimed to be the messenger of God. This fits Freud's model of the group members united with each other through a common deep attachment to the same leader, who is the source of the group's cohesiveness and, in fact, the reason why the group exists in the first place.[16] Often, people drawn to such groups have been alienated and powerless, such as peasants, unemployed workers, and the poor who were isolated and confronted with a bleak and uncertain future.

Led out of Germany by Barbara Heineman, who was called the "Instrument" of God, the Inspirationalists settled in Iowa; marriage was discouraged and they led an austere and pious life. The work and their relationships with each other must have been very satisfying, for the young people did not leave and members tended to live to an old age.[17] Among the Shakers at Niskeyuna, New York, there was a parenting–maternal role bestowed on all females in their relationship to the men. Each "sister" was assigned a "brother" for whom she was responsible. Another form of nurturance came from the joy and solidarity the group shared during orgiastic dancing.[18]

The kibbutzim of Israel are the only communes in the world where egalitarian socialism and self-management are fully lived out. Provision for creative, independent development is built into the social setting. Strong attachment to the kibbutz creates a a powerful sense of self. The true meaning of the experience of being a kibbutznik is caught in the words of one member who expressed it this way:

> The kibbutz has its own rules and you can't play kibbutz outside of a kibbutz. If you want to talk about self-realization, I will have to ask, "What is the self?" because the self in the collective is not the same. The self is derived from the collective; this is the essence of the kibbutz. In this sense I am the kibbutz! The kibbutz is a social entity oriented toward goals and if a person doesn't share these goals, he or she is not a member of the kibbutz. The kibbutz is a whole and not an aggregate. There can be no self realization except as a whole, together. The kibbutz can be understood as a process and a system. Nothing is ever frozen in place.[19]

The Israeli kibbutz is a caring, egalitarian community where the division between the rule and the ruled has been abolished, direct participation in decision making by all in a general assembly has been established, and all authority roles (officers) are filled by rotation.[20] There are few role distinctions[21] and the people share their lives at work and at home. It is a social system built on "voluntary participation, voluntary cooperation, and mutual control." It operates on the principle "from each according to his ability, to each according to his needs."[22]

"I-Death"

The Brudenhof community highlighted the personal changes necessary to fit into a collective life. The emphasis was on a war between good and evil and the need to renounce the ego that is brought from the outside in order to become a fully loving person. Zablocki referred to the death of personality as the final elimination of previous conditioning. Toward this aim, the initiate goes through a strenuous preparation, learning to do difficult things including carrying out painful or repetitive exercises. The struggle, which takes several years, results in a rebirth that frees the individual of all past attachments and ambitions. When this occurs, there is an upsurge of the greatest joy. What seems to happen is the severance from values, ways of being and behaving that were learned in the competitive, self-involved, selfish world outside the commune.[23]

So impressed was Zablocki with the atmosphere of the Brudenhof commune, that he wrote, "never before or since have I felt the presence of brotherly love so permeating a place that I felt I was breathing it."[24] He raised the question of whether community is at all possible without the loss of the self. The same question could be raised in respect to what happens to the self in in-depth relationships. Buber referred to the loss of boundaries in the I–Thou experience where the other becomes part of the self rather than simply an object. We are faced with the probability that all mutually reciprocal exchanges of the highest intensity are similarly built on a breaking down of individuality. Although Zablocki had strong reservations about the death of the personality, he commented on how rich the life of the Brudenhof is, "a favorite Brudenhof aphorism is that the personality flourishes in the absence of the ego." In fact, the people at the Brudenhof have very unique and colorful personalities.[25] The "dead" personality is, after all, the end of patterns of behavior learned in a social setting that is no longer relevant to the commune member.

Judson used the term "I-Death" to refer to this personality change. One of the initial confrontations with change of the self pertains to occupational identity that has much to do with how we are defined, how we behave, and how other people expect us to behave. In the effort to relinquish such established roles, new commune members resist even acknowledging the skills and abilities they may have. After they have begun to build genuine relationships within the commune, however, they may "liberate" these skills. Judson gave an example, in which one commune member whose domineering behavior was increasingly under attack preferred to leave the commune rather than strip himself of this personality characteristic that gave him a great deal of security.[26] A vivid example of what I-Death might mean is revealed in a woman's effort to account for the failure of a commune. She said,

> We had plowed and begun to plant the earth but we had not pierced our own ego skins. . . . We must apply the blade to ourselves and cut back the outer skin to expose the pulsating flesh. And then we must harrow and pulverize the outer skin and use our egos for compost. Then, in the new flesh, we must plant the seeds of the people we wish to become.[27]

One of the aims of personality change in the commune is to do away with predictability, the one factor that ensures regularity and continuity. This is beneficial when what is predictable is undesirable. Suddenly, there is nothing a person is supposed to be and no particular achievement is expected. The change is a discontinuation of the established self. It is then "a leap into the truly unknown, with unknown consequences for the person involved."[28] Of course, this is not quite so, since in some communes the members are expected to conform to a very specific way of being, and the end of one community's pressures becomes that of another's. If there was not an immediate community of values and norms imposing itself on us, would we not seek them out? Is there one form of nurturance, the intense mutual exchange, that transcends all social orders, or is it possible only in the most egalitarian setting and one where the expected norms are also the least clearly defined?

In a group therapy setting, an effort is made to release the members from unrewarding, incapacitating behaviors. This is accomplished, however, by making mutual exchange acceptable, desirable, and predictable. The old predictabilities are replaced by the new group predictabilities of acceptance and support. The dialectics of opposites, destroying one predictability and creating another, operate in therapy groups as well as communes.

AT THE WORKPLACE

Grzyb defined work culture "as the ways of living on the job (and often off the job as well) that workers devise in their informal groups. It includes all the various group components—norms, beliefs, traditions, rituals, etc."[29] The work culture may then be seen as an alternative to the depersonalized work situation that leaves workers feeling stripped of their humanity. Some see the work culture as a challenge to the notion that people can be objects or commodities that must obey. In his study of informal work groups, Kornblum found that these groups could be of greater importance to the individuals than their other primary groups outside the workplace.[30]

Weir described how interactions between workers enabled them to give meaning to the work experience and to establish a viable "subculture" that provided support and means of dealing with the stresses produced by managerial tactics. The work group manifested many of the characteristics of any effective small group including role divisions among the members. Individual workers were often given nicknames that represented some distinctive quality the individual had. There were also roles that might or might not be associated with the nicknames, such as that of comedian, which could serve to relieve mounting tensions as well as give one person a special place in the group. Another observed role was that associated with "Silent Louie" played by someone who listened, summarized, and helped the group reach conclusions. "They laugh, slap him on the back and kid him about being their leader."[31]

In marked contrast to the grass-roots development of the work culture, management often tries to impose a culture on work groups that is labeled "participatory democracy" but that, in fact, keeps workers in their place. Work group responsibility is translated to mean working in such ways as to be consistent with managerial goals. The group is autonomous or participatory mainly in deciding if it is acting to achieve a narrowly defined goal, the firm's interests as defined by management.[32] Workers can take on the values of the organization to such an extent, that institutional directives can be demeaning and lead to pseudobehaviors interferring with self-esteem. As Grzyb put it, in accordance with institutional goals, workers are "supposed to pat their own back, slap their own wrists, and kick their own behinds— rather like children being expected to internalize values."[33]

Alienation on the job occurs when people feel cut off from their own feelings of compassion, fear, and anger at work. A job can deaden a person's emotional responses and increase withdrawal, passivity, and "robopathic" behavior. The "growing dehumanization of people" can reach "the point where they have become the walking dead."[34] The sense of not being oneself while on the job can contribute to an experience of a "split of the self." This occurs in other spheres of life as well, although the job is often the primary source of such splitting. Yablonsky noted that,

> . . . the final irony of a social machine society may be that even these constructed "humanistic" social interaction patterns sometimes deteriorate into forms of interaction where some of the participants, who might be called "therapeutic groupies," cry, laugh, open up, and even have insights on cue.[35]

The system of human relationships in organizations fostered by a capitalist or autocratic so-called Communist society rests heavily on the maintenance of the nurturance exchange at an infantile level for the majority at the lower ends of the hierarchy, in order that those with power can retain it. Independent autonomous people wanting to control their own lives at work and at home threaten systems that favor control by the few at the top. Workers are expected to maintain loyalty to the organization, fit into technical contingencies, and defer to authority. The personality of workers and officials are molded to meet these criteria. Above all, they are expected to accept uncritically the legitimacy of the organization and the rationality by which it operates.[36]

Jacques explained worker involvement at the workplace as a continuation of the splitting of projection and identification processes.[37] He proposed that, in this way, workers were able to adapt to the conflicts and struggles at the workplace where it sometimes was necessary to align with other workers, and sometimes compelling to identify with management.[38] He claimed that the workers ward off anxiety, provoked by life in the organization, by the introjection or identification of good and bad parts of the manager and projection onto the manager of good and bad parts of the self. It is common for workers to be unified in their shared hostility toward a boss who not only exploits, but is the object of their shared projections of unacceptable parts of self. Occasionally, a person other than a supervisor or boss is the object of a group projection that brings some solidarity to the group. Jacques observed that workers saw the managers that they worked with daily as good because the work they did under their direction had to be done. On the other hand, the managers who were negotiating with their plant representative were seen as bad, although they represented the same management.[39] This view of projection and introjection operations is of interest because it provides a basis for some form of reciprocal relationships among workers. Unity against a supervisor is an action producing nurturance in a situation where it would otherwise be absent. Additionally, projection of self onto others is a way of connecting.

Piaget, and other cognitive theoreticians, would take an entirely different position on the nature of the mental processes, since the basic idea behind his studies is that the human being functions in an integrated total manner. Applied to the workplace, the worker's or the manager's behavior would only have meaning as reactions to the total workplace situation and its general meaning. A rational process rather than the analysis of unconscious forces would place greater emphasis on ways of knowing and thinking, levels of awareness, and perceptual modes.

A group which functions on the basis of reciprocal nurturance and the unique value of the individuals and the specific group has its own internal controls. A group that receives its goals from outside and is managed by a representative of a power base in a community or institution is inevitably going to be subject to a molding that has little to do with who the members are. Manipulation of the identification-projection processes may be attempted by anyone in the position to control others. Sociotherapy, a treatment named by Mertens, epitomizes such abuses. Showing full knowledge of the basic theory and practice of group therapy, he proceeded to demonstrate how it can be used to change the personality of workers so that they can better fit into the organization in which they work. This type of misuse of the therapeutic group climate can lead to brainwashing and the destruction of freedom. It is inconceivable to consider such an approach within a moral framework that honors and respects the rights of people to be who they are, to make decisions about their own lives, and to be free from coercion.

His purported purpose was to increase efficiency, and decrease organizational stress in the enterprise. To accomplish this, he dealt with workers as if they were patients who needed to be adapted to the strictures of a mental institution.[40] Using group therapy sessions, i.e., some sort of T-group with all the coating of therapy, he deliberately planned to make the workers "more normative, more inceptive, and more perceptive." The desire for change came from Mertens and the employer, not from the workers. The purpose of the change was for the betterment of the institution, not the worker. The exploitive assumptions made are that what is good for the institution is good for everybody who works there and that change directed from above is "therapeutic." The end product is "reciprocal identification . . . group functionality and receptivity to change"[41] in which the workers accept and identify with the source of information that, in this case, represents management. The analysis of "the transference relationships" with the agent helps the workers accept the social model advocated.[42]

Sociotherapy is part of Organizational Development (OD) that "is a social movement, or a passing fad, or an important profession, depending upon one's perspective."[43] Thayer noted that OD was and is an effort to democratize and humanize work and it emphasizes team and group work. It was an outgrowth of Maslow's humanistic psychology and self-actualization, which Thayer thought was faulty because it portrayed self-actualized people as superior people and leader material[44] and directed management and human relations experts to manipulate workers and middle managers to achieve predetermined notions of potential that will increase the profits of the firm. The assault on people at the workplace is most devastating when OD is combined with the theory and practice of individual and group therapy. "When hierarchy and intensive psychological involvement are combined, it becomes relatively easy to advance from manipulation to out-and-out brainwashing (without realizing it)."[45]

CONCLUSIONS

People have banded together to form their own communities throughout history. In this way they have attempted to establish a secure and nurturing world of their own outside the general stream of things. When people intentionally go about creating their own society within a society, they make a bold move to control their lives, to live in ways that take into account their individuality, and to provide for collective caring and work with others. As in group therapy, they establish a group culture, norms, and communication networks.

Some collectives have been relatively temporary, in which women, men, and children have set up living arrangements that have lasted briefly. Others have thrived and become permanent communities for living and working together. Most entail some therapy-like activities; members meet regularly to discuss what is happening to them, how they are feeling, and what to do to help each other. Such arrangements are extensions of the family.

It is remarkable that a number of intentional communities take strong positions against the traditional family. Most pertinent is the discovery that various degress of personality change take place. The questions raised by such ventures have direct implications for the structure and functions of therapy groups. In particular, the relation of the individual to the pressures of the group is a pivotal problem.

Within the complex society, the social institutions, particularly those of the workplace, create cultures of their own that can have a profound influence on our sense of self and our ability to participate in egalitarian relationships. The stratification by power and powerlessness and the corresponsing distribution of positive and negative self-images pervasive in our world appears in most small group settings. Unless the harm of such cultural standards are recognized, they can continue to do their damage even in therapy groups.

NOTES

1. Fairfield, R. (1972). *Communes USA*. Baltimore: Penguin.
2. Kahler, E. (1961). *Man the measure: A new approach to history*. New York: George Braziller, p. 139.
3. More, T. (1964/1518). *Utopia*. New Haven, Conn.: Yale University Press.
4. Kropotkin, P. (1972). *Mutual aid: A factor in evolution*. New York: New York University Press, pp. 194–225.
5. Kanter, R. M. (1973). *Communes*. New York: Harper & Row, p. 16.
6. Plath, D. (1971). *Aware of utopia*. Urbana, Ill.: University of Illinois Press, pp. 1–17.
7. Ibid., op. cit., p. 21.
8. Kanter, R. M., op. cit., pp. 22–3; Plath, D., op. cit.
9. Judson, J. (1974). *Families of Eden: Communes and the new anarchism*. New York: Seabury Press, p. 183.
10. Kropotkin, P., op. cit., pp. 195, 197.
11. Kirschner, W. (1966). *Western civilization since 1950*. New York: Barnes & Noble, p. 156.
12. Laidler, H. W. (1968). *History of socialism*. New York: Thomas Y. Crowell, p. 760.
13. Ibid., p. 529.
14. Schiffman, J. (1961). Introduction, In L. Swift (Ed.), *Brook Farm*. New York: Corinth, p. II.
15. Laidler, H. W., op. cit., pp. 87–8, 97.
16. Freud, S. (1940/1922). *Group psychology and the analysis of the ego*. London: Hogarth Press, pp. 49, 52.
17. Lawson, D. (1972) *Brothers and sisters all over this land*. New York: Praeger, p. 35.
18. Ibid., pp. 44, 47.
19. Greenberg-Edelstein, R. (1977). Based on conversation with Alexander Barzel, at Conference on the Quality of Worklife and the Kibbutz. Haifa: Haifa University.
20. Rosner, M., & Cohen, N. (1978). *Is direct democracy feasible in modern society? the lesson of the kibbutz experience*. Haifa: Givat Haviva.
21. Fine, K. S. (1973). Worker participation in Israel. In G. Hunnius, G. D. Garson, & J. Case (Eds.), *Workers' control*. New York: Random House, pp. 243–44.
22. Melman, S. (1975). Industrial efficiency under managerial versus cooperative decision-making. In B. Horvat, M. Markovic, & R. Supek (Eds.), *Self-governing socialism*. New York: International Arts and Sciences, pp. 218–19.
23. Zablocki, B. D. (1971). *The joyful community*. Baltimore, Md.: Penguin, pp. 264–65.
24. Ibid., Introduction.
25. Ibid., p. 277.
26. Judson, J. (1974). *Families of Eden and the new anarchism*. New York: Seabury, pp. 172–73.
27. Ibid., pp. 174–75.
28. Ibid., p. 176.

29. Grzyb, G. J. (1981). Decollectivization and recollectivization in the workplace. *Economic and Industrial Democracy,* 2:455–82, p. 460.
30. Kornblum, W. (1974). *Blue collar community.* Chicago: University of Chicago Press.
31. Weir, S. L. (1974). *A study of the work culture of San Francisco longshoremen.* Unpublished Master's Thesis, University of Illinois.
32. Grzyb, G. J. op. cit., p. 472.
33. Ibid., p. 473.
34. Yablonsky, L. *Robopaths.* New York: Bobbs-Merrill, p. 6.
35. Ibid., p. 101.
36. Presthus, R. V. (1978). *The organizational society.* New York: St. Martin's Press.
37. Discussed earlier in Chapter 4 under Therapeutic Empathy.
38. Jacques, E. (1974). Social systems as a defense against persecutory and depressive anxiety. In G. S. Gibbard, J. J. Hartman, & R. D. Mann (Eds.), *Analysis of groups.* San Francisco, Calif.: Jossey-Bass, pp. 277–88.
39. Ibid., pp. 289–93.
40. Mertens, C. J. (1976). From theory to practice: The meaning of sociotherapy. In B. H. Kaplan, R. N. Wilson, & A. H. Leighton (Eds.), *Further exploration in social psychiatry.* New York: Basic Books, p. 245.
41. Ibid., p. 255.
42. Ibid., p. 258.
43. Thayer, C. T. (1973). *An end to hierarchy! An end to competition!* New York: New Viewpoints, A Division of Franklin Watts, p. 30.
44. Maslow, A. (1962). *Toward a psychology of being.* Princeton, N.J.: Van Nostrand.
45. Thayer, C. T., op. cit., p. 26.

10
Forms of Nurturance in History

Briffault came to the conclusion, in his monumental work *The Mothers*,[1] that feminine "sentiment" binds societies together. As early as the fourth century B.C., Herodotus studied social elements by reviewing the place and behavior of women in various parts of the Persian Empire and the Greek states.[2] The forms of nurturance propagated by men and by religious and social movements have often been ignored because women have been considered the conveyers of nurturance. The isolation of this fundamental element of humanness to one sex has been a major barrier to its effective use as a therapeutic agent. This chapter reviews very briefly the multidimensional forms of nurturance in history for the purpose of understanding their social potentials.

EARLY COMMUNITIES

The pervasive influence of nurturance is evident in the artifacts representing the mother as nurturer that appear early in prehistoric findings. Stone-age sculptures of the Great Mother as a goddess, the earliest cult works and art known aside from the cave paintings, were symbols of fertility, shelter, protection, and nurturance.[3] Early people, however, were also concerned with fate and death, for in the neolithic villages the dead were buried carefully in formal positions and provided with goods and weapons.[4] In the less distant past, the Egyptians splendidly stocked magnificent tombs, which they built to fulfill the wish for rebirth and eternal nurturance. The nurturance of the dead is one of our earliest signs of people caring about one another.

The old Sumerian Gilgamesh epic, which goes back to 1600 B.C. and antedates the Old Testament, dealt with the dialectical opposition between the enticement of the unconditional timeless nurturance of childhood and the challenge that fostered movement toward independence and eventual death. In the epic, Gilgamesh refuses to grow up because maturity would bring death closer. Although the father tries to help Gilgamesh take on marriage, responsibility, and independence, his mother aides him in remaining a child and avoiding marriage by furnishing him with a friend ("compeer") to become attached to instead.[5]

Some believe that during the early years of the human race when goddesses were prominent, women nurtured, tamed, and educated men to be more peaceful and social.[6] Engels believed that there was a natural relationship between a nurturing, democratic society and greater influence of women.[7] Dreams of a simple and ideal life led to the belief, shared by Greek and Christian traditions, that advanced civilization with its technology, science, and laws is a corrupting influence, and that history shows the retrogression of humankind rather than its progress. In early Egyptian civilization (about 3000 B.C.), which was contemporary with Sumer, women had an equitable place, monogamy was the rule, and there was no class stratification. The Sumerians are also believed to have had a more democratic society in their early years.[8]

The matriarch of yore did not always represent nurturance. In fact, she was sometimes a fearful figure, threatening and destructive. Some of the early societies were hierarchic, glorifying the matriarch and degrading the servants. A woman monarch at Sakkara was buried in the tradition of a pharoah: the tomb contained the bones of male servants, apparently sacrificed.[9] The people of the matriarchal city, Catal Huyak, 10,000 years ago, buried women in such a way as to indicate high reverence, whereas they showed no care for the men whose bones they threw into a charnel house.[10] The Sumerian society became more oppressive as it advanced and grew more bountiful. Wealth and power were possessed by the privileged few. The fact that the Sumerian people believed that they had been created to be the slaves of the gods helped the ruling class maintain its power.[11]

Evidence of the revolt against goddess worship appears in the Hebraic Old Testament in 40 places. Some believe that during the time of Moses, the Hebrew deity was the Goddess that created the world.[12] With the decline of the Mother Goddess and the rise of male religious leaders came alternate forms of support and nurturance and greater individuation. Humankind was considered to have progressed toward a greater maturity. This progress was associated with less dependence on the powerful mother of earlier times. The ascension of the God of Israel, Yahweh, represented the achievement of male independence and a dynamic open dialogue with God. Micah, a

Hebrew prophet living about the eighth century B.C., is credited with developing further the idea of the social contract and reciprocal relationships with God.[13]

Some of the new religions that arose during the years 800 to 200 B.C., represented a new type of nurturance which placed emphasis on individuality and self awareness. For instance Guatama Buddha's teachings emphasized "becoming" and, for women, this meant self-fulfillment outside their constrained family life.[14] Also following in this direction were Zoroaster in Iran and Confucious in China. These religions were masculine-oriented revolutionary movements that eventually replaced the dominance of the maternal principle.[15] People have separated nurturance from maturity and independence at least since ancient times. One of the reasons for this is probably the traditional division of labor between women and men: one assigned individualized caring and supportive work, the other social leadership and community based work. This seems to have resulted in the latter becoming dissociated from nurturance even though clearly belonging under the rubric of nurturance.

ANCIENT TIMES

The conflict between the feminine and masculine forms of nurturance are remarkably symbolized in the work of ancient historians and writers. Close in time to the writing of the Old Testament was Hesiod's work, *Theolog,* a Greek accounting of man's feminization in the struggle to deal with fatherhood, not unlike the father in the Old Testament who struggles to share in the care and protection of his children.[16] In the *Theolog* the father–husband places children and wives in his belly in order to prevent the children from growing up and taking power. As a consequence, a generic form of solidarity and revolt against oppression occurs when the children unite with the mother against the father. The eternal family triangle is enacted in this extremely ancient document when the father is castrated by his son Kronis, with the help of the mother.[17] In another incident, a husband, Zeus, swallows his wife, Metis, to retain control over her outstanding abilities.[18]

Odysseus, the hero of the Greek epic poem by Homer, faces his inner conflicts through his encounters with good and evil goddesses. This famous figure of Western literature exemplifies the dialectical struggle between the longing for a nurturing home and hearth and the desire to travel and experience the world.[19] Homer's other epic poem, the *Iliad* (c. 800 B.C.), portrays, on the one hand, women as objects or prizes as well as sources of wealth, and on the other hand, as powerful mother–goddesses who nurture, direct, and protect.[20]

In the rigid military state of ancient Sparta, the state was central and women's nurturing capacities were subverted to its needs. Sons were taken away from their mothers at the age of seven and women had to teach their daughters to repress every emotion of womanly tenderness, to consider the state first and foremost in their lives, and to accept that their prime function was to bear sons to be soldiers. They suffered the exposure of their infants in a public place where children were either judged frail and thrown off a cliff or returned to them if they were considered healthy.[21] Another extremely antinurturant practice was the annual flagellation of boys at the alter. The boys were beaten mercilessly and they frequently died of the ordeal.[22]

Regardless of the narrow channeling of their nurturing capacities, women did manage to develop an interpersonal support system, giving the rigid Spartan authoritarian order just enough flexibility to enable it to survive. Toynbee viewed Spartan women as the backup strength of a militaristic society when it began to topple. The women seem to have managed to develop a high resiliency and personal stamina that enabled them to adapt to change more readily than the men. Toynbee thought that the women's strength was derived from their lack of specialization, which contributed to their elasticity and adaptability.[23] The stern state system could not prevent women from developing nurturing abilities that helped sustain the society when it started to crumble.

The potential political power of women in their sexually nurturing capacity was presented by Aristophanes in his play *Lysistrata* (c. 412 B.C.). Lysistrata proposes that the women take a stand against the Peloponnesian War by going on a marital strike, "If we really want our men to make an armistice, we must be ready to . . . give up sleeping with our men."[24] The women vow to impose nonnurturant attitudes and behavior in the hope that their men will stop the war, "I will not give myself . . . and if he constrains me . . . I will be as cold as ice and never move . . ."[25]

In Athens, Plato wanted to eliminate the emotionality and personalized nurturance that are characteristic of the family. He proposed that the state replace the family by having all women and children in common and eliminating the specific parent and child relation. All children born during a specific period would be the daughters and sons of a particular group of men, and brothers and sisters to each other.[26] This resembles the "consanguine" family Morgan described as the oldest form of society. A group of males would agree to a contract for the "joint subsistence of the group, and for the defense of the common wives against the violence of society."[27]

Among the ancient Greeks, the courtesans were often outstanding women, highly educated and talented, and sought out as companions by the men. Husbands often did not socialize with their wives whose primary purpose was childbearing and rearing.[28] Aspagia is one such brilliant courtesan, mistress to Socrates and Pericles. In *Menexenus,* Plato reports Socrates as saying that Aspagia wrote Pericles' famous speeches and then proceeds to present one of them. Her references to the nurturing role of the state are of interest. Motherhood and government are described as the same because the government can also nurture.

. . . we and our citizens are brethren, the children of one mother, and we do not think it right to be one another's masters or servants, but the natural equality of birth compels us to seek for legal equality, and to recognize no superiority except in the reputation of virtue and wisdom. [Let the state] . . . cherish the old age of our parents, and bring up our sons in the right way . . . we will nourish your age, and take care of you publicly and privately. [The city] . . . is to the dead in the place of a son and heir, and to their sons in the place of a father, and to their parents and elder kindred in the place of a guardian—ever and always caring for them.[29]

Although in Plato's *The Republic* (c. 358 B.C.) the state is chief benefactor and nurturer of children, not all children are to be cared for.

The offspring of the good . . . they will take to the pen or creche, to certain nurses who live apart in a quarter of the city, but the offspring of the inferior . . . they will be properly disposed of in secret . . .[30]

Plato's plan for the division of labor emphasizes specialization and some have thought this would result in people becoming dependent and powerless, adding to the already overdependence on the nurturing functions of the state.[31] High levels of specialization are concordant with the dualistic view of intellect and spirit expressed by the Neoplatonist, Plotinus (c. 250 B.C.), who described intellect as the specialty of males and spiritually the province of females.[32]

The famous epic poem, *The Aeneid,* by the Roman, Virgil (c. 19 B.C.), is about male conflict between caring for people held close and the quest for public acclaim.[33] The nurturance of the home, hearth, and family actually played a nuclear role in early Rome. Nevertheless, the earliest constitution gave the father supreme power. He possessed all properties, even of married sons, and was able to sell into slavery, if he so willed it, any member of his household including his wife and children.[34] Regardless of the legal power of the man, the woman did run the household.[35] Worship of the nurturing spirits of the household and store chamber, which included Vesta, probably had the deepest hold on the people. The first duty of the father upon entering the home was to express his devotions to them. Public worship of Vesta was in the care of the vestal virgins, who dressed like brides and served 30 years under a strict rule of chastity.[36] Thus, a religious form of caring and giving was substituted for a maternal one.

Class wars helped liberalize Roman society in the fifth and fourth centuries B.C. The ruling class was forced to recognize the lower class's demands for (1) the greater sharing of information about laws, which the patricians had kept to themselves, (2) greater power for the assembly as against the aristocrats in the senate, (3) an end to the enslavement of debtors, and (4) limitations on the amount of property the patricians could own. One of the consequences of this liberalization was the elimination of the law that prohibited marriages between patricians and plebians. The opening up of marriage alternatives made a wider range of relationships possible for women as well as men.[37] It is noteworthy that the prostitute, as in Greece, had much greater freedom than wives. Some Roman matrons, in fact, registered themselves as prostitutes because only prostitutes had the legal right to multiple sexual experiences.[38]

According to Mommsen, the emancipation of Roman women began in earnest about 180 B.C.[39] Familial nurturance decreased as public and peer-related forms increased.[40] Nurturance exchange between women appeared in shared breast feeding by Roman matrons and their female slaves: some nursed their children in common and interchangeably.[41]

CHRISTIANITY

The early Christian movement fostered a cluster of nurturing activities that enabled men and women to develop a new faith and new types of relationships. In contrast to later development, early Christianity permitted the return to the "natural." The collective communities that were formed were nurturant and supportive. The devotion of lives to helping others wherever they might be, with whatever they might need—such as physical care, support, instruction, nourishment, and guidance—was emphasized. The celibacy that was practiced in the communes was a means of eliminating the property tag that placed women in stereotyped nurturing roles. They also changed their traditional ways of dressing. These violations of community norms met with great hostility and thousands of young women were imprisoned; some died violent deaths at the hands of furious fathers, husbands, and fiancés.[42]

Later, the monastic movement represented a new social form and became a challenge to the ecclesiastical hierarchy in Rome. People were able to build alternatives to the family by establishing orders in which parental roles were taken over by the abbess or abbott. These new family arrangements particularly provided women with unique opportunities to develop scholarly or administrative skills and nurturing skills different from those the family required. Many of the early Christians became teachers and healers.[43] The outstanding success of the nuns and abbesses was possible because of their release from the norms dictating female behavior.[44]

In the church, Jesus was a nurturing figure and he put faith in the people helping themselves. In contrast, Paul was stern and punitive and held that power resided only in God and existing rulers. Paul's theology provided the basis for a sacred autocracy, the divine right of kings, and acceptance of the slavery that existed. He taught that male and female were one, that woman existed for man, and that she should demonstrate her subjection by keeping her head covered in church. This dichotomy contrasted nurturing Christianity with a stern and punitive one.

An increase in the bureaucratization of Christianity became evident about the eleventh century. The homes of religious people were closed when the double monasteries of men and women were demolished. Women lost the support of the church and found themselves, once again, restricted to the traditional family setting and the limited nurturing opportunities it allowed. With these negative developments, came the effort of church authorities to eliminate the Mother of God as a major religious figure.[45]

A countermove to these repressive forces was the development of a new source of nurturance through the emerging universities in the twelfth century, particularly in Paris and Oxford. Both poor and rich were admitted to the faculty and the student body, and there was also an expansion of opportunities for work and growth. Peasants were able to leave the manorial grounds and to avoid compulsory labor. The cooperative mutual aid societies for merchants and guilds for the crafts offered nurturance and support among peers.[46]

The progressive suppression of women continued into the late Middle Ages and was so extreme that women were, in most matters, treated as members of a separate and inferior race. Those who were not passive, silent, and self-effacing, nurturant mothers and wives were seen as a threat to the existing male-dominated system of the traditional family, community, and church. The proportion of women to men who were burned alive as witches, from about 800 to 1800 A.D., was as much as 10,000 to 1.[47] The female creature, the source of carnal pleasure, and the mother of everybody, became someone to be feared and despised. The wholesale destruction of women was the result of the anxiety she provoked and the danger she posed to male authorities.[48]

The writings of the Renaissance, which frequently portrayed women as being born inferior, trivialized the nurturing process with which they were so intimately associated. Although this was pervasive, there were women who shared in the individualistic spirit that was evident in the breakdown of the feudal class structure, in the ventures in developing business and commerce, and in the spread of the scientific attitude.

One remarkable person of this period was Teresa of Avila, born in 1515, who was canonized. Her work emphasized spiritual experiences and the extreme importance of nurturance in helping people. Her work was distinctive because of its great ardor and candor. She objected to the Apostle Paul's double standard for men and women, particularly his insistence on chastity for women but not for men. She maintained that there was great value in women's proclivity for being loving, taking time to share their concerns, conversing with people, and forming close relationships.[49] The artist–nun, Caterina Vigri, made paintings with which she hoped to heal the sick, an activity that was a remarkable amalgamation of art and nurturance. These paintings were usually versions of the Holy Child and they were reported to help cure the sick.[50] A comprehensive history of the healers and health care givers that came forth during this period was recorded by the nurse scholars, Nutting and Dock.[51]

MODERN TIMES

The Islamic Ottoman empire, that existed between the fourteenth and twentieth centuries, replaced the family with the state. It was a gigantic paternalistic state offering nurturance, protection, and education in return for loyalty and service. The state provided a great military state school that, in comprehensiveness of curriculum and length and severity of training, appears to be without parallel in the general history of education. Children, who were removed from their families at an early age, came from the conquered lands as prisoners of war or were purchased as slaves.[52] The conquering Ottoman soldier was given the absolute right to own his captives unless they converted to Islam. Handpicked men, who were to serve the Sultan personally, were not permitted to marry or hold property.[53] Mothering was replaced by the state's schools, harem, army, and civil service. Any boy within its domain could become a general, a prime minister, any girl, one of the wives of the Sultan. The training was so severe that a man had to be treated as an isolated individual unattached to any background or family in order to ensure his submission to the rigors of the system. The women of the harem were educated and taught skills.[54] The children thus nurtured by the state became totally dedicated and completely loyal to it. In this way, the state developed ferociously committed soldiers and civil servants.

The royal slave–concubine could rise to prominence based on the type of relationship she had with the Sultan. The nurturing role of the woman as mother of the prince and wife of the Sultan enabled her to wield various amounts of power and control, depending on her personality, charm, and intelligence. There were alliances between mothers and sons, as in earlier societies. Often, the mother used her relationship with the Sultan to obtain personal power and to try to gain advantages for her son, preferably ascension to the throne. Roxelana, a slave girl from Russia, managed to use her nurturing abilities and persuasive talents with the Sultan so well that he created the title of Empress for her.[55] Using similiar tactics, a peasant girl developed a close relationship with the Czar and eventually succeeded Peter the Great to become Catherine I of Russia in 1725.[56]

The Reformation, which began in the early sixteenth century, brought with it many revolts against existing religious practices and a reconsideration of some of the nurturing potentials. Martin Luther, an Augustine monk in Wittenburg, Saxony, had proclaimed, among other things, that everyone could be his or her own priest and master. His attack on the authority of the Roman Catholic Church led to demands that dogmas, sacraments, and traditional worship be abolished. This emergence of Protestantism was associated with greater freedom for women to adapt their nurturing capacities to religion. A number of women religious leaders appeared in different countries brandishing their own version of Protestantism. They were often branded heretics and witches and suffered various forms of atrocious punishment including death. For instance, Isabel de la Cruz in Spain, who preached the love of God and the interiorization of religion, found guilty of heresy and imprisoned. There seemed to be an equal number of women and men condemned for heresy in the various countries.[57]

Knights rebelled against their overlords and peasants rose up against serfdom, extravagant taxes, and restriction of their privileges, and demanded the right to worship God in their own way. In reaction to this, Luther defended the authorities saying that rebellion was not justified even if the rulers were wrong. Because of his support of the authorities, he was accused of subordinating religion to the existing political order.[58] In explaining his position, Luther maintained that the order of the state was primary, that Christian love should be subordinate to it, and that the authorities should be loved as parents because they cared for the lower classes.[59]

Radical followers of the Reformation took up Luther's repudiation of the sacramental basis of marriage and also extended the priesthood to women. The Radical Reformation, which included among its adherents, Erasmas, was characterized by espousal of radical rupture with the immediate past and all its institutions. People wanted to restore the primitive church.[60] Some were inspired to live in collectives which replaced the family. Among the Hutterites, a wife was called "marital sister"; people were members of the collective first, and only secondarily, a husband or wife.[61]

John Calvin added repressive features to the break-off religion. Most serious was the denigration of the nurturing attitude and warning against emotional indulgences in personal life. People were told to avoid close relations with even their best friends. Going among the people was said to be like going "into a wild forest full of dangers."[62] Calvin also preached complete abandonment to God and the authority of the church, prohibition of all luxuries and amusements, and the absolute necessity of prayer and work. The doctrine of predestination led to the feeling that everything was hopeless. People were doomed even if they obeyed God's commandments.[63] Exploitation on the job was also supported, for he proclaimed it was a sin to waste time, to be social, to sleep too long, and to engage in religious contemplation at the expense of daily work.[64] He also taught that people were to support unconditionally whatever their government imposed on them.[65] Such nonnurturant approaches to religion were bound to produce a counterreaction.

There is little wonder that there developed an overwhelming need for a supportive deity. This was achieved by the return of the cult of Mary, the Mother of Jesus, which became very popular, particularly in Northern and Western Europe. At this time, paintings of Mary emphasized feminine and motherly features: mercy, kindness, tenderness, and nurturance. She became "Our Blessed Lady," "Notre Dame," and "Madonna." Mary represented mercy and forgiveness and the value of tenderness and nurturance, whereas God the Father appeared unapproachable and terrible.[66]

Women were the major means by which greater permissiveness and acceptance of children were achieved in England and colonial America. The increased freedom of women in the colonies was associated with this softening influence in the family. Women's tendencies to be accepting and to give unqualified love could be more readily expressed in the colonies. The movement toward greater closeness between children and parents was gained more slowly in England. There, the relationship to children remained formal and cold for a longer period of time.[67]

A loosening of the autocratic structure of the family led to the increased opportunity for women to bring greater humanity into the family. This was enhanced by the greater choice they had in what they could do other than being wives. In other words, improved "working conditions" for wives was the result of improved working conditions in areas of work outside the home and greater freedom of the worker–wife to contract for better conditions of "employment."

At the end of the eighteenth century, the American and French Revolutions celebrated greater freedom and liberty for the people and concommitantly fostered more opportunities for voluntary nurturing relationships at different levels. At about this time in England, Wollstonecraft stated, in a book that is now considered a classic, that the nurturing, supporting, and teaching role expected from the woman–mother cannot be forthcoming if she remains ignorant, uneducated, and without equal rights.[68]

Until very recently, the American legal system supported the dependence of the wife on her husband and her retention of a childlike role in relation to the nurturing or punitive husband. In the nineteenth century, as in early Roman times, the husband owned the wife's property, even her personal jewels, and had a legal right to the children, of whom he could dispose as he wished. Husband and wife were conceived of as one legal person and they could not enter into contracts with each other.[69] In such a legal system, even the nurturing functions of the married woman were the property of the husband. American lawyers, who fastidiously followed these legalities that were based on Blackstone's *Commentaries* did not seem to appreciate that he had been dedicated to the maintenance of the rigid English class system and that the English legal system was being recast under the leadership of people like Jeremy Bentham.[70] The voice of Florence Nightingale, celebrated English nurse in the Crimean War, was heard in America by women in all walks of life when she called on women to better their lives and stop subordinating their existence to their husband's lives.[71]

During the middle of the nineteenth century, when women were organizing to get their legal rights and especially the vote, a range of socialistic and religious ventures into new ways of living was tried in Europe, America, and England. These communes laid down new patterns of living that emphasized shared community, nurturance, and mutual aid societies that abandoned the traditional patriarchal hierarchy. They arose in reaction to the inhumanities of the industrial revolution and the mechanization of industry, which diminished the functions of the family as a source of security, nurturance, and support.[72] Basic to these ventures was a belief that a person can develop more fully by living and working in small groups.

The extension of women's nurturing capacities into the community at large began in earnest in the nineteenth century. Women feminized religions when they became volunteers teaching Christianity and forming reform societies to help the unfortunate.[73] Women who had gone to college found there was no place to apply their knowledge. They initiated the women's club movement to support one another. Some established settlement houses and public health nursing agencies where they could care for, teach, and help the poor.[74] By the end of the century, more than half the teachers were women, although in the 1800s there were scarcely any.[75]

CONCLUSIONS

Generic maternal nurturance occurs in new and different forms in the family, religion, and the state. Conflicts between the desire for unconditional nurturance and the wish to attain public acclaim reflect what appear to be unending interactions between personal needs and social pressures. The backup role of the "nonspecialist" nurturant women in holding societies together supports the theory that nurturance is the underbase of any society and that, when a human system becomes malfunctional, it is the process that will provide the continuity needed while adaptive forces do their work.

The Mother Goddess in early civilizations and in the ancient world symbolized the central need for continued nurturance. Whereas female deities and oracles were important in ancient Greece and Rome, the power structure was in the hands of the men. It took a social revolution to release the nurturance potential in the public domain.

The ancient Hebrews emphasized a more egalitarian exchange with the deity and more mature forms of nurturance. The Christian movement fostered collectives where people devoted their lives toward helping others. People sought out the Mother Goddess in the form of the cult of Mary, mother of God, when religious forms became nonnurturant and punitive.

The state as nurturer may seriously imperil independence and the opportunity to develop in multiple ways. Egalitarian arrangements have encouraged people to give greater importance to caring relationships. The small, intimate work groups in early monasteries, among the Radical Reformation communities, and the religious or socialistic collectives in the nineteenth century fostered reciprocal nurturing activities among peers and some of the solidarity and cohesiveness that occur in families. These formats are being applied today to the achievement of therapeutic goals for individuals through one-to-one and group methods.

NOTES

1. Briffault, R. (1927). *The mothers: A study of the origin of sentiments and institutions* (Vol. 3). London: George Allen, p. 509.
2. Herodotus. (1930). *The histories* (9 vols.). (W. Beloe, Trans.). London: Jones Temple of the Muses, Finsbury Square.
3. Neumann, E. (1944). *The great mother.* (R. Manheim, Trans.). New York: Pantheon Books, pp. 94–96.
4. Muller, H. J. (1961). *Freedom in the ancient world.* New York: Harper & Brothers, pp. 4, 8.
5. Jacobsen, T. (1976). *The treasure of darkness: The history of Mesopotamian religion.* New Haven, Conn.: Yale University Press, pp. 195–97.
6. Davis, E. G. (1911). *The first sex.* New York: G. Putnam's Sons, pp. 17, 49.
7. Engels, F. (1972/1884). *The origin of the family, private property and the state.* New York: Pathfinder Press.
8. Kirchner, W. (1960). *Western civilization to 1500.* New York: Barnes & Noble, pp. 6–13.
9. Cottrell, L. (1965). *The land of the Shinar.* London: Souvenir Press, p. 116.
10. Mellaart, J. (1967). *Catal Huyak.* New York: McGraw-Hill, pp. 204–26.
11. Ibid.
12. Patai, R. (1968). *The Hebrew goddess.* New York: Farrar, pp. 55–61.
13. Kahler, E. (1961). *Man the measure: A new approach to history.* New York: George Braziller, p. 139.
14. Boulding, E. (1976). *The underside of history: A view of women through time.* Boulder, Colo.: Westview Press, p. 401.
15. Muller, H. J. op. cit., p. 109.
16. Bakan, D. (1979). *And they took themselves wives.* New York: Harper & Row, p. 165.
17. Hesiod. (1983). *Theogony; work and days; shield.* (A.N. Athanassakis, Trans.). Baltimore, Md.: John Hopkins University Press, p. 24.
18. Ibid., p. 35.
19. Homer. (1980). *The odyssey.* (W. Shewring, Trans.). Oxford: Oxford University Press, pp. 118–119.
20. Homer. (1950). *The iliad.* (E. V. Rieu, Trans.). Harmondsworth, Middlesex, Eng., Penguin Book: p. 23.
21. Carroll, M. (1907–1908). *Women: In all ages and in all countries.* Philadephia, Penn.: G. Barrie & Sons, p. 137.
22. Seltman, C. (1956). *Women in antiquity.* London & New York: Thames and Hudson, p. 68.
23. Toynbee, A. J. (1948–1961). *A study of history* (Vol. 3). London: Oxford University Press, p. 75.
24. Aristophanes. (1954). *Lysistrata.* An English version by D. Fitts, New York: Harcourt, Brace, p. 11.
25. Ibid., pp. 17–18.
26. Plato. (1930). *The republic* (2 vols.). (P. Shorney, Trans.). Cambridge, Mass.: Harvard University Press, p. 467.
27. Morgan, L. H. (1877). *Ancient society.* Cambridge, Mass.: Harvard University Press, p. 501.
28. Grote, G. (1857). *A history of Greece* (Vol. 5). London: J. Murray, p. 100.

29. Plato. (1938). *The dialogues.* (B. Jowell, Trans.). New York: Random House, pp. 777–78.
30. Plato. op. cit., p. 463.
31. Diamond, S. (1969). Plato and the definition of the primitive. In S. Diamond (Ed.), *Primitive views of the world.* New York: Columbia University Press, p. 173.
32. Plotinus. (1967). *Complete works.* (A.H. Armstrong, Trans.). Cambridge, Mass.: Harvard University Press, p. 197.
33. Virgil. (1908). *Aeneid.* (T.C. Williams, Trans.). New York: Houghton Mifflin.
34. Mommsen, T. (1908). *The history of Rome.* (Vol. 1). New York: Charles Scribner's, p. 76.
35. How, W. W. (1907). *A history of Rome.* New York: Longmans, Green, p. 401.
36. Lloyd, R. B. (1969). Vestal virgins. *Encyclopaedia Britannica* (Vol. 22). p. 1012.
37. Kirchner, W., op. cit., p. 82.
38. Boulding, E., op. cit., p. 346.
39. Mommsen, T., op. cit., Vol. 3, p. 121.
40. Ibid., pp. 121–23; Vol. 5, p. 516.
41. Ibid., Vol. 5, p. 118.
42. Boulding, E., op. cit., p. 359.
43. Ibid., pp. 360–79.
44. Stuard, S. M. (1976). *Women in medieval society.* Philadelphia: University of Pennsylvania Press, p. 3.
45. Ibid., p. 8.
46. Kirchner, W., op. cit., p. 205.
47. Davis, E. G., op. cit., p. 256.
48. Horney, K. (1937). *The neurotic personality of our time.* New York: W.W. Norton, p. 113.
49. Bainton, R. H. (1977). *Women of the Reformation.* Minneapolis, Minn.: Augsburg Publishing House, pp. 47–67.
50. Greer, G. (1979). *The obstacle race.* New York: Farrar Straus Giraux, p. 174.
51. Nutting, M. A., & Dock, L. L. (1907–1912). *A history of nursing* (4 vols.). New York: G. P. Putnam's Sons.
52. Miller, B. (1970/1931). *Beyond the sublime parte: The grand seraglio of stambul.* New York: Amsterdam Press, pp. 50–1.
53. Kinross, L. (1977). *The Ottoman centuries: The rise and fall of the Turkish empire.* New York: William Morrow.
54. Miller, E., op. cit., pp. 52–3.
55. Ibid., pp. 86–94.
56. Lockhart, L. (1969). Catherine I. *Encyclopaedia Brittanica* (Vol. 5). p. 77.
57. Bainton, R. H. (1977). *Women of the Reformation.* Minneapolis, Minn.: Augsburg Publishing House, p. 45.
58. Pascal, R. (1971/1933). *The social basis of the German Reformation.* New York: Augustus Kelly, p. 127.
59. Ibid., p. 177.
60. Williams, G. H. (1975). *The Radical Reformation.* Philadelphia: Westminster Press, p. 505.
61. Ibid., p. 514.
62. Weber, M. (1930). *The Protestant ethic and the spirit of capitalism.* London: G. Allen & Unwin, p. 224.

63. Bendix, R. (1962). *Max Weber: An intellectual portrait.* New York: Doubleday, p. 590.

64. Weber, M. (1930). *The Protestant ethic and the spirit of capitalism.* London: G. Allen & Unwin, pp. 114–18.

65. Kahler, E., op. cit., pp. 396–97.

66. Briffault, R., op. cit., Vol. 3., pp. 499–500.

67. Thompson, R. (1974). *Women in Stuart England and America.* London: Routledge & Kegan, pp. 156–57.

68. Wollstonecraft, M. (1967/1790). *A vindication of the rights of woman.* New York: W. W. Norton, p. 283.

69. Beard, M. R. (1946). *Woman as force in history: A study in traditions and realities.* New York: Macmillan, p. 162.

70. Miller, V. Y. (1969). Sir William Blackstone. *Encyclopaedia Brittannica* (Vol. 3), p. 749.

71. Spender, D. (1982). *Women of ideas.* Boston, Mass.: Ark Paperbacks, pp. 403–04.

72. Kirchner, W. (1966). *Western civilization since 1500.* New York: Barnes & Noble, p. 156.

73. Clinton, C. (1984). *The other civil war: American women in the nineteenth century.* New York: Hill & Wang, pp. 11, 61.

74. Hymowitz, C. & Weissman, M. (1978). *A history of women in America.* New York: Bantam Books, pp. 222–33.

75. Clinton, C., op. cit., p. 46.

Epilogue

Ultimately it is within small groups, at work, in the community, and the clinic, that change takes place. However, the way we relate to one another, care about one another, and exchange nurturance is influenced by the structure of modern society. Most prevailing economic systems have social priorities which do not reflect the basic concerns of the majority of the people. Embroiled as we are in the economic system in which we live, major obstacles exist to our developing a universally nurturing world ethic. The domination by subsystems of economy, technology, and science submerge the entire notion of personal identity and the potential of discovering universal ethical ways of behavior.[1]

Habermas' "characteristics of a new identity which is at least possible in complex societies and at the same time compatible with universalistic ego structures" has powerful implications for solving the modern preponderant needs for meaning and authentic love. If his five points, which are directed at attaining more genuine human relations, were applied to reciprocity of nurturance and groups we would have the following:

1. Universal values bond us together in reciprocal nurturance.
2. We need to engage in reciprocal nurturance on a continuous basis.
3. Fixed modes of relating which are based on traditional authority interfere with the development of new awareness and unique experiences.
4. Political processes which subvert free reciprocity between individuals and groups and maintain "systematic mechanisms of control which

express the interests of the few" impede the development of mutual positive reciprocity.

5. The future will be based on the development of universalistic forms of positive reciprocity.[2]

The early industrial consciousness in the United States, as described by Charles Reich,[3] focused on a nonnurturant mentality which included such features as: self-interest, competition, the belief that success is determined by hard work, self-denial, character, and morality. Associated features were suspiciousness, isolation of self, and excessive repression. Nurturing relationships were probably predominantly parental and asymmetrical. With the advance of technology, there was increased emphasis on discipline, hierarchy, meritocracy, and the manipulation of nurturing relationships to attain personal success. With emphasis on the social nature of society, equality and reciprocal nurturance become central. The theme of the post-industrial era is more socially conscious and, according to Hughes,[4] it calls for the integration of the rational and affective. This can pave the way for reciprocal nurturance at personal, group, and community levels to become the predominant mode of relating. It is interesting to note that Kropotkin called the nurturance factor "mutual aid" and set forth to show that the cooperative communities that existed demonstrated that mutual aid is far more important than mutual struggle, and that this was especially important for the progressive evolution of the species.[5]

Acceptance of nurturance as the root of human groups leads to a perspective of a caring society as a collection of cohesive supportive small groups. Within each of these groups lies the essence of what it means to coexist with others in time. Some supportive groups, however, do not permit variations and developments beyond the status quo. They lack the conflict and disharmony which are essential for growth and change. Without negative exchanges there is no movement and we are left frozen in narrow paths of repetitive and monotonous continuity. Also, excessive and unresolvable conflicts lead to limited and unflexible adaptations. Sometimes the remedy is the therapy group, which provides the vehicle for release from the destructive effects of some natural groups. Groups set up for this purpose do not always achieve their goal because the members sometimes are unable to develop a nurturance exchange network. Just as other alternate groups do not always provide the milieu for sufficient growth, so therapy groups may also be limited by leadership, membership, and environmental factors.

Some cults and collectives have been therapeutic ventures offering participants release and freedom from the constraints of an exploitive social order. Ultimately it is the relationship between the individual and the group that differentiates between the various social forms that therapy groups, cults, collectives, and society may take. More often collectives are politically democratic while cults center on a dominant figure and a hierarchical order. Both attempt to develop what is seen as a better society within a corrupt, troubled world; the cult, however, specifically attempts to start a new religious tradition.[6] Some levels of the nurturance exchange are restrictive and foster a selfless exchange which debases the individual personality. The meaning of democracy is then drastically altered to provide for a type of sharing and caring in which the self as we know it disappears or is never allowed to emerge.

Although the nurturing moment is never recreated, it bears the imprint of the past and has its imprint on the future. The nuturing interrelationship comes into being by virtue of the meaning of the moment and its special place in our existence. Bergson takes the position that the experienced moment is both unique and different from the constructs we create to look at our history, where we are going, and what will happen.[7] This existential position holds that the moment can only be fully lived if we can disconnect ourselves from the past and the future. But then from whence does the moment get its meaning in the group?

The group provides the setting for the experience of a unique moment of reciprocal exchange with a number of others at a moment in time. This could be the experience that leads to the next, and then the next, so that eventually, having had a series of such experiences, we experience all other moments quite differently. Since this applies to an organic creative evolution, there is no way to put the process into a theory that explains, if A, B, and C are present, D will come to be. The essence of this evolution is a qualitative merging of moments and to break up the moments into quantities of caring, awareness, or any other attributes of these sorts, is to do violence to the idea altogether.

Even the identification of a nurturance need and a nurturance factor suggests a constancy that does not exist except for the purpose of categorical thinking. If we are concerned with the value and meaning of the moment of contact or exchange, we have to deemphasize logical and deductive approaches to group work. This is not something we do lightly. As a matter of fact, it takes a great deal of confidence in our own capacity to create and become without specific pointers and clear guidelines to lead the way.

Bergson noted that "we could know—causes in detail" and that "we could explain by them the form that has been produced; [but] foreseeing the form is out of the question."[8] "Repetition is therefore possible only in the abstract . . . concentrated on that which repeats, solely preoccupied in welding the same to the same, intellect turns away from the vision of time. It dislikes what is fluid, and solidifies everything it touches. We do not *think* real time. But we *live* it, because life transcends intellect . . ."[9] A dialectical approach to human creativity has to be associated with changing nurturing relationships and meaning that are relative and volatile. Both newly emerging selves and innovative forms are born in such exchanges.

NOTES

1. Habermas, J. (Spring, 1974). On social identity. *Telos, 19,* 19–103.
2. Ibid., pp. 101, 103.
3. Reich, C. (1970). *The greening of America.* New York: Random House.
4. Hughes, H. S. (1958). *Consciousness and society.* New York: Vintage Books.
5. Kropotkin, P. (1972). *Mutual aid: A factor in evolution.* New York: New York University Press, p. 19.
6. Bromsky, D. G., & Sharpe, A. D. (1981). *Strange gods. The American cult scare.* Boston: Beacon Press, p. 23.
7. Bergson, H. (1911). *Creative evolution.* New York: Holt.
8. Ibid., p. 27.
9. Ibid., p. 47.

Index